THE DYNAMICS OF A TRADITION

Kasturbhai Lalbhai

The Dynamics of a Tradition

Kasturbhai Lalbhai and his Entrepreneurship

DWIJENDRA TRIPATHI

MANOHAR
2025

First published 1981
Reprinted 2023, 2024, 2025

ISBN 978-93-94262-59-1

Published by
Ajay Kumar Jain *for*
Manohar Publishers & Distributors
4753/23 Ansari Road, Daryaganj
New Delhi 110 002

Printed at
Replika Press Pvt. Ltd.

For Ravi J. Matthai

Foreword

The present volume is a part of the IIMA's effort to promote research in Indian entrepreneurial history. Historical scrutinies into the business behaviour of a society may provide raw materials for building meaningful theories and constructs necessary for comprehending and explaining the present managerial behaviour. India has a rich tradition of historical research, but for various reasons, entrepreneurial history has received less attention than it deserves. Consequently the empirical base of our understanding of the managerial dynamics in India is not very strong. It is with a view to removing this lacuna that this Institute from its very inception has encouraged research and teaching in the field of entrepreneurial history.

Professor Tripathi in the present work has given an analytical and comprehensive account of the business career of one of the foremost business leaders of our times. Sheth Kasturbhai Lalbhai was not only a towering figure in the Indian business world, but also a great champion of social, educational, and cultural causes. He was a "mahajan" in the real sense of the term. The career of such a man would be a significant input in our understanding of the growth of Indian business. Based on primary documentary materials and interviews, and informed by appropriate theoretical constructs, Professor Tripathi's account would be of interest to the common reader and the scholarly public alike.

I commend the book and hope that it would give a new impetus to historical enquiry into Indian entrepreneurial and managerial dynamics.

V.S. Vyas
Director

Indian Institute of Management
Ahmedabad

Acknowledgements

Private business is not known for its willingness to open its records or share information regarding its performance to researchers. I had, however, full and free access to all sources of information thanks to the help and cooperation of Sheth Shrenik Kasturbhai. Not only did he and his associates freely give me all the records I asked for, but also put me in touch with persons and institutions who could provide additional information. Manubhai D. Shah, and B.V. Shah, General Managers of the Arvind Mills and of the Atul Products Limited respectively, acted as contact points between the employees of various companies and myself.

Records of a business organization seldom tell the complete story. Interviews with the members of Kasturbhai Lalbhai's family and with the executives of his companies formed very important sources of my information. Sheth Kasturbhai Lalbhai himself sat through a series of long and searching interviews. The members of the family who provided helpful information include Sheth Siddhartha Kasturbhai, Sheth Shrenik Kasturbhai, Sheth Chinubhai Manibhai, and Dr. (Mrs.) Vimla Siddharthabhai. Premvada K. Nagarsheth let me use some records in her possession bearing on the history of her illustrious family. B.K. Muzumdar, who among all his executives was closest to Sheth Kasturbhai Lalbhai, granted several interviews in spite of his failing health. Several current executives including Manubhai D. Shah and B.V. Shah, N.S. Johary, Chief Executive of the Atic Industries, A.R. Naik, General Manager of the Cibatul, R. Acharya, Production Manager of the Atul, B.P. Mistry, and T.P. Desai provided crucial data. I have also benefited from the records of interviews Sheth Kasturbhai Lalbhai had granted to S.P.S. Pruthi of the Indian Institute of Management, Ahmedabad, in 1964 and to Howard Spodek of the Temple University, Philadelphia, in 1975.

There is no way for me to repay the intellectual debt I owe

to my professional colleagues and friends. They include M.J. Mehta, Shirin M. Mehta, S.C. Misra, G.S. Gupta, Ramesh Gupta, H.N. Pathak, S. Sreenivas Rao, Ravi Acharya and many others whose names I cannot possibly mention without making this list unduly large. Bhagirathi Harihar compiled statistical data, and checked and rechecked the tables. Seminar reports written by two of my students Deepak Chawla and N.S. Laxmi Jayanti on Atul and the Arvind Mills respectively have also been helpful.

My debt to the Indian Institute of Management, Ahmedabad, is considerable indeed. I took up the study on the suggestion of Samuel Paul, who was then its Director. Both he and his successor, V.S. Vyas, provided every kind of institutional support I needed. The Institute's library and its staff, particularly J.F. Pandya and G.J. Trivedi, were most helpful in locating reference materials. Also helpful were the staff of the libraries of the Gujarat Vidya Sabha, Gujarat College, Ahmedabad Millowners' Association (all in Ahmedabad), National Archives of India, Jawaharlal Nehru Memorial Museum and Library (both in Delhi), and Maharashtra Government Records Office, Bombay.

V.N. Ganesan, M. Govindan, P. Vedachalam and V. Arumugam typed and retyped the manuscript. Maps and charts are the work of G.D. Patel.

But for the help of these individuals and organizations this work would never have been completed. To all of them I am most grateful.

DWIJENDRA TRIPATHI

Ahmedabad
20 January 1981

Contents

List of Charts and Maps

Introduction

THE history of big business in India is the history of a few business families. Literary and religious sources refer to several merchants and traders who dominated the business scene in olden days. Our knowledge of business leadership in India after the end of the 16th century, however, is based on more secure foundation. The names of premier merchants in different parts of the country are frequently mentioned in the records of the European East India Companies which had extensive dealings with Indian traders. As the balance of trade between India and European countries was always favourable to the former and the European countries frowned upon the export of billion, the European companies operating in India had to knock at the *pedhis* of the indigenous bankers for help to facilitate their commercial activities. The reports that their officials in India sent back home refer to a number of prominent businessmen of the time and supplement the information gleaned from indigenous sources or, in some cases, constitute the only authentic basis of our knowledge.

For obvious reasons, most of these merchants lived in major urban centres. Virji Vora (1590-1760), his contemporary

Haji Zahid Beg and several others had their headquarters in Surat, the most important port in India then and a window towards the west. About the same time business magnates like Shantidas Zaveri and Vanmalidas Tapidas lived in Ahmedabad. Travadi Arjunji Krishnaji Nathji (1750-1822) operated from Varanasi for a long time and then moved to Surat for some mysterious reasons. The Jagatseth family was firmly entrenched in the 18th century in eastern India with their seat of power at Murshidabad, then the capital of the province, and the house of the Malayas located at Pulicat dominated the southern region of the country. With their enormous financial power, these families occupied leadership position in social field and also exercised significant influence on political developments in their respective regions. Urban leadership in India before the rise of the British power was, in many cases, co-terminous with business leadership.

For various reasons a large number of these families lost their prominence before the British rose to pre-eminence. Some others failed to cope with the rising challenge of the British at the end of the 18th century. The situation had undergone such a radical change by the beginning of the 19th century that the influence of the merchant princes, or whatever was left of them, on Indian business and social life had been considerably eroded. In fact it would be no exaggeration to say that the first half of the 19th century, or the period immediately preceding the rise of industrialization in India was an era of petty traders and money-lenders who operated in a limited area and at a modest scale. Admittedly, a few big merchants and bankers still retained a part of their past strength and glory, but they also found themselves incapable of or unwilling to face the challenge posed by a rising industrial leadership in the latter half of the century. And in most of the cases, the industrial leaders did not come from the families which had been in the forefront of commercial life. It is significant that just a few decades ago, most of the industrial families which dominate the private sector today, exercised very little influence on the commercial or industrial life of the country or in their respective regions.

The family of Kasturbhai Lalbhai is among the exceptions. It has occupied the centre of stage in the business and social horizon of Ahmedabad and Gujarat for well over three centuries and a half. The family can justifiably trace its descent from Shantidas Zaveri who was the dominant figure in the business and civic life of the city during his lifetime and whose successors continued to enjoy this enviable position up to the closing years of the 19th century. And when the main branch lost its lustre, the splinter, branch, from which the Lalbhais sprang succeeded to its pre-eminence which they still enjoy. Few families in the world can match such a long and almost uninterrupted record of business leadership.

On this ground alone, an investigation into the processes and stages of evolution of the business power of this family would have been justified. In attempting this work, however, we have been guided by a more important consideration. The number of historical enquiries in Indian business is woefully small. Preoccupied as the Indian historical scholarship has been with political developments or with the analysis of aggregate social and economic phenomenon, the need for empirical studies of businessmen and their activities has suffered a grievous neglect. All that we have by way of Indian business history are a few monographs dealing with lives of business leaders and their exploits. Not only that most of these works lack scholarly rigour and objectivity, together they cover only a fringe of the entire canvas. Consequently, empirical foundation for any meaningful generalization about the business dynamics in India has been and continues to be extremely shaky. After all the only way to comprehend the behaviour pattern of a society in any sphere is only through a longitudinal search, and such a search is possible, as Alexander Gerschenkron puts it, only through "a great deal of patient monographical research"[1] into its past. If the generalizations about Indian business behaviour are to transcend their *a priori* and somewhat speculative character, we can no longer dispense with the responsibility to produce a larger number of empirical studies in the antecedents and evolution of various business units or groups. The present work is an attempt in this direction.

It is the story of a business group which occupies a prominent place in India's industrial life today. Consisting of seven textile mills, a starch company, and one of the largest and most sophisticated chemicals and pharmaceutical complex in the country, the group, in the words of R.K. Hazari, is "one of the most reputable"[2] business houses in the country. The present position of this group is due, to a large extent, to the leadership of Kasturbhai Lalbhai who presided over its growth and expansion for well over six decades. His business power coupled with his demonstrated concerns for the society surrounding him won for him a place in the community life which may be the envy of many of his contemporaries. The accent of the present work is on the growth of these industrial enterprises and their social impact under Kasturbhai's leadership. With a view to providing an appropriate backdrop to our account, however, we have traced a brief history of the family, its commercial interests and social leadership, and its entry into industrial field before Kasturbhai came to the helm of affairs.

The history of a business house, essentially, is the study of a series of entrepreneurial decisions. And the character of an entrepreneurial decision is related to the ability of the leadership to perceive opportunities, appreciate their potential for gain, and exploit them subject to the constraints placed, or assistance offered, by the wider environment. Admittedly, the innovative uses of productive function, as the powerful voice of Joseph Schumpeter has rightly emphasized, is the most distinguishing feature of an entrepreneurial decision but its full import cannot be properly appreciated without analyzing the context in which a decision is taken. In fact, in the words of another major theorist, "the act of innovation *per se* is very often less significant historically than the structural and environmental aspects of these situations in which the innovational act takes place."[3]

It may be easy to imagine, but not so easy to define, what constitutes "environment" at any given point of time. For, the environment is an amalgam of a host of constantly changing and mutually interacting forces, visible as well as invisible. As such, at a given point of time diferent individuals may have different perceptions of environment. This is because even though certain elements in the environment, such as economic and political conditions, social values and ethos, and religious and cultural influences may be common, personal values and attitudes differ from individual to individual. These values, again, are in a state of perpetual flux, as they, in the life of a single individual, are conditioned by his family affiliation, nature and level of his education or lack of it, nature and level of his contact with the outside world, his own experiences, the impact of the activities of others on him and, a host of several other factors. The interaction of these influences, specific to an individual, with the common features of the socio-economic horizon constitute what we would like to call constellation of forces. The concept of constellation of forces, we must clarify, encompasses not only the forces external to an enterprise, but also those operating within an enterprise and within the individuals responsible for strategic decisions.

It is the constellation of forces that affects an individual's ability to perceive an opportunity, assemble relevant facilities and resources, and create an organization to exploit the perceived opportunity. The nature of the opportunity perceived, the method of assembling required resources, and the character of the organization created are also determined by the constellation of forces of an individual at a given point of time. These activities together, if related to an industrial venture of some significance, mark the beginning of a qualitatively new career on the part of the individual concerned, or in other words, result in what may be called entrepreneurial initiative. Entrepreneurial initiative, thus, is a successful attempt to lay a secure foundation for an industrial enterprise on the part of an individual in response to his constellation of forces.

The constellation of forces, however, is by no means static. Change in the national or international landscape may create new opportunities and the experience of having exploited the initial opportunity may bring about a qualitative change in an individual's confidence and in his own ability to enter new avenues of profit. This may lead the individual to build a superstructure of business based on the initial foundation. A business leader, thus, may not remain content with the first step; he may continue to consolidate and expand his activities through a series of critical decisions in response to the change in the constellation of forces. For the sake of conceptual clarity the series of subsequent successful responses to industrial opportunities may be called entrepreneurial continuum. In other words, entrepreneurial initiative and entrepreneurial continuum denote different stages in the career of a business leader. A historical account of a business group, therefore, is the study of entrepreneurial initiative and entrepreneurial continuum.

Undeniably, it is the profit potential, or the expectancy of reward, which is the primary motive force behind all major business decisions. However, the value system and the personal beliefs of the major decision-maker may detract him from exploiting an opportunity even if it is profitable, and his social conscience may induce him to commit a part of his resources to purposes which may have little direct bearing on the quantum of his profits. In fact, in supporting public causes and purposes he may not seek or expect any personal gain at all. In evaluating the success or the failure of a business group social purpose and concerns are very often ignored or receive but insufficient attention, but the fact is that profit and social responsibility—these two seemingly conflicting objectives—constitute two ends of the same spectrum. And a business group must be evaluated on both these criteria.

We have made this somewhat long detour into theoretical discussion because of rather underdeveloped state of the concept of business history in the country. Most of the existing works on the biographies of prominent business leaders or dealing with the evolution of business undertakings have been attempted by general writers; historical scholarship has kept more or less aloof from the field. We wish to use the insights of history and the rigours of historical method on the study of a business undertaking informed by a conceptual framework. A schematic presentation of our conceptual position, outlined above, is given on the following page.

While attempting to approach our subject with the insights that historical discipline provides, we are aware of the dangers which are supposedly inherent in studying a phenomenon too close to our times. Kasturbhai was amidst us almost till yesterday, and his accomplishments are a part of contemporary life. Would not we, a skeptic may justifiably argue, be carried away by our own passion and subjectivity in dealing with our subject matter? It is no occasion to enter into a debate about the role of personal biases in historical writings no matter how far removed in point of time the writer may be from his subject. Suffice it to say that detachment, as S. Gopal has pointed out, "is a mood born out of self discipline and not a matter of remoteness in time." With his experience in the

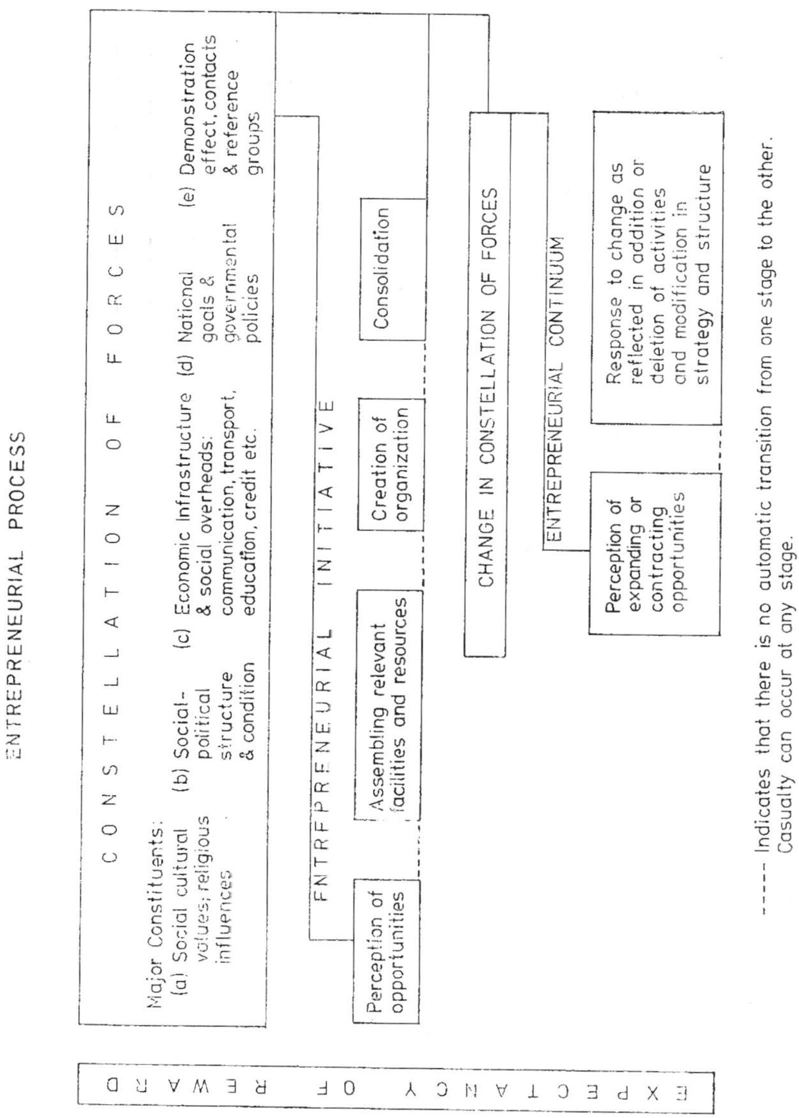
ENTREPRENEURIAL PROCESS
CONSTELLATION OF FORCES
Major Constituents:
(a) Social cultural values; religious influences
(b) Social-political structure & condition
(c) Economic Infrastructure & social overheads: communication, transport, education, credit etc.
(d) National goals & governmental policies
(e) Demonstration effect, contacts & reference groups
ENTREPRENEURIAL INITIATIVE
Perception of opportunities
Assembling relevant facilities and resources
Creation of organization
Consolidation
CHANGE IN CONSTELLATION OF FORCES
ENTREPRENEURIAL CONTINUUM
Perception of expanding or contracting opportunities
Response to change as reflected in addition or deletion of activities and modification in strategy and structure
EXPECTANCY OF REWARD
----- Indicates that there is no automatic transition from one stage to the other. Casualty can occur at any stage.

area of contemporary history he has also drawn our attention to some "positive advantages", including "abundance of oral testimony and participant observation",[4] in attempting a historical treatment of a contemporary theme.

There may be room for honest differences on whether these advantages offset the disadvantages in dealing with other aspects of contemporary life, but in writing the history of business organizations, these advantages clearly outweigh other considerations. Reasons behind some of the crucial business decisions are seldom committed to comprehensive documentation. Testimonies of main decision-makers, under such a situation, provide more than mere icing to the cake of historical writing; judiciously used they constitute the primary, and sometimes the only, source of our knowledge. Also most of the Indian business organizations have not been known for maintaining their records for a long time till the "detached" historian of a distant future would be ready to use them. Under these conditions it is necessary to use these records and gather additional insights into the affairs of a firm or group through interviews before it is too late. To let go the opportunity to present a comprehensive account of a historically significant phenomenon because of a somewhat puritanical approach to historical research is no real service to the discipline.

It is these considerations which led us to undertake this work much before Kasturbhai's unfortunate death on 20 January 1980. We were, therefore, fortunate to have the benefit of extensive interviews with him. The terminal point of our study, however, is 1976 because the business magnate had retired from the active leadership of his enterprises in early 1977. It was under his command that a predominantly commercial house became a prominent industrial group; it was due to his efforts that the leadership of the city reverted to the family; and it was his commitment to certain values that made him one of the most respected figures in the Indian business world. The society has a right to a comprehensive view of the factors which brought Kasturbhai and his family to this enviable position. Also at a time when we are engaged in augmenting the entrepreneurial resources of the country, a systematic study of the entrepreneurial ventures of one of the outstanding business leaders of our times should be of some practical value.

CHAPTER I

Farewell to Sand

KASTURBHAI Lalbhai belonged to a family of Oswal Jains. James Tod reckoned the Oswals among the "richest and most numerous of the eighty-four mercantile tribes of India."[5] According to the Jain traditions, the Oswals were originally Kshatriyas who got converted to Jainism in very ancient times. They are divided into two major groups. While those who claim their descent from the original converts are known as *Visa* Oswals, all others are called *Dasa* Oswals. Kasturbhai Lalbhai was a Visa Oswal.

The Oswal Jainism has taken its name from the place of its birth, Osian, where the original conversion is believed to have taken place. Osian is now a small railway station and tehsil headquarter in Rajasthan about 45 kilometres in the northwest of Jodhpur, but the Oswals claim that in ancient times it was a large and prominent city and the capital of Marwar. Older residents of the place still assert that several adjoining places situated 25 to 30 kilometres away from the present town were the suburbs of the metropolis. Given the primitive means of communication it is improbable that a city of such a size could develop then, but certain archaeological finds and the ruins of a huge lake are reminders of the antiquity and ancient glory of Osian.

The fact of the Osian conversion has been corroborated by certain Rajasthani literary sources. Gaurishankar Oza has cited an inscription, found on a pillar near a Jain temple in Osian, which refers to this event. The remnants of several Jain temples and monuments and the presence of a magnificent Jain shrine, said to be an ancient structure renovated in the latter half of the 19th century, seem to add credence to the belief of Oswal Jains that Osian was the birth place of their faith. We do not know when the original conversion took place. The Jain traditions would have us believe that it was around 500 B.C. that the conversion by a preacher of the king of the region along with his subjects marked the beginning of the Oswal Jainism.

The Kshatriya connection of the Oswals has never been questioned. This does not mean that they are in the direct line of the Vedic Kshatriyas. According to Tod they were Rajputs and most of the Oswals claim to have hailed from the Sisodias, Solankis, Parmars, and Bhatti clans of Rajasthan Rajputs. The origin of these clans, it has been conclusively established, "dates from the Shaka or Kushan invasion which began about the middle of the second century B.C. or more certainly from that of the white Huns who destroyed the Gupta empire about 480 A.D."[6] These invaders, who came in small numbers and did not have a great culture to boast of, got assimilated in the Hindu society. Being conquerors and rulers they identified themselves with the Kshatriyas who under the *Varnashrama* scheme were charged with martial functions. The Oswal affiliation with the ancient Kshatriyas, thus, is through a circuitous route.

If this is so, the Oswal Jainism cannot be as old as the traditions would have us believe. For, the sect itself could not have originated prior to the origin of the Rajput clans. In fact the early history of Kasturbhai's ancestors suggests that the Osian conversion took place much later. The family claims its descent from the Sisodia Rajputs, a branch of which occupied the throne of Mewar in the early years of the 8th century. The editor of the *Jain Rasmala* has testified to Kasturbhai's forefathers belonging to the "Kakola" branch of the Sisodias and having close ties of kinship with the Mewar Ranas. According to Tod and D.R. Bhandarkar, the Sisodias hailed from the

Huns or their kinsmen or their allies, who settled down in Saurashtra with their capital at Valabhiputra (the present Walai, ten miles from Bhavnagar, according to Tod). But after sometime, perhaps in the first half of the 6th century, the sack of Valabhiputra by a group of 'barbarians' forced them to leave Saurashtra and found a kingdom at Bhinmal about 75 kilometres in the northwest of Mount Abu in Rajasthan. A branch of the Bhinmal rulers later founded the kingdom of Mewar. According to the Jain tradition, the prince who led his people into Oswal Jainism belonged to the ruling family of Bhinmal. He had earlier carved out a principality for himself and developed Osian as his capital.

This gives credence to the claim of blood relationship between the Mewar rulers and Kasturbhai Lalbhai's ancestors. More importantly, this indicates that the birth of the Oswal sect cannot be placed earlier than the 6th century for, Kasturbhai Lalbhai's ancestors were among the original converts to Oswalism. Some archaeological evidences also support this hypothesis. The earliest specimens of the Jain temples at Osian were built not earlier than the 7th century and an inscription in the Jain Mahavir temple speaks of the shrine as existing in the time of Vatsaraja who reigned in the last quarter of the 8th century, though the temple in its present form is of much later date. All this goes to confirm the impression that the Oswal Jainism was born around the 7th or the 8th century. Most religious traditions tend to invest their faith with the dignity of much greater antiquity than historical facts would warrant. Oswal traditions are no exception.

Even though they embraced a new faith, the Rajput converts retained whatever they could of their pre-conversion customs and traditions. It is evident from the fact that the Oswals still retain the trappings of some of the old Rajput customs. But in essence, the conversion meant to these Rajputs the adoption of a new way of life. The occupational arrangements of the Hindu society were still, to a large extent, regulated by the *Varnashrama* scheme which assigned martial activities to the Kshatriyas, whereas non-violence was an article of faith with the new converts. Also Jainism, being a protest movement against the supremacy of the Brahmans, prevented the converts' upward mobility in the *Varnashrama* hierarchy. Consequently, they adopted agricultural and mercantile pursuits. It is by this process perhaps that Jainism gradually came to be dominated by commercial and business groups.

The new sect did not remain confined to Osian and its environs; it spread gradually to other parts of Rajasthan and India through migration and conversion. For the people of Marwar, the region in which the birth place of the Oswal Jainism was situated, the urge to migrate to other places must have been natural. A corruption of Maruwar (derived from Sanskrit *Marusthan* or desert land), the region bears the most appropriate name for, a large part of it comprises the great Indian desert which has never been known for a climate hospitable to human habitation. The river Luni, which virtually divides the region into two parts, is probably the only redeeming feature of a land dominated by a sandy and rocky monotony. The soil, particularly of the northern part where Osian is situated, is mostly infertile and unproductive. Frequent failure of rains must have added to the hardships of the people. A Marwari proverb, "expect one lean year in three, and one famine year in every five", still reminds us of the dreadful old days. Tod called Marwar "the region of death"[7] perhaps because of the sterility of the soil and the severity of the climate.

The children of the soil, perhaps, would have been less oppressed than was the British Officer by the rigours of the desert climate, and yet it is a fact that over the last several centuries, a large number of people gradually moved out of Marwar to settle elsewhere. The nature of the climate and the soil must have been prominent factors in migration. Many competent authorities, including Abul Fazl, have testified that whenever there was a famine in Marwar, the people moved to other places. Other factors which strengthened the migratory trends from time to time included unsettled political conditions, frequent wars and strifes, internecine quarrels, unjust laws, and tyrannical regimes. For, almost till the occupation of the region by the Mughals, these evils in varying degrees troubled the social and economic life of Marwar. Some people, of course, left their homeland only temporarily to return after the source of their transitory distress was eliminated. But a sizable number made a permanent break from their original homeland, though in most cases the break came in stages rather than abruptly.

It is not easy to determine with any degree of certitude the social and economic background of the Marwari migrants who settled elsewhere. It seems logical, however, to believe that the merchant classes were the most predominant. Most of these had trade and money-lending as their principal occupation. Some possessed a little land or took land on tenancy basis to carry on trade and agriculture simultaneously, but even for the cultivator merchants, the land was too infertile to create in them any great sense of attachment to it in view of the fact that agriculture was a less important source of livelihood for them. Thus, for most of the merchants, exploitable market was more important, and in a region with scanty population such a market was limited indeed. Natural calamities and manmade hardships shrank these markets still further. The decline of a city or trading centre intensified the desire on the part of its merchant community to explore commercially more attractive places. All these factors either individually or collectively lured the Marwari businessmen away from their region. The means of communications being what they were, the migrants found it difficult to return to their original homeland frequently. Thus, gradually they made new business centres their homes.

Of course, migratory urge was not limited to the people of Marwar alone. Merchants from other parts of Rajasthan, where conditions were not too dissimilar from those prevailing in Marwar, also left their homeland with the hope of improving their lot elsewhere. But the process was probably initiated by the Marwari merchants. This is suggested by the fact that today all people of Rajasthani descent engaged in any kind of business out of Rajasthan are known by the generic name of Marwari. It is possible that the earlier migrants attracted later groups out of Rajasthan by virtue of the ties of religion and kinship. And these groups developed a sense of affiliation with each other because of the strong attachment that the members of a minority group normally feel towards one another at a new place. The early explorers, thus, probably formed some sort of a resource group to mitigate, at least to some extent, the feeling of insecurity on the part of later migrants caused by unfamiliar, and in some cases, hostile environments.

There were two major directions in which the Rajasthani merchants went—in the east, and in the south and south-west.

In what direction did individuals or groups go depended on availability of trade routes, and their perception of profitable opportunities at the new place based on information from kinsmen, relatives, or friends who had preceded them there. Some merchants had developed close business connections in other parts of the country and these connections played a major role in their choice of a place of domicile.

We find the names of a large number of Oswal Jains among the Marwari migrants. There is no way to know when and under what circumstances did the process of migration from Osian begin. Perhaps it had something to do with the decline of the city. The monuments there indicate that the city was still flourishing in the 11th and the 12th centuries. Thereafter the decline seems to have set in, and with that the contraction in business opportunities. There must have been a time-lag between these developments and the merchants' decision to explore new opportunities and finally move to more tempting commercial centres. According to a recent study, Rajasthani migrant communities began to grow outside their homeland during the Mughal period. It is possible that the political unification achieved by the Mughals and comparatively greater safety in the movement of goods and people provided by their rule reinforced the migratory urge. This assumption would put the date of the Oswal migration not earlier than the latter half of the 16th century.

How many Oswals left their homeland so early is not known but the ancestors of Kasturbhai Lalbhai, as we shall see later, seem to have been among them.

II

Many vital facts about these ancestors are shrouded in mystery. Though it is clear from the above discussion that the family embraced Jainism in the 7th or the 8th century (at the time of the original conversion), the name of the person who led the family into the new faith would perhaps always remain unknown to history. Nor are we certain about when and under whose leadership did the family migrate out of Rajasthan, and what the actual circumstances were which made him decide to bid farewell to his homeland.

The *Jain Rasmala* provides some clues. It describes, among other things, the accomplishments of Sheth Shantidas, who as we shall see later, was among the most notable personalities in the history of the family. According to one version of the family genealogy given in the *Rasmala*, the earliest known member of the family was Padmasha (Padma Shah) and his son was Vachasha (or Vatsa Shah) whose son Sahasra Kiran (or Sesakaran) was Shantidas' father.

All accounts agree that Shantidas was born around 1590 in Gujarat. This means that the family could not have moved to Gujarat later than the last quarter of the 16th century. Nor could this event have taken place much earlier if we believe the traditions which credit Sahasra Kiran with having led the family to its new habitat. It is quite possible that Sahasra Kiran's decision to settle down in Gujarat was encouraged by and followed the acquisition of Rajasthan and Gujarat by Akbar and the establishment of tranquillity in the region which businessmen cherish so much.

If this is so, several generations must have elapsed between the 7th or the 8th century, when the family embraced Jainism, and the end of the 16th century when it emigrated out of its original habitat. Sahasra Kiran's choice of Gujarat for his future settlement had several justifications. Gujarat was one of the richest regions of India. It was probably the busiest centre of trade and commerce. Surat and Cambay, the main outlets for Indian exports, were among the best ports of India. The region had already developed sizable and influential business and mercantile communities and its several cities including the above port towns pulsated with environment conducive to profitable business activities.

In addition, considerable measure of cultural integration had already taken place between the land of Sahasra Kiran's birth and that of his adoption. Beginning with the end of the 9th century, when the Gurjara Prathiharas were at the zenith of their power, and almost up to the middle of the 13th century, when the Solanki power disintegrated both Gujarat and Southern Rajasthan, including Marwar, were under the control of the same imperial authorities. This encouraged interaction of various kinds between the two regions. Documentary evidences draw our attention to the business intercourse that existed between the two regions. Several Rajasthani bankers maintained their branches in Gujarat and vice versa. Marwari and Gujarati languages borrowed from each other to the advantages of both. These borrowings were so extensive that even today a large number of words are common in both the languages, and Mirabai, the celebrated poetess of the Bhakti cult, is claimed by both. Traces of cultural integration between the two regions can also be found in dress habits and folk culture of these two regions.

For a Jain, Gujarat was by no means a strange land. Much before the closing years of the 16th century, Jainism had made considerable headway in Gujarat. The Solanki rulers were great patrons of this faith, and one of the most prominent of them, Kumarpala, had probably himself embraced this religion. At any rate he offered various kinds of encouragement and protection to Jain monks and teachers and during his days "Gujarat became a stronghold of Jainism in respect of followers as well as institutions."[8] A large number of Jain temples and monuments found in Gujarat testify to this fact.

Geographical proximity and comparatively better means of communication between the two regions were yet other factors which could induce a Marwari businessman to migrate to Gujarat. Marwar region was connected with Gujarat through several trade routes. As the map on page 17 indicates, two major routes—one from Agra to Ahmedabad and the other from Multan to Ahmedabad—passed through Marwar. Some sort of a country road running between Pali on the Agra-Ahmedabad line and Jaisalmer on the Multan-Ahmedabad route joined the two. There were several by-roads to connect the interior of Marwar to the Pali-Jaisalmer road and through this to the two trunk lines. The inhabitants of Osian, Sahasra Kiran's place of birth, had access to both the major routes through two by-roads connecting the city to the Pali-Jaisalmer road—one to Phalodi, 30 kilometres away in the southwest and the other to Jodhpur—though the Osian-Jodhpur-Pali-Ahmedabad route was a much shorter distance.

III

Conceivably, Sahasra Kiran came to Gujarat by the shorter

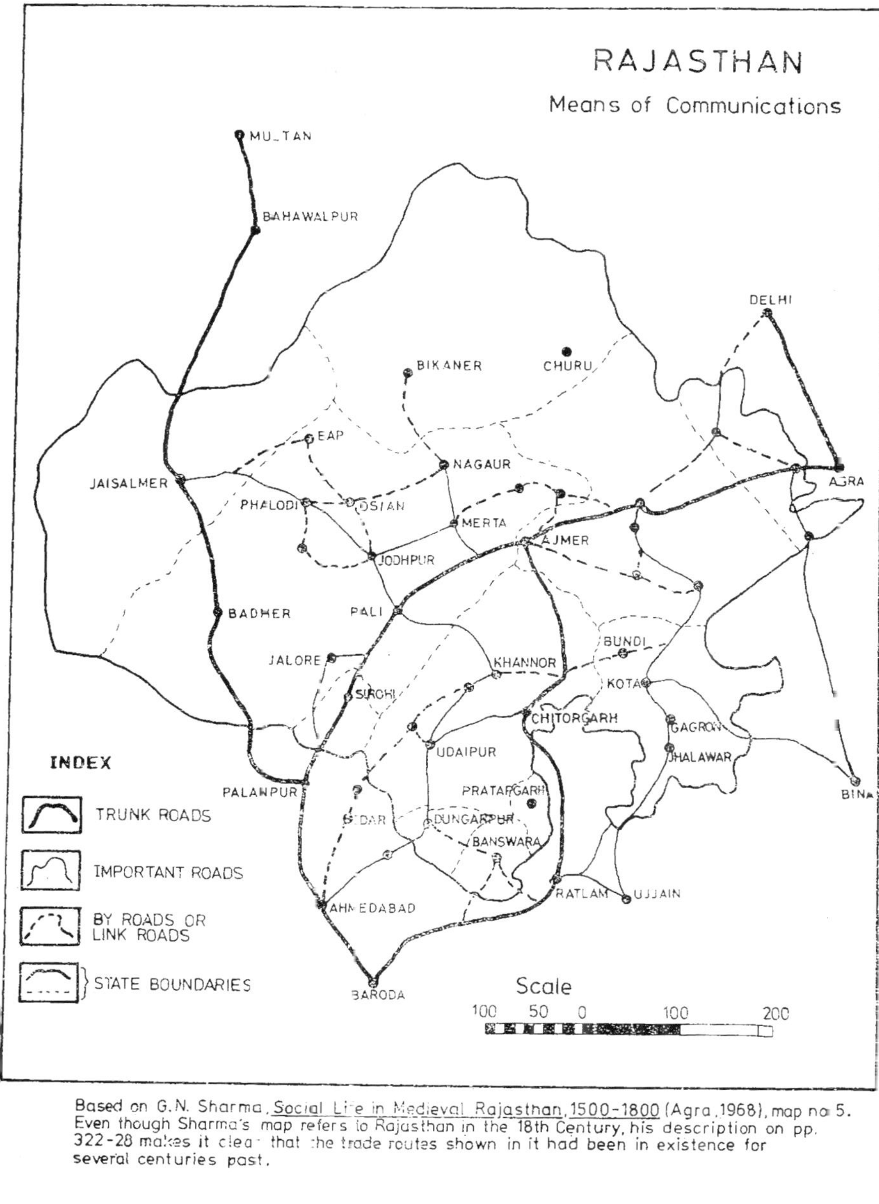

Based on G.N. Sharma, Social Life in Medieval Rajasthan, 1500-1800 (Agra, 1968), map no. 5. Even though Sharma's map refers to Rajasthan in the 18th Century, his description on pp. 322-28 makes it clear that the trade routes shown in it had been in existence for several centuries past.

route. It is also reasonably certain that he settled down at Ahmedabad. Like most Marwari emigrants, he was a man of modest means, but if the motive behind his leaving the arid desert was to better his fortunes, he could have hardly chosen a better place in Gujarat to settle down. For, Ahmedabad was a principal city not only in Gujarat but the whole of India, and probably the most important centre of trade and commerce in the country.

Founded in 1411, Ahmedabad then was less than two hundred years old in a country where several cities could boast of a much longer history. In Gujarat itself, Surat, Cambay, Anhilwara Patan, and Broach, to name only a few, could easily mock at the relative youth of Ahmedabad. But perhaps none could surpass it in beauty and grandeur. It is believed that Sultan Ahmad Shah, the founder of the city, wanted to recreate in his new capital the lost glory of Anhilwara Patan, for long the capital of the Solanki rulers of Gujarat, which in its heyday had few rivals in splendour. He spared no effort and grudged no expenditure to realize his dream, and his descendants continued to follow his example. They beautified the city with "imposing mosques, palaces, and market places", beautiful lakes and reservoirs, wide roads and streets, and strong fortifications and formidable gates.[9] So lavishly did they bestow their attention upon their new capital that before the middle of the 16th century, Ahmedabad had become a model for city builders. That its splendour and grandeur had an enduring quality is clear from the fact that the rule of the weak Sultans in the middle of the 16th century and the temporary transfer of capital to Champaner near Baroda had little adverse effect on the glory of Ahmedabad.

Eye witness accounts bear this out. Portuguese traveller Barbosa who visited Gujarat after the Sultans had moved to Champaner found Ahmedabad "rich and well supplied".[10] Abul Fazl, Akbar's celebrated courtier, found Ahmedabad to be a "noble city in the high state of prosperity which for the pleasantness of its climate and display of its choicest productions of the whole globe . . . is almost unrivalled . . . ."[11] The author of *Haft-Iqlim*, a Persian work of the early 17th century, expressed similar views. According to him "Ahmedabad is unique in India in the matter of neatness and flourishing condition, and is superior to other cities in the excellence of its monuments. It would be no exaggeration to say that in the whole of the world there exists no town so grand and beautiful . . . . Its shops with two or three storeys each are finely built, and its inhabitants, both men and women, are graceful. . . ."[12]

The authors of *Ain-i-Akbari* and *Haft-Iqlim* had little acquaintance with principal urban centres in the world and they could have been legitimately partial to the beauty of a place which was regarded as a centre of Islamic culture. But the accounts of more unbiased observers, and more conversant with several other parts of the world, free these writers from the odium of partiality. The foreign travellers, who visited Ahmedabad roughly about the time when the above two treatises were written, were full of praise for the beauty and grandeur of the city. John Jourdain, an Englishman who visited the city in 1611, characterized it as "one of the fairest cities in all the Indies both for building and strength as also for beauty and situated in a pleasant soil. . . ."[13] In the same year another Englishman, William Finch, found Ahmedabad a "goodly city, [with] buildings comparable to any city in Asia or Africa, the streets large and well paved. . . ."[14] Four years later Ahmedabad impressed Nicholas Downton as a "great and populous city, the metropolis of all these parts of Gujarat, famous for nobility and gentry. . . ."[15]

Ahmedabad was also a large and populous city. With a circumference of about twenty miles and a population of about 200,000, it was one of the biggest cities not only in India but also in the world. The city had as many as 84 wards and 1000 mosques when Abul Fazl visited it, and Nicholas Withington found it nearly "as big as London" in 1613.[16] Other travellers who came a little later found that the city was "completely large with great suburbs"[17] and that it had as many as 25 great towns under its jurisdiction. In many respects, it surpassed the great imperial cities of Delhi and Agra.

Apart from the grandeur and size, Ahmedabad had other more important attractions for a merchant. Starting as an administrative and military headquarters of the province, it had by the end of the 16th century become a great manufacturing and commercial centre. It was famous for its cotton, silken, and a variety of woollen goods. Its gold and silver brocades were in great demand in India as well as abroad, and the gold and silver jewelleries made by its craftsmen were among the best specimens of manual dexterity. Other flourishing industries included dyeing and bleaching, embroidery and needle work, and inlaying of precious stones. One of the principal commodities of the Ahmedabad market was indigo, and the town of Sarkhej (now a suburb of Ahmedabad) was a major centre of indigo trade in the country. The Sarkhej indigo was so much valued by the foreigners that an English traveller in the beginning of the 17th century strongly recommended the appointment of "four or five factors"[18] at Ahmedabad to facilitate the purchase of this coveted commodity. Another article which was in great demand at home as well as abroad was saltpetre, an indispensable ingredient of gun-powder. Ahmedabad supplied plenty of it.

As a centre of trade and commerce, both inland and foreign, Ahmedabad had few rivals. Major trade routes connected it with other major inland commercial cities like Multan in the north and Agra in the east, and with principal port towns like Cambay in the west and Surat in the south. In fact, it was connected by direct trade routes with every part of the country. As a consequence, the capital city of Gujarat gradually emerged as an emporium of goods from various parts of India and the world. The result was that "there is not in a manner in any nation nor merchandise in all Asia which may not be had in Ahmedabad. . . "[19] and it was well on its way to becoming "a general confluence of most nations in the world, English, Dutch, Portuguese, Jews, Armenians, Medes, and Persians, Turks, and Tartarians. . . ."[20] Thus, the city distributed not only its own productions and those of other parts of Gujarat, but also the goods produced in far-off regions like Sind, Kashmir, Bengal, and Malabar coast, and to a certain degree, the imports from the countries of Asia and Europe. In 1611, William Finch found that as many as two hundred coaches "richly laden with merchandise"[21] used to leave for Cambay, the nearest port, every ten days. Other writers, too, have referred to the extensive trading activities in the city.

All this made Ahmedabad an enormously prosperous place by contemporary standards. According to Abul Fazl, the city yielded an annual revenue of about 600 thousand rupees which was about 12 per cent of the total revenue of the province of Gujarat. Significantly enough, the revenue from Surat, the principal port in India then, was less than 150 thousand rupees. It is no surprise, therefore, that the city could boast of a rich and variegated mercantile class with large quantities of capital.

In short, Ahmedabad in the last quarter of the 16th century possessed everything which would attract a merchant interested in materially profitable pursuits. Throughout its brief history, its rulers had offered various kinds of encouragement to the merchants and traders to settle down in the city. More importantly, it was still a fast growing city; no other city in Gujarat was growing as rapidly so much so that by the end of the next century, its circumference would increase by more than 50 per cent and its population would be doubled. And with its physical growth, the business opportunities in the city were bound to grow.

Sahasra Kiran could not have asked for a better compensation for having bid farewell to the sandy land of his forefathers.

CHAPTER II

The Heir to a Heritage

SAHASRA Kiran's decision to make Ahmedabad his home must have been influenced by its commercial importance. But mere logic is seldom the sole determinant of human choices, and it is quite possible that certain purely fortuitous circumstances justified his perference for the city. At least the traditional Jain sources make us believe that it was so. According to these, the Marwari emigrant was very young, about 19 or 20 years of age, when he arrived in Ahmedabad. Looking for the source of livelihood, he stumbled into the shop of a jeweller or *Jauhari* who also hailed from Marwar. The jeweller appointed the immigrant as an all-purpose assistant. The assistant was young and energetic. More importantly, he displayed an uncanny knack of business situations, intuitive insight into the market conditions, and remarkable understanding of commercial details. Above all, he impressed his master by his unquestionable integrity. Consequently, the jeweller slowly and gradually inducted Sahasra Kiran into the highly specialized jewellery business. Soon the apprentice became an expert.

This must have relieved the Marwari sheth from some of his responsibilities, but more significantly, it solved the problem of an heir for the sonless businessman. The jeweller married off his only daughter to Sahasra Kiran and bequeathed his entire assets and liabilities to his daughter and son-in-law. We have no way to determine the historicity of this account, but the instances of matrimony changing the fortunes of a family are not uncommon. Ahmedabad jewellery works enjoyed a great reputation for the quality of the materials and dexterity of designs and were in great demand in the royal and noble families. It is not unlikely that Sahasra Kiran rode the road to prosperity on the coattails of a fellow Marwari who had preceded him to the land of opportunity. He adopted not only his mentor's occupation but also the last name "Zaveri" or "Jauhari" indicative of the profession of a jeweller.

This story of Sahasra Kiran's apprenticeship and consequent acquisition of wealth sounds credible as it conforms to the stories of the rise of many a Marwari family. But there is yet another tradition, perhaps more popular, which assigns a little later date for the beginning of the family prosperity and attributes it to non-temporal designs. According to it, Sahasra Kiran's son, Shantidas, was endowed by sheer accident with miraculous powers of the *Chintamani Mantra* through the spiritual endeavours of a great Jain monk. Aided by the *mantra*, Shantidas displayed remarkable qualities as a jeweller and won the favour of the Mughal emperors whose patronage turned the fortunes of the family.

The modern mind will surely be skeptical of the supernatural explanation of Shantidas's wealth. Some aspects of this story, however, do have historical basis. It is a fact that the name of Sahasra Kiran's son was Shantidas and it is the latter who, by all accounts, was the real founder of the family fortunes. A series of *farmans* or royal charters issued by the Mughal emperors testify to the esteem and honour in which he was held in the imperial court. Jehangir offered royal protection to him and Shah Jahan instructed his officials to ensure that neither the material interest of Shantidas were to be jeopardized nor his religious susceptibilities offended in any way. The imperial bureaucracy was to facilitate the work of his business agents at various ports and offer them safe conduct throughout the territories under their jurisdiction. The royal servants in Ahmedabad were ordered to show respect and deference to the Jain merchant, protect his property from infringement, ensure its bequest to his heirs after his death, and help him collect his dues from his debtors. One of Shah Jahan's *farmans* of 1635-36 indicates that either he or his predecessor had granted properties to Shantidas in Ahmedabad including houses, shops, *havelis* (mansions) and gardens. Another order refers to the grant in perpetuity of the entire Sankheswar village near Radhanpur for the paltry sum of Rs. 1,050 in annual revenue. Shah Jahan went to the extent of conferring a rich robe of honour on Shantidas as a token of his patronage in 1656. There is no independent evidence to support the claim made in the Jain traditions that the Rajput mother of Emperor Jehangir, regarded the great jeweller as her brother and, therefore, the Emperor treated the Jain as his maternal uncle, but there is no doubt that the Mughal court did extend to Shantidas great respect and consideration. In the records of the East India Company he is described as the "chief *bania*"[22] and very powerful at the court.

Both Jehangir and Shah Jahan followed in the footsteps of their illustrious predecessor, Akbar, in adopting a policy of catholicity and tolerance towards the Jain faith. The Jains enjoyed complete freedom of worship throughout the empire and Jain monks were honoured by these emperors in various ways. The Mughal attitude to Shantidas, however, had very little to do with his religious affiliation. He seems to have developed his influence in the imperial court as a result of his great and unfailing skill in judging the quality of precious jewels. Jehangir's *farman* of 1622 has added the word "Zaveri"[23] with Shantidas' name indicating his association with the business of jewels, and an English document of 1627, the year of Jehangir's death, refers to him as "the deceased king's jeweller."[24] The rulers, nobles, and courtiers, in those days were excessively fond of precious jewels and dealers in these commodities were greatly in demand. Shantidas seems to have developed an unassailable position in this line and built up a reputation for integrity and fair business dealings so much so that even when he occasionally supplied goods which offered less than entire satisfaction to his royal customers, they voiced only a feeble remonstrance, as Shah Jahan did in 1656 when he found the quality of the jewels supplied to him rather inferior.

Shantidas, on his part, continued to cement his relations with the imperial court by regular supplies of expensive gifts.

The success of Shantidas' jewellery business was largely due to the way in which he organized it. He normally acquired his commodities in the regions and places in which they could be had at competitive prices. For this purpose he deputed his agents or *gumashtas* in far-off places. There was hardly any prominent port in Gujarat where his agents were not active. The ability to judge the quality of the goods is of decisive significance in this kind of business and Shantidas was endowed with this in full measure. Perhaps he was a good judge of men also which helped him select competent persons to help him. Most probably his brother Vardhaman, whose name is mentioned in at least one Mughal *farman*, assisted him in his business.

Jewellery was not the only line in which Shantidas was interested though this, without question, was the sheetanchor of his prosperity. The days of business specialization were still far-off, and an enterprising businessman could deal in several profitable activities simultaneously. He could be a general merchant buying and selling a variety of goods. At the same time, he could perform the role of a banker and earn considerable profit by way of interest or through commission by exchanging one kind of currency into another, or by issuing *hundies* or drafts to facilitate the remittance of money to far-off places. The rate of interest was usually high—between 12 to 18 per cent—and money-lending was always a great source of wealth. This line of business received a great fillip as a result of the operations of the European companies in India as they were usually short of purchasing power and almost perpetually dependent on the Indian merchants for help. The latter always extended their generosity as long as they were assured of liberal interest. The activities of the European companies created a new class of businessmen known as brokers. Unfamiliar with the ways and customs of the land, the Europeans had to depend on the guidance of Indians in their business dealings. Each European establishment, therefore, appointed an Indian merchant as its broker to perform a variety of functions. The broker advised his patrons about the state of markets, acted as an intermediary between the European and Indian businessmen, helped the former to circumvent governmental regulations, and take care of a host of sundry matters. The broker was "an essential factor for European trade to operate and thrive in India".[25]

We do not have much evidence to suggest that Shantidas took any interest in general trading activities. Perhaps his trading was limited to jewellery alone. But he did act as a broker and banker. In a document of the English East India Company of 1636, he is referred to as the "Governor's broker".[26] Perhaps the Mughal governor could easily trust someone who was so close to the imperial court. Whether Shantidas performed any service to any of the European companies as a broker is doubtful, but he frequently did come to their rescue when they were short of funds. In 1628, for instance, the agent of the English East India Company borrowed Rs. 10,000 from him at an interest of 12 per cent per annum. These, however, did not represent the principal lines of Shantidas' business, and there were others who were far ahead of him in these fields—Virji Vora, Hari Vaishya, Mohandas Parekh, and Haji Zahid Beg in Surat; Surjit Naik at Sarkhej; and Mahidas Surjit, Hardev Pande, Balchand, and Sinha Shah at Ahmedabad. It was in the jewellery business that Shantidas reigned supreme, and none of his contemporaries could ever pose a threat to him in this field.

Whatever his source of profit, Shantidas had surely amassed a considerable fortune by the end of the second decade of the 17th century. He had acquired by this time huge immovable properties consisting of *havelis*, shops and gardens in the present Saraspur area of Ahmedabad, some of which had been received as grants from the Mughal emperors. In this area he built a gigantic Jain temple. The Chintamani Temple, as it came to be known, was an imposing structure made of marble whose walls and ceilings were inlaid with the pieces of *akik*, a special variety of stone found near Cambay. Behind huge and high walls were several big quadrangles with impressive corridors around them. In the front were two huge statues of elephants which seemed to guard the entrance to virtue. By all accounts it was a magnificent specimen of temple architecture, "without dispute one of the noblest structures"[27] to quote a German traveller, J. Albert de Mandelslo, who visited Gujarat in 1638.

Shantidas' services to Jainism increased as the business expanded and the profits swelled. It was largely due to his influence in the imperial court that Shah Jahan confirmed in 1630 the rights of the Jains over the ancient shrines on the Shatrunjaya Hills near Bhavnagar, at Sankheshwar near Palanpur, and the celebrated Keshariyaji temple near Udaipur in Rajasthan. He is also known to have maintained *pinjarapoles* or veterinary hospitals in different parts of Gujarat—in Surat, Cambay, and Radhanpur.

Shantidas' religious endeavours received a setback when Aurangzeb came to Ahmedabad as the governor or *subedar* of Gujarat. Being a bigot, he could not tolerate that the most imposing building of the city should be a Jain temple—the one that Shantidas had built about two decades ago. On Aurangzeb's orders the Chintamani temple was converted into a Muslim mosque. The aggrieved Jeweller represented to Shah Jahan directly on whose orders the sacred property was returned to its builder along with "the complete restitution for the damage"[28] done to it. The order, however, could not undo the consequences of Aurangzeb's bigotry because orthodox Jain monks would not permit the use of the building as a Jain shrine once it had been defiled. But the message of Shah Jahan's gesture was unmistakable. The Jeweller had sufficient leverage with the Emperor to have the prince overruled. Shah Jahan's order was almost unprecedented in the history of Islam. He was a more strict and less tolerant Sunni Muslim than Jehangir and his decision was clearly against the popular interpretation of the laws of orthodox Islam. The basis of his decision that the construction of a mosque on somebody else's property was illegal was somewhat specious and would have done little to assuage the feelings of his more orthodox and less tolerant son. But Shah Jahan could not afford to displease the Sheth who had helped the empire with large loans in the hour of need. It is said that Shantidas had contributed a great deal towards financing Shah Jahan's invasion of Quandhar and the Jeweller had secured some of the choicest pieces for his jewel-studded Peacock throne.

The Chintamani temple episode, however, shook Shantidas' trust in imperial assurances as contained in Shah Jahan's proclamations that purity of the Jain shrines in Gujarat would be respected by his representatives and successors. It was perhaps because of this consideration that the Jeweller decided to bring the temples at Shankheshwar and the Shatrunjaya Hills under his firmer control. He obtained a long-term lease of the entire village of Shankheshwar, secured the village of Palitana as an award or *inam*, and purchased for rupees two lakhs the whole of the Shatrunjaya Hills. At the same time, he continued to acquire properties of temporal character either through royal grants or purchase. Among such properties was a tract of land comprising thirty *bighas* in Asarva village (now a part of Ahmedabad) which Shah Jahan had given in gift, and a grand mansion which the Jeweller had bought for Rs. 6,000—the highest price anybody was willing to pay. There is no evidence to suggest that these acquisitions were motivated by the desire to promote business in real estate in a big way, but he is known to have given several buildings on rent. On several occasions, Shah Jahan instructed his officials in Ahmedabad to help the Jeweller in collecting his rent from defaulting tenants.

The imperial patronage and support was one of the crucial factors in Shantidas' business success. He must have trembled, therefore, at the success of Aurangzeb, the third son of Shah Jahan, in the war of succession among his four sons following the Emperor's seemingly incurable illness in 1656. The Jeweller had associated himself rather too closely with the deposed Emperor who had been put in prison. It was not long ago that Aurangzeb, as the Governor of Gujarat, had suffered discomfiture because of Shantidas' influence on his father. And to make the matter worse, the Jeweller's "brothers and sons"[29] had loaned a sum of Rs. 5,50,000 to Murad Baksh—the youngest prince who was then the governor of Gujarat—in his bid to capture the imperial throne for himself. To placate the new Emperor, therefore, the Jeweller visited his court and was pleasantly surprised to find that his fears were unfounded.

Auranzeb showed as much civility and courtesy to him as the Jeweller had been used to in the courts of his predecessors, and honoured him with "an award and a robe".[30] More importantly, it was through him, "the best among campeers", that the new Emperor, still in search of legitimacy, conveyed his assurances of "conciliation and consolation", to "all merchant *mahajans*, common inhabitants, and general residents"[31] of the Ahmedabad region. He also took the rather unusual step of ordering an immediate payment of one lakh of rupees towards settling Murad's debt to the Jeweller without any verification of the Jeweller's claim so that "he may carry on his business and profit by it."[32] The remaining amount was to be paid after verification. The "highest officers" of Ahmedabad were instructed to consider Shantidas as "the old servant of the court . . . and to discharge the obligations of good dealings and kind treatment [towards him and] help him in his financial affairs."[33] It is obvious that whatever might have been Aurangzeb's animosity towards the heretic businessman in the past, in his new capacity, the former needed to cultivate the latter as much as the latter needed to befriend the former.

The new Emperor displayed a conciliatory attitude towards Shantidas' religion also. Barely a week after his first accession he issued a *farman* which reconfirmed the grant of Palitana *pargana* to the Jeweller and his descendants. Less than two years later, Shantidas received another order granting him again the village, the hills, and the temples of Palitana. Why this second confirmation was necessary is not clear, but it is possible that the Emperor after his formal coronation thought it necessary to repeat an order issued at a time when his own legal position as an emperor was not beyond doubt. This *farman* also gave the hill and temples of Girnar and Abuji to the Jeweller in perpetual grant.

All this indicates how keen Aurangzeb was to placate the Jeweller and keep him on his side. It was not Shantidas' money alone which made the Emperor suppress his past hostility towards the Jain merchant, though Aurangzeb needed money. There were several other merchants in Ahmedabad to whom the Emperor could turn in need. After all, the Jeweller's relatives had contributed only a little more than ten per cent of the loan which Murad had raised to equip his army for the succession battles. Though none in Ahmedabad individually surpassed Shantidas' wealth, there were merchants in other parts of the province whose resources equalled and in some cases even surpassed Shantidas'. The financial resources of Virji Vora of Surat were definitely greater than the Ahmedabad Jeweller's. Aurangzeb, thus, did not entirely have to depend on the Ahmedabad merchant. Nor could Shantidas' past loyalties and services to the empire have been a sufficient basis for the claim of Aurangzeb's support. For, the new incumbent to the Mughal throne was no respector of sentimental ties.

What perhaps was crucial in bringing the new emperor and the old merchant closer was the latter's social position and prestige in the religious and commercial circles of the province. Because of his services to his religion, Shantidas had by then come to be regarded as the secular head of the Jain community not only in Ahmedabad but the whole of Gujarat and perhaps even beyond. But his influence was by no means limited to the Jain community. He had, in fact, become a leader of the whole population of the city. The fact that Aurangzeb chose Shantidas to bring the message of conciliation to the city population after winning the throne for himself is indicative of the Jeweller's unique position. His influence and riches had definitely made him the unofficial spokesman of the city as a whole.

II

It is popularly believed that Shantidas had been conferred the title of Nagarsheth by Jehangir, but the claim can hardly stand historical scrutiny. Had it been so, there would have been a *farman* to support it, but Shantidas is nowhere mentioned as Nagarsheth in any contemporary record. The fact is that during the lifetime of Shantidas, the position was still evolving itself. For, no city in Gujarat is known to have had a Nagarsheth then. Even though *mahajans* or trade guilds representing various crafts or occupations, each headed by a *shresthin* or *sheth*, had existed in cities of Gujarat for a long time, there is no evidence to suggest that any city prior to 1660 had a Nagarsheth who could speak for the entire city. Occasionally, a prominent and wealthy head of an individual *mahajan* performed this role, as Virji Vora did in Surat, but the Nagarsheth was yet to emerge as a formal and distinct position in the management structure of the city.

The process of formalization seems to have started around the middle of the 17th century in Ahmedabad. The city was still fairly young and its urban institutions were still evolving. As the city grew in size, its commercial population became more heterogeneous and its business life more complex. This might have created the need to establish some link between the individual *mahajans* to attend to the matters cutting across them. As in the case of Surat, Shantidas, as the wealthiest and by far the most influential merchant, provided such a link which invested him with a position of informal leadership.

The earliest mention of a Nagarsheth in Ahmedabad is in a sale deed of 1660 where it has been added to the name of one Sundardas. By this time Shantidas had died. Sundardas was Shantidas' brother who survived him; the other brother Vardhaman had predeceased the better known member of the family. It is possible that Shantidas' powerful personality had prevented Sundardas from making any mark on the life of the city during the former's lifetime. In search of some impressive prop to symbolize his rise to the position left vacant by his illustrious brother, Sundardas might have adopted this title. It is also possible that the family feud, which had started during the lifetime of the Jain magnate, led Sundardas to assume this title to denote the supremacy of his line against the direct descendants of his deceased brother. Significantly, none of Shantidas' five sons have ever been referred to as Nagarsheth in any contemporary record. As we shall see later, it is only after a generation, during the time of Shantidas' grandson, Khushalchand, that the position got stabilized. The *Mirat-i-Ahmadi*, which has seldom mentioned the name of Khushalchand without prefixing Nagarsheth with it, has never used this title for Shantidas or his son Lakshmichand, or for that matter, anyone else antedating Khushalchand. Obviously, the position of Nagarsheth was not an official creation nor was it a part of the Mughal bureaucratic structure. The Mughal emperors could appoint their own officials or confer titles of decoration on non-officials. They could not have conferred a title which came to denote in due course the leadership of the city. And no official fiat could create such a position or interfere with the selection of an incumbent when the position itself was still in an embryonic stage.

There is no denying the fact, however, that Shantidas commanded great influence and prestige in the community. It was because of the power of his wealth and influence that he, like Virji Vora in Surat, acted as an intermediary between the government and the city merchants even without occupying any formal position except the headship of the jewellers' *mahajan*.

It is quite possible that the recognition of his successors as Nagarsheths after the position became an integral part of the urban institutions of Ahmedabad in later years was a mere formalization of the informal role that Shantidas played in the civic affairs in his lifetime.

The great Jeweller, thus, had an eventful and successful career. According to traditional Jain sources, Shantidas died in 1659. More reliable sources support this for, the last Mughal *farman* issued for Shantidas, probably posthumously, bears the date of 12 March 1660. Though the son of an immigrant into Ahmedabad, he had fully integrated himself with the culture of the city and left behind a family which identified itself with the life and culture of Gujarat rather than Marwar. In fact, Shantidas and his descendants identified themselves with Gujarat so closely that their Marwari connection was all but forgotten. And this identification with their new habitat was not an insignificant factor in their rise to supremacy.

III

According to the *Jain Rasmala*, Sheth Shantidas had five sons: Panaji, Ratanji, Lakshmichand, Manekchand, and Hemchand. Of these, Panaji, Lakshmichand, and Manekchand have been mentioned in contemporary records. Panaji predeceased his father but the other four sons, it seems, had taken over, or at least started sharing, the management of the business towards the close of Santidas' life. Murad's as well as Aurangzeb's *farmans* clearly inform us that it was Manekchand and his brothers, and not Shantidas directly, who had loaned the campaign money to Murad to fight for succession. There is no doubt, however, that the advice of the patriarch continued to be available to the sons. Also the old Jeweller did not hesitate to interrupt the placidity of his retirement during times of crisis. Aurangzeb's order to repay at least a part of the money Murad had borrowed from the Sheth's sons was issued after Shantidas' personal visit to the new incumbent to the Mughal throne.

Murad's and Aurangzeb's early *farmans* do not mention by name any of Shantidas' sons except Manekchand; others have been referred to as "his brothers."[34] It is possible that initially it was Manekchand who, though younger, had an upper hand in the management of family affairs. If this was so, Manekchand's supremacy was short-lived for, in the very first year of his reign Aurangzeb issued a *farman* asking his officers in Gujarat to help Lakshmichand recover his loans from some defaulters. Also we do not find the mention of Manekchand in any other contemporary record. According to a later document the descendants of Manekchand were living in Surat in the 19th century. It is quite possible that Manekchand himself had settled down in Surat either because an efficient management of the business in the port city demanded personal supervision of one of the brothers, or because his absence from Ahmedabad was considered to be a convenient solution of the possible differences between the two brothers.

Whatever may have been the case, the mantle of Shantidas eventually fell on Lakshmichand. Our knowledge of the state of business under him is scanty. Most likely it flourished, as he continued to enjoy the imperial patronage. Money-lending and trading, particularly in jewelleries, remained the mainstay of the business, and Shantidas' successor continued to be the head of the jewellers' *mahajan* and perhaps the principal merchant of the city. According to some sources, he sided with Muazzam in the struggle for the Mughal throne among Aurangzeb's sons following the Emperor's death. Naturally, therefore, during the reign of Bahadurshah—or Shah Alam I, the name adopted by the Prince on ascending the imperial throne—Lakshmichand could depend on imperial favours and consequent benefits.

After Bahadurshah's death in 1712, there was again a struggle for succession among his sons, and again the Ahmedabad Sheth is said to have sided with the winner—Jahandar Shah. The new Emperor, however, disgraced his position and was removed and slain by his nephew Farrukhsiyar barely ten months after assuming power. Farrukhsiyar's principal supporters in his bid for the throne—Hussain Ali and Abdullah Khan or the Saiyyad Brothers, as they are known to history—were assisted by Lakshmichand's money in raising the army and provisions for the succession battle.

During Lakshmichand's time or sometime before Shantidas' death, the family seems to have shifted its residence from Saraspur to Jhaverivada. We may recall that it was in Saraspur, situated out of the city wall, that Shantidas owned shops and properties, had some land gifted to him from the Mughals and built his famous Chintamani Temple. Obviously, his residence would not have been far removed from these properties. Later, as a result of the growing volume of business and with the growing social eminence of the family, it might have been considered necessary to move to a more appropriate location. The new residence was very close to the Bhadra Fort, the seat of the provincial administration, and situated within the city walls, Jhaverivada was a much safer place to live. To strengthen their security, the Sheths also employed armed retainers to guard their residence.

It is quite possible that the name Jhaverivada given to the locality was due to the famous Jhaveri family having made it its home. But Shantidas' successors were not the only prominent jewellers living there. Others such as Padam Gopal and Kapurchand Bhansali also had their *havelis* in Jhaverivada and they too possessed sufficient wealth and social position to justify having status symbols such as keeping their own armed soldiers for protection. Doubtlessly, merchants belonging to other communities lived in the ward occupied by the Sheths.

Whatever might have been the attitude of these merchants towards Shantidas, they, it seems, began to challenge the supremacy of his successors in the city's business and social life soon after the Jain magnate's death. For, some sale deeds of the period refer to one Vanmalidas Tapidas and his son, Kika, as Nagarsheths. It is also significant that following a communal riot in 1714 in the city, it was Kapurchand Bhansali and not any of Shantidas' successors, who went to the imperial court to explain the Hindu side of the situation. Bhansali was a leading citizen of Ahmedabad and according to *Mirat-i-Ahmadi*, the Nagarsheth in 1720 when he was killed as a result of a conspiracy hatched by the deputy governor of the province who resented Bhansali's eminence. The Nagarshethship had yet to develop around itself any specific function, authority, or privilege. Perhaps it signified no more than an informal supremacy in the civic life. Perhaps it came to be associated with a person or persons who acquired considerable social influence as a result of his riches, munificence, and charities, and demonstrated concern for the welfare of the city and its people. Bhansali's charities might have earned the unique distinction for him for, he is known to have built several *pinjarapoles*.

The battle for the title continued during the days of Lakshmichand's son and successor—Sheth Khushalchand. We do not know for sure when he came to the helm of affairs, but he had certainly become a force in the business and social life of the city before 1725. By that time the Saiyyad Brothers, who since the death of Bahadur Shah I had made and unmade emperors as a child does a toy house, had been removed from the scene, and Muhammad Shah, whose rule lasted up to 1748, had come to occupy the imperial throne. The empire, however, was definitely on the downhill road. In the wake of the constantly weakening central authority, the provincial officials were indulging in intrigues and conspiracies against one another. What is worse, the dark clouds of the Maratha power, whom Aurangzeb despite all his deficiencies had kept at bay, were gathering strength in the western part of the empire.

The Maratha raids on Gujarat cities started in 1706. After 1719 the invaders came almost every year. They posed one of the most serious threats to the Mughal power in the province in December 1724. The Marathas advanced into north Gujarat, defeated and killed several imperial officers including the deputy governor, and overran the cities of Cambay and Ahmedabad. By the middle of February, the Maratha forces were definitely in command of the situation; their forces were spread in every nook and corner of the capital city like "swarms of ants and locusts."[35] Their presence created great deal of consternation among the people, and business came to a standstill. The city would have definitely been sacked by the needy invaders but for the timely action of Khushalchand who paid a huge amount to the invaders from his personal pocket to save the city from destruction.

Khushalchand's gracious and generous act won for him the gratitude of the city population, specially of the business class which was the hardest hit by the Maratha presence. As mentioned before the business life of the city was dominated by a number of trade guilds, known as the *mahajans*, each one representing a particular trade or craft. Following the departure of the Maratha forces, the heads of "all the Mahajans of the city of Ahmedabad",[36] representing all trades and crafts and various castes and communities—both Indian and foreign—decided upon a novel method to express their gratitude to the Sheth for his noble act. They resolved that henceforward Khushalchand and his descendants would receive in perpetuity a small part of the amount collected as town duties on goods entering the city. This was a great compensation indeed. More importantly, it was a great recognition, because the *mahajans*' action virtually amounted to acknowledging the Jain Sheth's supremacy in the civic affairs. Significantly enough, the first mention of Khushalchand's name in *Mirat-i-Ahmadi* with Nagarsheth prefix coincides with the reference to this incident.

Under normal conditions Khushalchand's position, power, and prestige would have remained unchallenged after his great sacrifice for the city, but the political climate after the death of Aurangzeb in 1707 was anything but normal. The central authority had been considerably weakened and the administration of provinces was characterized by intrigues and counter-intrigues. Gujarat, too, was affected by this unfortunate development. In the new environment, the provincial authorities, which had so far stood scrupulously aloof from the struggle between rival groups for supremacy in the city, were only too willing to throw their weight on one side or the other with a view to controlling the principal merchant.

It was easy for Khushalchand's rivals under these conditions to invoke the power of the state in their favour. They poisoned the ears of the governor against the Sheth. It was believed in certain quarters that the Maratha forces had entered the city with the connivance of Khushalchand, and it is possible that his enemies exploited this rumour in their bid to turn the governor against the Sheth. Whatever the truth, the governor took the unusual step of putting Khushalchand behind the bars and appointing in his place one Gangadas as the new Nagarsheth. Gangadas, however, could not last long. When a new governor assumed power in 1731, he, emulating his predecessor's example, decided to have a Nagarsheth of his own choice. On his orders, Gangadas had to make room for one Ahmad who was the head of the Bohra community.

The imposed Nagarsheths seem to have enjoyed little popular support. Khushalchand, having bought his release in the meantime, had fled to Delhi. He still retained the respect and confidence of the various *mahajans* and the general populace of the city. But he needed something more for a *de jure* recognition of his leadership; he needed the supersession by a superior authority of the governor's derecognition of his position. The emperor still was such an authority in spite of his influence having been greatly eroded. While in Delhi, therefore, Khushalchand obtained an imperial *farman* stating that the emperor had appointed the Jain Sheth as the Nagarsheth and charged him with the responsibility "to attend to welfare of the people, prosperity of the city, well-being of the common folk, and manage affairs with such diligence that persons may devote themselves with satisfaction to their respective work and profession."[37] The imperial order virtually legitimized Khushalchand's position as the leader of the city and its business communities. The Nagarsheth still had to struggle hard to win back his place, but his and his descendants' right to Nagarshethship was never challenged again.

IV

After Khushalchand, the position of Nagarsheth became hereditary. Never in future would the family face any serious challenge to its supremacy in the affairs of the city and this was not only due to the legitimacy acquired through the imperial *farman*. Khushalchand's successors continued to prove worthy of this position because of their prosperity, charity, and concern for the city and the community to which they belonged. Their position and influence in the mercantile life of the city was unrivalled. By all accounts, Khushalchand's perennial troubles with the authorities and his long absence from the city had little effect on the fortunes and the prosperity of his business. The prestige and power of the family further increased under the leadership of his sons and successors, Nathusha (1720-1793), and Wakhatchand (1740-1814). Banking and trading remained the mainstay of their business. The house paid large sums of money to ruling powers or settled the claims of governments for tributes and land revenue from feudal chiefs. In this process, they earned considerable profits by way of interest. They also augmented their earnings by dealing in various expensive articles which were in great demand in the households of the nobles or royal families. A Gujarati verse written in the late 18th century gives the following description of the nature and extent of their business activities:

> The firm of Nagarsheth possessed reputable shops in different parts of the country like Dacca and Bengal. The Sheths buy a variety of textile goods which are light in weight but heavy in price. The commodities sold by them are famous far and wide—in Delhi, Agra, Kota, Bundi and Sorath. In recognition of their services to the state, the government has awarded them the grant of Palitana and Racharda. At present they exercise authority over ten to twelve villages which are leased to them. The Sheths act as advisers to the state and have acquired incredible wealth. During the time of famines, they show great sympathy for the poor and the helpless and save their lives by their munificence.[38]

It is significant that these lines depict the picture of a period when Ahmedabad presented a scene of political disorder and economic insecurity as a consequence of the disintegration of the Mughal power. The Maratha raids depressed the business and created an exodus of the population out of the city. And finally when the city fell under the Maratha occupation in 1758, Ahmedabad entered perhaps the worst phase in its history. The new rulers extracted large sums of money from the merchants, destroyed many of its beautiful buildings, and created an atmosphere of fear and consternation. They, however, treated the Nagarsheth family with deference and respect, and extended their patronage to the illustrious Sheths. This is clear from the fact that four successive Gaekwad rulers conferred on Wakhatchand several symbolic honours such as umbrella (*chhatra*), torch (*mashal*), and palanquin (*palaki*). As a gesture of goodwill, the Gaekwad rulers maintained these paraphernalia of distinction for the Sheths at state expense. Several decades later when the city came under the British rule, the new government continued to maintain good relations with the family as its predecessor governments had done.

Wakhatchand's stewardship of the family affairs was a watershed in its history. Visible cracks in its unity appeared either duriug his Nagarshethship or soon after his exit from the scene. The family had maintained a tradition of cohesiveness ever since the days of Shantidas. Wakhatchand's seven sons found it difficult to continue this tradition. Perhaps the family had become too large for unity and its unusual prosperity and unchallenged supremacy in the city removed that sense of insecurity which had held its members together in the past. The result was that while Wakhatchand's fifth son Hemabhai (1785-1858) succeeded to the Nagarshethship after his death, some of his other sons founded their own separate branches.

The founder of one of the splinter branches was Motibhai, Wakhatchand's third son. Five generations later Kasturbhai, was born in Motibhai's family. Though the Nagarshethship always remained with the parent stock, the Motibhai branch, as also other splinter branches, partook of the glorious family heritage as much as Hemabhai and his successors.

CHAPTER III

Entrepreneurial Initiative and Consolidation

MANY vital facts about Motibhai are unknown. We have no idea precisely when and why he decided to leave the sheltering umbrella of the illustrious Nagarsheth family. In fact, our knowledge of the affairs of the Motibhai branch during the first three generations is almost nil. Obviously, while the main stock under the leadership of Nagarsheth Hemabhai was enjoying the power and glory of its position, the splinter branch remained in relative obscurity for several decades. One thing is certain, however, Motibhai and his immediate descendants made no attempt to try out their luck in any area of activity other than the ones which merchant population those days generally embraced, and in which the Nagarsheth branch had excelled. Money-lending and trading claimed all their attention but as their resources were limited, the scale of their operation was necessarily modest.

This was the situation when the outbreak of the Civil War in the United States in 1861 cut off the supply of raw cotton to Great Britain. Textile industry was then the backbone of the British economy. Naturally an anxious British Government encouraged the supply of raw material from its colonies among whom India was the principal cotton growing country. This shot up the price of Indian staple to an unprecedented degree and generated a speculation mania in 1864-65 the like of which India has never witnessed before or since. Bombay, being the principal cotton mart, was worst affected where few escaped the temptation to gamble, but some Ahmedabad merchants also threw off their usual caution for the sake of quick gain.

Two generations had already passed since Motibhai's separation from the parent stock. The head of the splinter branch was Dalpatbhai. Motibhai, his son Fatehbhai, and grandson Bhagubhai, had died in quick succession. Premabhai (1815-1887), on the other hand, had succeeded as the head of the Nagarsheth line after his father's death in 1858. Premabhai and Dalpatbhai both indulged in speculation. But when the cessation of hostilities in America in 1865 created an unprecedented slump in the Indian cotton trade, Premabhai suffered a considerable loss whereas Dalpatbhai was lucky enough to earn a huge profit. Premabhai's losses had little adverse effect on his standing in the city; he had sufficient financial strength to withstand a temporary setback. But for Dalpatbhai's family, the share mania proved a turning point. Almost overnight he became a man of lakhs. He, however, never speculated again. Instead, he reorganized his money-lending business, and put it on a more sound footing by starting a *pedhi* (banking firm) under the style of Dalpatbhai Bhagubhai. By all accounts, the *pedhi* yielded excellent returns and enabled its founder to consolidate his position.

Dalpatbhai's newly acquired wealth enhanced his social standing. He now began to associate himself with a number of social welfare and educational activities. He was a founder member of the *Vidyabhyasak Mandali* (an association for promoting education and learning) and participated in relief works of various kinds. He was also active in the programmes of the Gujarat Vernacular Society founded in 1848 by some well-meaning Englishmen and enlightened Indians to promote social reforms. By the beginning of the 1860s the Society had become the most effective instrument of social regeneration in Gujarat. Prominent citizens and merchants including Nagarsheth Premabhai supported the Society in various ways. Dalpatbhai's joining this group was symbolic of his new status.

His charities and donations for the cause of Jain religion improved his standing among his co-religionists. By the time Dalpatbhai died in 1886, his family had definitely come out of the relative obscurity from which it suffered in the early part of his life.

Lalbhai, who now took over the management of the family affairs, was the eldest among Dalpatbhai's three sons; the other two were Manibhai and Jagabhai. He was born in 1863 when his father was nothing more than an ordinary trader and money-lender. But the prosperity which descended on the family after 1865 and the growing appreciation of modern education on the part of the mercantile communities of the city influenced his father's decision to send Lalbhai to English schools. Having passed his intermediate examination in 1885, the young-man was studying for his Bachelor's degree when his father's health began to deteriorate. A reluctant Lalbhai had to discontinue his education in order to take charge of the family business.

II

By this time the environment in the country had undergone a radical change. The establishment of the British rule brought infrastructural changes of far-reaching consequences. The introduction of a uniform currency replaced nearly a thousand legal tenders which circulated in the country previously. Innumerable custom barriers, which had created serious impediments in the growth of trade and commerce earlier, were abolished. The construction of roads and railways and the development of post and telegraph made communication between various parts of the country far easier. The establishment of the new legal-administrative structure reduced, if not entirely ended, the severity of insecurity and arbitrariness which had threatened the people under the previous regimes. At the same time the spread of English education on secular lines, the growing impact of European liberalism on the Indian mind, and the rise of social reform movements in various parts of the country including Gujarat were challenging some of the traditional props of the Indian society. Consequently, the caste system and the resultant occupational immobility, which had hindered the expansion of the social base of entrepreneurship, began to experience increasing strains. These changes, together, were creating a new kind of environment conducive to new possibilities on business front in India.

The demonstration effect of the rising British enterprise in India reinforced the impact of these changes. The British agency houses and free merchants which took great risks to exploit hitherto unfamiliar avenues of profit opened up new vistas for profits. In addition, their operations brought the Indians face to face with a superior technology, and assured the availability of personnel to handle the new machines. More importantly, in the process of developing their own enterprise, the alien businessmen contributed to the development of a unique system of corporate management—the managing agency system. It was possible under this system for a few individuals or families to float and manage a host of enterprises.

The cumulative effect of all this ushered India into the industrial age. This was reflected most convincingly in the starting of the cotton textile industry in the middle of the 19th century under Indian management and with Indian capital. Bombay naturally led the way as it had long experienced the impact of the new forces. The pioneers were the Parsees who had traditionally acted as the middlemen of the English businessmen in India and thus were quick to appreciate the potentialities of industrial ventures.

Well entrenched as bankers and traders at a time when the interest rates ranged between 12 to 19 per cent, the Ahmedabad business elite was slow to perceive the new opportunities. The merchants, of course, had welcomed the establishment of the British rule. They had supported social and educational reforms and rejoiced over the expansion of English education in Gujarat. They must have felt happy when Ahmedabad was connected by railways in 1864 and new roads established better links between the city and the outside world. It must have been obvious to them, as it was to many contemporary observers, that the constantly increasing volume of imports of machine-made yarn and cloth was having a ruinous effect on the calling of local spinners and weavers. But the thought of setting up textile ventures on modern lines seldom occurred to them even though their city lay in the vicinity of the cotton growing areas.

In fact so slow were the mercantile groups to realize the profitable possibilities of modern industries that when Ranchhodlal Chhotalal, a former civil servant, decided to set up a textile mill, he received very little encouragement from the business leaders. The *Nagar* entrepreneur, however, went ahead with his plans with a remarkable doggedness and his Ahmedabad Spinning and Weaving Mill started production in 1861. Even then, the Jains and Vaishnava *banias*, who were in the forefront of mercantile activities, kept aloof and continued to do so until 1877 when Mansukhbhai Bhagubhai, a Jain merchant, established the Gujarat Spinning and Weaving Company in the teeth of opposition from his community. The thought that an industrial undertaking would involve some kind of violence, imperceptible though it may be, disturbed his co-religionists.

At first, the traditional mercantile groups did not realize that their indifference towards industrial ventures would have patently adverse effect on their position in the life of the city. As we have seen earlier, almost since the birth of Ahmedabad, these groups had enjoyed a position of supremacy not only in business life but also in social matters. The coming of the British rule did not bring about an immediate change in the situation. Nagarsheths Hemabhai and Premabhai, symbolizing the mercantile leadership, continued to enjoy undisputed supremacy in the civic life. Then the early leaders of the textile industry began, though unwittingly, to stake their claim to this leadership. It is significant that next to the Nagarsheth the most active participants in the deliberations of the Ahmedabad Municipal Committee established in 1857, were Ranchhodlal Chhotalal and Bechardas Ambaidas Laskari. Belonging to a *Patidar* or landholding family the latter was the founder of the second textile mill in the city. Later in 1883 when it was decided to have a non-official chairman of the Committee, the mantle fell on Ranchhodlal, Premabhai having declined the honour because of his old age. In 1885 the *Nagar* entrepreneur was appointed the president of the Committee and held this position till his death in 1897. In fact, after Premabhai's death in 1887, the *Nagar* industrialist came to occupy the kind of position in the life of the city which Nagarsheths had occupied previously.

III

When Lalbhai Dalpatbhai came to the helm of the family affairs, it was clear to perceptive observers that the future belonged to industrial ventures. The new and relatively inexperienced head of the family, however, needed time to gain experience in the intricacies of business. His father had left a flourishing banking business but it was necessary for Lalbhai to improve his resources and standing in the market before he could think of branching off into a new and far more risky line than money-lending and trading. By all accounts he was extremely hard-working, careful about the minutest details, and meticulous and honest in his dealings. His education, which must be considered fairly high by the then existing standards, was an asset to him in his interaction with officials and fellow businessmen. He used these resources to expand his business and place it on a more sound footing. Consequently the Dalpatbhai Bhagubhai Pedhi made enormous profits under his leadership.

The Ahmedabad textile industry in the meantime, had made triumphant progress. As industrial ventures proved profitable, the Jains and Vaishnava *banias* cast off their hesitation and came forward in increasing numbers to partake of the opportunities that textiles offered. In fact, during the twenty years following the entry of the first Jain into the industry, practically all the cotton mills in the city were floated by the Jains or Vaishnava *banias*. Obviously the Jain community which had opposed Mansukhbhai's venture in 1877 had come to compromise with its religious inhibitions. The Jain entrants in the industry included, besides Mansukhbhai, the descendants of Karamchand Premchand or the forerunners of the famous Sarabhai house, and Premabhai Hemabhai. The former acquired a cloth printing mill in 1879 and converted it into a manufacturing concern under the name of Ahmedabad Manufacturing and Calico Printing Company, and the latter founded the Hathising Manufacturing Company in 1895. The Vaishnava *banias* made their debut in textile manufacturing in 1888, and within a short period at least 6 mills were floated by the members of these communities. Some of the Vaishnava *banias* who were lured into manufacturing activities included distinguished leaders of their communities.

Strangely enough, most of the Jain and Vaishnava *bania* mills were floated during a rather unfavourable period for the textile industry. The 1890s were marked by several natural calamities and business recession. To make the matter worse, the government imposed in 1892 heavy excise duty on the production of Indian mills. These adverse factors told heavily on the profits of the textile industry, and some of the companies suffered heavy losses or made indifferent progress. It was during these adverse times that Lalbhai decided to join the new group of industrialists and floated his Saraspur Manufacturing Company in 1897 in association with his brothers. Ahmedabad then had as many as 21 textile companies with a total of 418,922 spindles and 5,466 looms. About two-thirds of these mills were controlled by the Vaishnava *banias*; five Jain families had already preceded Lalbhai in establishing manufacturing units. In the strict sense of the term, therefore, his venture may not be called entrepreneurial. But in view of the fact that the Ahmedabad industry had yet to reach a saturation point and the transition from a commercial and financial career to an industrial undertaking still involved a certain degree of risk, Lalbhai's attempt undoubtedly contained some elements of entrepreneurial initiative.

But if the timing of floating the mill reflects Lalbhai's business courage and his confidence in his ability, some other aspects were indicative of his caution and concern for details. Like most of the Ahmedabad mills, the Saraspur Company started with a small share capital of Rs. 500,000 divided into 500 shares of Rs. 1,000 each. Rather than assuming the formal leadership himself, he invited Premabhai's son, Manibhai, to be the first chairman. Besides carrying the halo of the Nagarsheth family around him, Manibhai occupied an influential position in the life of the city as the Vice President of the Ahmedabad Municipality. The directors of the company included an Englishman, A.T. Vital, who could facilitate communication with the government, and Virchand Deepchand, who had been connected with some of the most reputed mills in Bombay and had wide experience in managing textile companies.

The management structure of the new company ran on conventional lines. Managing agency system, by this time, had become the most popular form of management for India's cotton industry—in fact for all modern industry. Lalbhai adopted this form of management for his industrial undertaking, and entrusted the affairs of the mill to a managing agency firm under the style of Lalbhai Dalpatbhai and Company. It was a partnership in which all the three brothers had equal shares. As in the case of management structure, the production strategy of the new company reflected little innovation. Most of the Ahmedabad mills were still concentrating on spinning alone. As many as 9 out of the 21 mills had no looms at all and the number of looms operated by the remaining 12 together was very small indeed. The Saraspur Mill, too, had no looms to begin with, but with 21,516 spindles it was the eighth largest spinning unit in the city at the time of its birth. In the very first year of its production in 1899, the company sold yarn worth Rs. 4,72,000, made a profit of Rs. 51,700 and declared a dividend of 4 per cent. The next year the sales almost doubled. Even though there was no appreciable increase in the profits—it rose by less than Rs. 2,000—the managing agents declared 7 per cent dividend, forgoing a part of their commission. The same year Manibhai Premabhai died suddenly, and Lalbhai assumed the chairmanship of the young undertaking.

The business strategy of the mill underwent little change for some time, and concentration on the production of yarn continued. Perhaps the company would have sooner or later started weaving department anyway, but the rise of the Swadeshi Movement in 1905 hastened the move. Opinion leaders in Ahmedabad had been propagating the virtue of Swadeshi for quite some time; in fact some whispering in this regard had been heard even before Ranchhodlal's first mill was founded. A number of leading citizens had established the *Swadeshi Udyog Vardhak Mandali* in 1875 in order to systematize the campaign to spread the Swadeshi consciousness. Lord Curzon's decision to divide Bengal in 1904, however, did more to arouse the feeling of Swadeshi than the propaganda of the last several decades. All of a sudden the country realized that its salvation lay in the maximum possible use of home-made goods.

The Swadeshi Movement had a profound effect on the textile industry and the number of mills, spindles, and looms increased. In Ahmedabad itself at least ten mill companies were started between 1905 and 1909, and the older ones increased their spinning or weaving capacities or both. Taking advantage of the spurt in demand for indigenous production, Lalbhai decided to start a weaving department in his mill in 1907. Initially he set up only 520 looms but the number was increased successively in the subsequent years. The result was that very soon the proceeds from the sale of its cloth outstripped the value of the yarn sold as the following table clearly shows:

TABLE III.1

The Saraspur Manufacturing Company: 1906-1911

(*Rs. in lakhs*)

Year	*Value of yarn sold*	*Value of cloth sold*
1906	15.85	Nil
1907	7.18	4.98
1908	5.84	7.30
1909	6.69	7.36
1910	6.85	10.55
1911	5.75	11.89

In the meantime, Lalbhai and his brothers had established one more mill – the Raipur Mills—in 1905. The rising spirit of Swadeshi might have had some effect on their decision, but the experience and profits that they had gained in their first textile venture were no less decisive factors. The new mill, like its predecessor made a small beginning with a small paid-up capital of Rs. 500,000 divided into 500 shares of Rs. 1,000 each. These shares were very closely held. Lalbhai had a majority interest with 251 shares. The rest were distributed among his brothers and close relatives and friends. Because of his personal influence and the reputation of good management demonstrated in the performance of the Saraspur Mills, Lalbhai had no difficulty in arranging capital for the venture and the subscriptions for the Raipur Mills were closed in three days! The basic strategies of the new company were almost the same as those of his earlier unit. Its management was entrusted to the same managing agency, and its sole product initially was yarn as there was no weaving department.

The company started production in 1909 and made a small profit at the end of the year. And yet to inspire confidence in the investing public, the management declared a dividend of 4.5 per cent. As in the case of the Saraspur Mills earlier, the managing agents decided to forgo a part of their commission to make dividend declaration possible. But the company started production at a time when the Swadeshi momentum was sagging and there was a general slump in the industry. In this context the performance of the new company in comparison with its older sister was not too unsatisfactory as table III.2 indicates. But the Raipur had yet to establish itself and its reputation in 1912 whereas the Saraspur had already come into its own. The result was that the latter's shares were being quoted for as much as Rs. 2,300 each for which only Rs. 1,000 had been paid initially while there was no appreciation in the value of the Raipur scrips.

TABLE III.2

Comparative Performance of the Saraspur and Raipur Mills from the First Year of Production to 1911

Year		*Sales*	*Profit**	*Profit as percentage of sales (%)*	*Dividend (%)*
		(Rs. in lakhs)			
1905	Saraspur	16.72	3.19	19 08	8.5
	Raipur	—	—	—	—
1906	Saraspur	16.01	1.83	11.43	8.5
	Raipur	—	—	—	—
1907	Saraspur	11.37	.77	6.49	8.5
	Raipur	—	—	—	—
1908	Saraspur	13.20	.37	2.80	7.5
	Raipur	—	—	—	—
1909	Saraspur	14.12	.35	2.48	7.0
	Raipur	11.31	.29	2.56	4.5
1910	Saraspur	17.50	.42	2.40	8.5
	Raipur	13.40	.26	1.94	5.1
1911	Saraspur	17.76	.47	2.65	9.5
	Raipur	12.38	.25	2.02	5.0

*Indicating profit before taxes but after depreciation.

All profit figures used in this work are calculated on the basis of the assumption that depreciation represents a part of production costs.

While the business affairs were making smooth progress, the family was passing through deep trouble. Lalbhai and his brothers were not getting along and eventually their disputes assumed such a proportion that division in the family was considered to be the only solution. The older and more established of the two mill companies went to the share of Manibhai and Jagabhai, and Lalbhai had to settle for the younger concern whose future was still uncertain. The division was a great tragedy for the family, but a greater calamity was in store. Just a few months after the family split, Lalbhai succumbed to a serious heart attack on 5 June 1912.

Less than 50 years in age, Lalbhhai was at the peak of his career and prestige when death took him away. He had established a firm reputation in the business world as "a prominent and successful millowner".[39] Like his father, he had spent a part of his profits to support the social, educational, and religious causes including the construction of a *dharmashala* (a free lodge for travellers) in the memory of his father, and the establishment of a girls' school in the name of his mother. His services to Jainism had endeared him to his co-religionists. He had acted as the secretary of the Shvetambara Jain Conference from 1903 to 1908 and also as the president of the Anandji Kalyanji Trust—on organization founded in the 1720s for managing Jain temples and institutions.* When the Europeans proposed to acquire housing sites near the celebrated Jain shrines on the Parshvanath Hills, Lalbhai was one of the members of the deputation which waited on the lieutenant-governor of Bengal against this move. His general standing and reputation in the society was reflected in the decision of the government a few months before his death to confer on him the title of "Sardar of the First Class of Gujarat." The *Prajabandhu*, a well-known Gujarati journal of the times, called him "a thorough businessman."[40]

With Lalbhai's death ended a chapter in the family history.

IV

Fate could not have chosen a worse moment to deny Lalbhai's family the benefits of his leadership. The family had yet to recover from the shock and consequence of the recent division. All his three sons were still young; only one, Chimanbhai, was an adult, but his knowledge and experience of business matters were too inadequate to meet the crisis. By way of assets, the family held about three-fourth of the share capital in the Raipur Mills—the only industrial concern left with it after the recent division—and of course the goodwill that Lalbhai had left behind. But no goodwill, unless constantly replenished, goes very far, and the Raipur's affairs were yet to be placed on secure grounds. On top of it, the family had little liquid capital which could enable it to stabilize its young manufacturing concern and overcome the crisis.

Under these conditions, the family had to take some hard decisions. One of these was to advise Lalbhai's second son and fourth child, Kasturbhai, to discontinue his education. Born on 19 December 1894, he was little more than seventeen years old then, and had just started his collegiate education in the then prestigious Gujarat College. Kasturbhai protested against the suggestion on the ground that "inadequate education would be a great handicap" in his future career. But he finally yielded to the persuasion of his mother who argued that looking after the business was more important.

In no sphere of activity till then had the young boy distinguished himself. Nothing more than an average student, he spent more time in playing cricket or flying kites. But his performance in the field of sports also was, at best, mediocre. As a school boy, he often indulged in practical jokes or pranks or outright mischief. Once, for no ostensible reason except to enjoy the discomfiture of his home tutor, he threw down the latter's headgear from the first floor. His performance in the high school examination, however, indicated that he was capable of achieving good results once he had decided to do so. Most of his teachers at the Ranchhodlal Chhotalal Government High School did not expect him to do very well. But Kasturbhai decided to prove to them and to his family and friends that he was not wanting in intelligence as they had thought. He worked hard and passed the examination in the second class. Very few students secured first class in those days and the second class had not yet been downgraded to its present position in popular imagination

The playful and mischievous boy, in fact, had a serious mind. He was conscious of his parentage and family background. On his father's side he often related himself to the position and prestige which Shantidas and his descendants had enjoyed in the city and outside for about three centuries. His mother Mohiniben, came from the Hutheesing family which had been long held in great esteem in the social and commercial circles on account of its wealth and charity. He also knew that Mohiniben had brought with her the tradition associated with her own grandmother, Harkunwar, who had donated lakhs of rupees for public purposes in her times and who was affectionately called *Rani* (queen) in Ahmedabad because of her munificence. Young Kasturbhai looked upon himself as the heir to these glorious traditions of his family and sometimes wondered whether he would be able to prove worthy of his heritage.

He had grown up in the large house built by his grandfather and in a large household. Dalpatbhai's three sons had maintained the unity of the joint family and lived together almost till the end of Lalbhai's life. The result was that more than thirty persons—men, women, children and servants—lived under one roof and under one command. Lalbhai, as the head of the joint family, was not expected to show any kind of preference for or shower extra affection on his own children. It was considered less than proper in those days to display one's affection for one's own sons and daughters, and most men in general maintained certain distance from the children in the family. In any case Lalbhai did, so much so that he and his eldest son used to go to the mill separately after the latter had been inducted into the business. Chimanbhai managed some aspects of the mills as he was asked to do, but seldom did his father discuss business or social matters with him or with other younger children in the family, including Kasturbhai.

Such a father could generate awe or fear among his children but would not create conditions for relaxed relationship with them. And this is precisely what Lalbhai did. The sound of his horse-drawn carriage was a signal to the children to hide themselves or start doing their lessons. They dared not seek his permission for going to circus, drama, or picnic. Though Kasturbhai was greatly interested in kite flying, he could not gather enough courage in the presence of his father to run after a falling kite as kite fliers generally do. As a stern disciplinarian, Lalbhai demanded complete submission to his orders and none could ever take liberties with him.

The atmosphere in the family over which such a stern person presided was generally authoritarian. There were certain other traits of Lalbhai's character which his children could not have failed to admire. He was very punctual. "Time is money", he often used to say. So jealously did he guard against the possibility of wasting a single moment that his horse-drawn carriage must start moving as soon as he stepped in it; he could not tolerate even a small interval. Extremely industrious by nature he started his day early in the morning and worked till late in the evening. Though aloof from his children, he was very good at cultivating and maintaining good social relations. Consequently he had a large number of friends including several British officers.

The general atmosphere of the household in which Kasturbhai spent his boyhood was imbued with the spirit of Jain ethics. Lalbhai insisted on strict observance of religious rituals and every member of the family spent some time in the prayer room of the house. Though very meticulous about his clothes and fond of good food, Lalbhai was frugal in his personal living. The family ate simple food and only on special occasions would the children find any change in the menu. Tea was taboo, as it was in most Indian homes then, and milk was served at supper. The head of the family was very careful about money matters and could not countenance any kind of extravagance so much so that his children could seldom expect to get more than 2 paise each (a rupee was equal to 64 paise then) a day for their afternoon snacks in the school. The children of less wealthy families were often more lucky.

Kasturbhai's mother, Mohiniben, shared the religious zeal of her husband. She visited religious temples, spent considerable time in prayer, and went on pilgrimage to the Palitana Jain shrines twice or three times a year. She also gave a large amount of money in donation to the Jain shrines. She was, however, not half as stern as Lalbhai. Mild, well mannered, and gentle, she maintained excellent relations with all members of the family, and was very affectionate in her dealings with the children. Though she had little or no formal education, she possessed a robust common sense, and managed the household affairs with tact and intelligence. Kasturbhai felt relaxed in the company of his mother with whom he often shared his feelings and anxities.

Another person with whom young Kasturbhai had some rapport was one of his teachers at the Ranchhodlal High School—Keshav Harshad Dhruva. The teacher was known for his proficiency in English and Sanskrit. Somehow the playful Kasturbhai developed very high regard for Dhruva. It was due to Dhruva's impact on him that Kasturbhai started taking his studies more seriously and passed the high school examination creditably. It was also because of his influence that Kasturbhai developed some taste for extra-curricular readings, and read the biographies of Mahavir, Swami Vivekanand, and Abraham Lincoln. On the whole, however, the atmosphere in the school was not very different from that at home. The headmaster was a learned Parsi, who like most of the headmasters of the day, placed great accent on discipline. Opportunities for self-development were limited indeed.

Kasturbhai's early life and thinking process, thus, were shaped by the atmosphere in a joint family system with its hierarchical relationship, a busy and industrious but stern and aloof father who valued integrity, discipline, hard work and frugality no less than worldly success, and an affectionate mother who along with her husband attached great importance to strict observance of the principles and rituals of a religious system which reinforced their beliefs and practices. Significantly enough, the Gujarati social system in general greatly valued some of the traits of Kasturbhai's father. The external environment which could have counteracted the impact of family influences on his early socialization were feeble and ineffective indeed.

V

The sudden disappearance of the protective presence of their father was a traumatic experience for Lalbhai's children. They felt terribly insecure but they had no option but to shoulder the responsibility of the family affairs. Of particular importance was the management of the mill in which a large part of their money was tied up. They were old enough to realize that if the mill did not make profits, they and their family would face serious hardships. Somewhat nervously Lalbhai's eldest son, Chimanbhai, assumed the chairmanship of the young concern. Kasturbhai's knowledge of the mill industry was practically nil. He was, therefore, entrusted with a minor responsibility. As a time-keeper, his job was to check workers' attendance and prepare pay slips. Chandulal Zaveri, the second son-in-law of Lalbhai, helped the boys in various ways in managing their affairs.

Chimanbhai and Kasturbhai, assisted by their brother-in-law, approached their job sincerely and earnestly. But the textile industry was still not quite out of the recession that had set in after 1908 and no one knew for sure when complete recovery would take place. The performance of the Raipur Mills conformed to the general trend. The next three years were a period of declining sales, fluctuating rate of returns, and low volume of profits. The young managers of the mill sought the advice of their uncles in their bid to improve the affairs but to no effect. In those days Kasturbhai often wished that his father had left his money in the form of cash and not shares so that it would have yielded a higher amount by way of interest than the profits from the mill. But since this soft option was no more open, the brothers decided to diversify production by starting weaving in the hope of using their yarn for producing cloth. They also decided to expand the spinning capacity of the mill. Work on installing 336 looms and additional 4690 spindles started immediately. But the impact of these actions on the fortune of the mill was still uncertain.

Then the First World War came with its dramatic effect on Indian industrial situation. Most of the Indian industries were still young and incapable of meeting foreign competition. The Government had all along pursued a policy of *laissez-faire* which was unquestionably prejudicial to the Indian industries as it could offer no protection against the challenge of import. No sign of change in the government attitude was in sight when the war drastically reduced imports of industrial goods from abroad. Demand for Indian products picked up and Indian industry gained in strength. The Government had turned a deaf ear to the demand for protection all these years; the destiny unwittingly granted it through a bloody instrument.

The textile industry was a beneficiary of the new situation. Though there was some shock and panic when the war broke out, within a year the fortunes of the industry showed an upward trend. There was a great spurt in demand, wages remained almost constant, and the total cost of production rose slowly. Beginning with the year 1916 the industry enjoyed an unmixed prosperity and made unprecedented profits. The decision of the Government to increase import duties under financial compulsion helped the cotton mills to consolidate themselves still further.

The Raipur Mills reaped the benefits of the new conditions in the industry. By the time the war broke out, cloth production had already started. Beginning with 1914, the share of cloth in the total sales registered a successive increase. Like the Saraspur Mills, the Raipur concentrated on the production of coarse and medium cloth. The mill span and weaved cnly one kind of warp and weft in the beginning so as to establish its product and quality. Partly because of these strategies, but mainly due to the war conditions, the profits increased—gradually in the beginning but very speedily after 1915, as is clear from table III.3. Only in 1918, the profit spree of the mill was checked, but that was the case with the entire industry. The release of the accumulated stocks and the fear of Government control depressed the prices and a protracted labour strike in Ahmedabad and an influenza epidemic in the country worsened the situation. The Raipur management, however, was quite sure that these difficulties were only temporary as is clear from the fact that they declared a large dividend that year even though the profits were considerably low. The mill also established a bleaching plant in 1918. The same year, a significant step was taken to attract small investors and reduce the risk. An ordinary share of the company, the value of which had been originally fixed at Rs. 1,000, was broken into 10 shares of Rs. 100 each.

While the Raipur Mill consolidated its position, Kasturbhai gained in maturity, experience, and stature. After staying at the routine and dull job of time-keeping only for six months he assumed the charge of the cotton purchase department. He

Saraspur Mills in 1920

Raipur Mills in 1920

TABLE III.3

Working of the Raipur Mills: 1912-1918

Year	*Sales*	*Profits*	*Profits as percentage of sales %*	*Dividend %*
	(Rs. in lakhs)			
1912	13.06	.30	2.30	3
1913	10 86	.25	2.30	5
1914	11.23	.28	2.49	5.5
1915	14.52	.34	2.34	6.5
1916	N.A.	N.A.	N.A.	N.A.
1917	22.09	4.3	19.46	30
1918	33.89	1.2	3.54	35

knew practically nothing about cotton. At the same time he had no doubt that the profitability of a textile mill largely depended on the quality of cotton used and the rate at which it was purchased. He, therefore, decided to see for himself where and how cotton was grown, how it was pressed and sent to the mart, what kind of impurities did it suffer from, and what were the prices of various varieties. To educate himself, Kasturbhai took a rather unusual step. He made an extensive tour of the villages and towns from where cotton was purchased. A salesman and a cook were the only two persons who accompanied him. This was unprecedented. Never before had a scion of a mill agent's family soiled his hand in his bid to study the intricacies of the basic raw material for his industry. Kasturbhai's exertions paid rich dividends. He soon became an expert on cotton unequalled by anyone else - an expertise which stood him in good stead throughout his industrial career.

An incident of Kasturbhai's tenure in the cotton purchase department gives a clue to the kind of personal ethics that would guide his business operations. He had entered into an oral agreement with a merchant to sell some cotton waste for Rs. 3,000. He later learnt from the general manager of the mill that he had been cheated, for the material was worth about Rs. 18,000. The manager also suggested to the youngman that he was not obligated to honour an oral contract with an unscrupulous person. Kasturbhai, however, refused to go back on his word and preferred to fulfil the contract though it meant a substantial loss. And throughout his life, he continued to enjoy the reputation for keeping his word once he had given it, no matter what the consequences.

While still in charge of cotton purchases, he got married. As was customary in those days, he had been betrothed at the young age of eight with a girl who was only two years old. He would have preferred to postpone the marriage for a few more years, but could not withstand the pressure from the girl's father. The marriage was solemnized in 1915. His wife, Sharadaben, had little education. Kasturbhai employed a tutor to teach her English, because he thought that her inability to communicate in English would be a serious handicap in future.

The year after his marriage witnessed Kasturbhai's induction into the formal decision-making body of his mill. He was appointed a member of the Board of Directors of the Raipur Mills. The offer of directorship of a company to the members of the promoting family was not always based on merit or ability. Kasturbhai, however, had given sufficient indication of his managerial talents to deserve this recognition. By dint of perseverance and hard work, he had developed keen insight into various aspects of textile production. Still an upstart in many ways, he gradually achieved mastery over the intricacies of his operations and came to be recognized as the principal voice in the management of his mill. Not only the members of his family, including his elder brother, but also perceptive observers in the city took notice of his potentialities and promise. One of them was Ambalal Sarabhai, a prominent leader of the Ahmedabad industry then, who would play a significant role in bringing Kasturbhai into public life.

By the time the war ended, the playful and mischievous boy had emerged as a confident and competent manager.

CHAPTER IV

Entrepreneurial Continuum: Expansion

THE benefits of the First World War to the textile industry were far more enduring than many during the bloody years would have thought. The war left the industry in a strong enough position to withstand the effect of the resumption of imports from England after the cessation of hostilities. Also, the sceptre of Japanese competition had little adverse impact on the fortunes of the industry. Exploiting the gap between the supplies and demand, Japan had stepped up its export of textile goods to India during the war. For a variety of reasons, Japan enjoyed a competitive advantage in Indian markets and demand for its goods rose successfully after the cessation of hostilities. And yet the combined English-Japanese commercial offensive did not affect the prosperity of the Indian mills adversely. In fact, the years immediately after the war witnessed an unprecedented boom during which textile manufacturers earned fabulous profits.

Conforming to the general trend, Kasturbhai's Raipur Mills continued to augment its profits so much so that the gross profits in 1919 were more than double the total paid-up capital of the company and the figure nearly tripled the next year. Success opened up additional and more attractive possibilities. Gone were the insecurity and hesitation that had characterized Kasturbhai and his brother during the early years of their industrial career. He decided to float a much bigger mill with a paid-up capital of Rs. 12 lakhs. But when the capital for the Asoka Mill, as the new company was named, was actually called, he realized how grossly unrealistic was his estimate of the investment climate. The Raipur Mills had yielded excellent returns during and after the war, and a general boom in the economy pointed to ready profits in the textiles. The result was that there was a veritable scramble for the Asoka scrips. Elated by this development, the managing agents decided to double the capital and establish a mill twice the size of what they had originally planned. The entire capital was subscribed within no time and a confident Kasturbhai placed orders with an English firm for 40,000 spindles and 1,000 looms instead of 20,000 spindles and 500 looms as contemplated earlier. Had Kasturbhai's plans materialized, only three mills in the city would have been ahead of the Asoka in terms of production capacity. The young millowner was undoubtedly thinking big.

Favourable rate of exchange, among other things, seems to have prompted him to place such a large order for, never before was the value of Indian rupees in terms of sterling as high as it was in the early part of 1920. Before and during the war years the exchange rate had fluctuated between 1 s. and 1.5 s. to a rupee, but in November 1919, it suddenly registered a steep rise because of decline in the world supply of silver. In the subsequent months it reached the level of 2 s. to a rupee and a special committee appointed by the Secretary of State for India under the chairmanship of Sir H. Babington Smith put the seal of expert approval at this rate. The Government of India seemed determined to stabilize the rupee at this rate and the prospects for the Indian importer looked bright indeed.

Full of confidence about the future and enriched by the war profits, the two brothers decided to broaden their knowledge and understanding of the world. In early 1920, they left for Europe to see new lands, new things, and new peoples. Besides England, where they made some valuable business contacts, they visited Belgium, France, Germany, and Italy. The things and articles in the European markets made a great impression on them. It was a trip aimed at the dual purpose of education and pleasure, but Kasturbhai used the opportunity to invest some fifty thousand rupees in the German and French stocks. The currencies in these countries were in a depressed state and Kasturbhai must have thought of the advantages that would accrue to him in the event of recovery. However, he gained only in his French investment which compensated for his loss in Germany whose currency continued to decline in value. The European trip did a lot of good to the young industrialist. He now had a better picture of the world, and a clearer understanding of the distance that separated India and Europe in the field of industrialization.

Kasturbhai returned home after eight carefree months abroad only to find that his new venture was in deep trouble. While he was away the market mechanism had thwarted the official determination to hold on to the 2s. exchange rate. Increased remittances to London by importers, speculators, and European community in India as a response to the favourable rate of exchange had reduced the market value of a rupee to 1 s. 3 d. by the end of 1920. Kasturbhai realized to his utter dismay that the equipments for his Asoka Mills would cost him considerably more than he had budgeted for.

This was the first major crisis that the young industrialist faced in his business career. He tried to meet the situation by cancelling a major part of his orders. But he had little control over the rumour-mongers who spread the news that the infant company was incapable of surviving the ordeal. The shareholders got panicky and the value of the scrips tumbled down to Rs. 40 from the original value of Rs. 100 each. There was little that the managing agents could immediately do to boost the confidence of the shareholders. A pseudo-poetic expression in Gujarati, "Asoka soka man nakhya" (The mill whose name literally means 'one who is free from grief' has actually plunged us in grief), heard frequently in the Ahmedabad Stock Exchange and business circles of the city, summed up the feelings of the repentant investors.

Kasturbhai was acutely aware that the collapse of the Asoka Mill would be much more than the collapse of an enterprise; it would mean a serious setback to his reputation as an industrialist and company promoter. He could not have postponed purchasing the machinery without jeopardizing further the credit of the company, and he was reluctant to suffer the loss caused by the fall in the exchange rate. In order to achieve his twin objectives, he hit upon a novel idea. He bought government securities and arranged for a large sterling loan against them from a London bank. The foreign exchange so arranged was used to pay for the reduced orders—13,000 spindles and 350 looms. Fortunately for him, the exchange rate improved to 1s. 4d. by the beginning of 1923 after which the debt was gradually repaid and the holding of the Government paper was eliminated. This strategy resulted in a substantial gain for the young enterprise and revived the confidence of the shareholders in the managing agents' competence and ability.

By the time the Asoka started production in February 1923, the textile industry as a whole had gotten into deep trouble. The post-war boom conditions did not last beyond 1922. If Manchester's re-entry into the Indian market, and Japanese commercial invasion of the country shrank the home market, a series of political troubles and development of indigenous industry in China drastically cut off a major foreign market for Indian yarn. These factors depressed the prices of Indian products. Lower movement of prices, however, failed to augment demand because of a general downward trend in the economy as a whole. To add to the woes of the Indian producers, the cost of production showed an upward trend in 1923 owing to, among other things, high cost of raw material following a crop failure in the United States that year.

Under these conditions, most of the mills suffered in various ways. It was impossible to maintain the level of profits made during the boom years; more disquietingly, only a few could make any profit at all. Kasturbhai's mills weathered the storm successfully. In 1923, the worst year after the boom, the Raipur earned more than Rs. 300,000 and declared 40 per cent dividend. Even the Asoka made small profit in spite of a labour strike which lasted for more than two months. During the next five years, the sales as well as the rate of profits in both the mills remained generally low, as is clear from Table IV.1.

TABLE IV.1

Working of Raipur and Asoka Mills: 1923-1928

Year		*Sales* (*Rs. in lakhs*)	*Profit* (*Rs. in lakhs*)	*Profit as percentage of sales* (%)	*Dividend* (%)
1923	Raipur	44.75	3.22	7.20	40
	Asoka	15.34	.05	0.33	0
1924	Raipur	57.89	4.31	7.45	40
	Asoka	50.21	1.23	2.45	5
1925	Raipur	49.26	5.81	11.79	50
	Asoka	42.57	1.74	4.09	6
1926	Raipur	40.06	5.48	13.68	50
	Asoka	N.A.	N.A.	N.A.	N.A.
1927	Raipur	N.A.	N.A.	N.A.	N.A.
	Asoka	35.54	2.77	7.79	7
1928	Raipur	N.A.	N.A.	N.A.	N.A.
	Asoka	40.14	2.85	7.10	0

It was by no means surprising that the Raipur which had firmly established itself in the market before the recession came earned better profits than its younger sister. But the speed with which the Asoka established itself must have surprised many. In the very first year it established a "fair reputation" for its products, and its profits successively increased. In fact, so confident of its future were the managing agents that in the very first year of production they added more than 13,000 spindles and 250 looms. As the rate of exchange improved favouring imports of machinery, the capacity was expanded still further with the result that by the beginning of 1925, the company had 31,024 spindles and 712 looms.

The most important factor in the success of Kasturbhai's two mills was their product-mix. The mills that were hardest hit during the recession were those which concentrated on the yarn production since the Chinese market had severely shrunk. The impact on weaving mills was far less. Fortunately for the Raipur Mills, its cloth production continued to rise throughout the 1920s till the ratio between the value of yarn sold to that of cloth increased from 1:3 in 1921 to just a trifle less than 1:15 in 1929. In the case of the Asoka this ratio went up from a little less than 1:5 in 1923 to almost 1:20 by the end of the decade.

II

In the meantime, the young industrialist had a rather unexpected opportunity to bring under his control the first mill floated by his father. Like most mills in the country, the Saraspur Manufacturing Company which Kasturbhai's uncles had claimed in the family division, made reasonably good profits during the war. Its top management, however, got involved in speculation and neglected the affairs of the company with the result that its liquidity position began to deteriorate after 1918. The attempt to arrest the process by increasing its paid-up capital by Rs. 100,000 in 1920 produced little impact. By 1922 its book debt had reached the staggering figure of more than Rs. 30,00,000 and its cash holdings were reduced to Rs. 7,600.

Such a company could hardly withstand the pressure of recession which set in the next year. It held on to its own for sometime but eventually the management had to decide in favour of liquidation. The proceedings for winding up the company started in June 1924 when the statutory application to the court was submitted. The directors asked Kasturbhai, whose managerial abilities had already won considerable acclaim, to be the interim manager of the company, while the court appointed an official liquidator.

Kasturbhai had some sentimental association with the first industrial venture of his father and did not countenance the idea of the company going out of the family's control. The liquidation scheme that he presented to the court guaranteed to safeguard the interests of the creditors and the shareholders. The scheme was considered to be the most advantageous to the company by the court. A meeting of the shareholders, creditors, and depositors, too accepted the scheme with little modification. A new management under the leadership of Kasturbhai was to take over the mill after settling the full claims of the creditors along with 3 per cent interest and after paying about Rs. 27,50,000 for the fixed assets and working capital. The shareholders were free to retain their shares at par or receive cash at the original value. Kasturbhai's scheme was highly satisfactory to all the claimants against the company and enhanced his prestige and reputation in the city's business circles. One may still meet a few depositors and shareholders of the Saraspur Manufacturing Company who remember Kasturbhai's role with gratitude in saving them from financial embarrassment.

While all formalities connected with the proposal to dissolve the old company could not be completed before 1953, most of the claims had been settled by the end of 1927. A new company under the style of the Saraspur Mills Ltd., was registered in January 1928 with Kasturbhai Lalbhai as Chairman, and under a new managing agency—Lalbhai Dalpatbhai Sons and Company—in which each of his two uncles retained 12.5 per cent share.

One of the first tasks that claimed Kasturbhai's attention was to modernize the machinery and the plant. The old management had continued to use the worn out and obsolete machinery during the war and after. It was clear to Kasturbhai that without a thorough overhaul of its equipments, the company could not hope to turn the corner. During the first two years, therefore, a comprehensive programme to replace the old machinery was undertaken on a priority basis. Several old spinning machines made room for new ones, and the whole of weaving equipment was changed. New spindles were added and weaving capacity was expanded so that by the end of 1929 the company had 33,000 spindles and 860 looms instead of 3,000 spindles and 630 looms which the new management had inherited from its predecessor. Expansion in the weaving capacity was proportionately larger to ensure the consumption of a large part of its yarn production by the mill itself and reduce dependence on an ever declining demand for yarn outside. Modernization cost the company a good amount of about Rs.8,00,000, but Kasturbhai was convinced that the money spent would be more than compensated by higher rate of returns in the future.

Not content with the acquisition of the Saraspur, the young industrialist started another mill in 1928 in collaboration with the Hutheesing family. Kasturbhai's eldest sister, Dahiben, had been married in this family and his brother-in-law,

Purshottam M. Hutheesing, was dead. The decision to float the new mill was partly influenced by Kasturbhai's concern for his young nephews, Surottam, Narottam, and Gunottam. Although the Hutheesing family had been given a small share in the managing agency of the Saraspur, it was necessary to provide for a larger income for Dahiben and her children. The Hutheesing family supplied a major part of the equity capital and the managing agency was entrusted to Messrs P.M. Hutheesing and Sons. Kasturbhai was appointed the Chairman of the Board. The Aruna Mill with 20,884 spindles and 576 looms started working, though partially, in August 1929 and commenced full production in the beginning of 1930. From the very outset the Aruna cloth "was favourably received in the market on account of its superior quality and variety of designs".

In order to reduce financial pressure consequent on the launching of the new projects, Kasturbhai adopted what may be called a strategy of divestment. As we have noted earlier, the Asoka Mills had started with a much larger paid-up capital than was usually the case with the Ahmedabad mills. The company had been floated during the boom years and the enthusiasm of the investing public had misled the young, and then somewhat inexperienced promoters, to increase the capital to Rs. 24,00,000. In a city where public deposits could provide working capital to the mill industry on more profitable terms, the Asoka was certainly overcapitalized. Soon after the mill was launched, Kasturbhai realized his mistake but any proposal to reduce the capital at a time when the Asoka was in trouble would have certainly led to a further erosion of confidence in its ability to survive. After the Asoka had been firmly established, it was decided to reduce its equity capital from Rs. 24,00,000 to Rs. 12,00,000. This was done by reducing the value of the outstanding shares of the company to half and returning the balance to the shareholders. The process started in 1929 and was completed in 1931.

In the meantime a great disaster, far greater in magnitude than the post-war recession, hit the industry, in fact the whole economy, in 1929. In India the onset of the Great Depression was attended or caused by a steep fall in the price of agricultural products in 1929-30, resulting in the severe contraction of the farmer's purchasing power and a general down-swnig of prices of all commodities. The impact of this unwelcome development on the mill industry was particularly severe because the demand for a large part of its production, being of coarse varieties, depended on the paying ability of the rural buyer.

The change in the attitude of the Government, however, gave some hope to the producer. As we have noted earlier, the Indian mill industry had to face from the very outset a veiled hostility of an alien Government. At any rate, it received no positive encouragement from the ruling power. Throughout the 1920s when the Japanese competition began to bite and Manchester renewed its challenge to the Indian producer, Indian public opinion clamoured for government intervention. As ws shall see later, Kasturbhai was in the forefront of the agitation against the official apathy. By 1927, the weight of Indian opinion produced some effect on the counsels of the government. In the first instance, a duty on the import of yarn was levied. As the depression deepened and the financial condition of the Government became more acute, revenue duty ranging between 11 to 15 per cent on the entry of all piece goods and an additional 5 per cent protective duty on the imports from countries other than England were imposed in 1930. In the subsequent year, the duty was again increased to 25 per cent on the British and 33¼ per cent on the non-British goods. These measures reduced the rigours of foreign competition so that while in 1928-29 the home production lagged slightly behind the figures of imports, by 1930-31 the ratio between the imports and indigenous production rose to nearly 1:3. The Indian manufacturer finally found some relief. More importantly, the acceptance of the principle of protection by a Government which had so far sworn by an altogether negative policy gave him some promise and hope.

The wave of Swadeshi sentiment which once again swept the nation in 1930-31 also served to prop up the sagging morale of the Indian industrialist. The new movement left much greater and more enduring impact on the country than its earlier counterpart. For, while the effect of the earlier Swadeshi movement was confined to the urban centres alone, the message of the new wave reached the rural masses as well. The organizers of the boycott of foreign goods appealed to the mills not to use imported yarn. A large number of mills, including even those managed by non-Indian interests, fell in line. Going one step further, the Ahmedabad millowners resolved to refrain from importing even machinery unless such import was absolutely indispensable to their operations. On the part of the masses there was an increased awareness of the benefits of using home-made products—a factor which could not fail to influence demand situation.

The situation in the beginning of the 1930s, thus, was a combination of favourable as well as unfavourable factors. It was, by no means, easy to assess with any degree of precision the overall meaning of these forces for the industry. Different entrepreneurs responded to the situation differently. While some, frightened by the uneven demand pattern, decided to reduce their operations or postpone their expansion plans waiting for better days to return, a few daring spirits expanded their production facilities in their bid to reduce the cost of production and, thus, the price of the final product. There were others who intensified their sale drive. Nobody probably knew what strategy would mitigate, if not altogether eliminate, the rigours of uncertainty afflicting the industry.

Kasturbhai was among those entrepreneurs who looked upon the 1930s as the years of opportunity and not of crisis. If the prices of the mill products were low, so was the cost of machinery. And thus, the saving in installing new equipments could partially offset low returns. More importantly, overhauling the machinery could lay the foundation for future prosperity when the economy would take a more favourable turn. Kasturbhai was not alone in this assessment. Many other persons felt that it was an opportune moment for expansion. Consequently, as many as 8 new mills were established in Ahmedabad in 1931, including two, the Arvind Mills and the Nutan Mills, by Kasturbhai himself.

Unlike Kasturbhai's earlier units, which concentrated, by and large, on the production of coarse goods, the Arvind was to cater to the demand for fine and superfine varieties. There was a growing consumers' preference for these varieties, which the Swadeshi wave had further accentuated. The only way to drive off foreign goods from the Indian market was to produce them at home, and there was no better moment to intensify the drive than the beginning of the 1930s when the middle class, the traditional user of such goods, was willing to accept indigenous production in preference to foreign goods. The Calico Mills was then the only company producing superfine goods in Ahmedabad, and the idea behind the establishment of the Arvind was to share an increasing market. Kasturbhai's new venture also conformed to the recommendation made by the Tariff Board in 1926 emphasizing the desirability of mills diversifying their production instead of concentrating on the coarse varieties.

With an initial share capital of Rs. 25,25,000 Arvind was a far bigger company than Kasturbhai's family had even promoted in the past, and the biggest of all the mills floated in Ahmedabad in 1931. The capital was divided into 5,250 ordinary and 20,000 preference shares of Rs. 100 each. The total capital except 250 ordinary shares were acquired by the Raipur Mills. This was, however, only a temporary expedient as the move mutilated against Kasturbhai's philosophy which viewed inter-corporate investment with disfavour. With the ultimate purpose of relieving the hold of the older company on the younger mill, Kasturbhai at the first stage increased the paid-up value of the former's 5,000 outstanding shares from Rs. 100 each to Rs. 600 each by capitalizing Rs. 25,00,000 from reserves. This was done in the year of the Arvind's registration. The following year the Raipur reduced the paid-up value of its outstanding shares to Rs. 200 each and distributed its holdings of the value of Rs. 20,00,000 in the Arvind to its own shareholders. The remaining holdings of Rs. 5,00,000 held by the Raipur in the Arvind were released in a like manner in 1937. Thus, Kasturbhai was able to kill two birds with one stone. He did not have to worry about arranging for the finance for his new venture and he could save the Raipur shareholders from incurring any tax liability on the funds received from the Raipur to be invested in the Arvind. In a real sense, thus, the Arvind was the Raipur's gift to its shareholders.

Kasturbhai could have achieved the same result even if the Raipur had retained its holdings in the other mill. But he considered inter-company investment, quite common those days, unethical. He did not want to control the management of the new company indirectly. In fact the management of the Arvind was entrusted to a new managing agency firm, Narottam Lalbhai and Company. In naming the managing agency of the Arvind after his younger brother, Kasturbhai's idea was to symbolize the involvement of another member of his family in managing the affairs of the business. He probably little anticipated the role that Narottambhai would play in shaping the destiny of the new company in future to make it the finest unit in the group.

The Arvind's twin sister, the Nutan, was founded with twin objectives. The primary purpose behind it was to draw the family of Kasturbhai's third sister, Kantaben, into the textile industry. She was married to Jagabhai Bhogilal Nanavaty who became the senior partner in a managing agency firm bearing his name. It is this firm that floated the Nutan Mills with Kasturbhai as its chairman. Another aim of the new company was to capture a segment of a market Kasturbhai had neglected so far. None of his mills was equipped to manufacture medium quality goods which seemed to have good prospects in the wake of the rising nationalist sentiment. The Nutan was to concentrate on producing such goods. But with an initial share capital of Rs. 5,00,000 it was to be a much smaller company than the Arvind.

One of the major factors which influenced Kasturbhai's choice of timing for launching these two ventures in spite of dangerously uncertain trends in the market was his hope to import the machinery at reduced rates. It seemed, however, in the beginning that his hope was not going to materialize. Sir Ness Wadia, whose Bombay firm was the agent of Messrs Platt Brothers of Oldham, England—the most reputable manufacturers of textile machinery—threw cold water on Kasturbhai's suggestion for a discount of 33⅓ per cent on his orders. The hope for anything more than ten per cent discount, according to Sir Ness, was nothing more than the day dream of a lunatic. However, on Kasturbhai's insistence, he agreed to refer Kasturbhai's orders to the English firm. If the manufacturers agreed to the suggested discount, Kasturbhai was to buy from them a total of 100,000 spindles and combers—40,000 immediately and the remaining within two years—under a mutually agreed schedule. So depressed was the world demand for machinery, that the Platt Brothers accepted Kasturbhai's terms. An astonished Sir Ness used this opportunity to order 50,000 spindles for his own mill—the Bombay Dyeing.

Like most of Kasturbhai's mills and those which started in the 1930s, both the Arvind and the Nutan were composite units. But the Arvind which was to cater to more affluent sections of the society had a more sophisticated technology. In addition to 52,560 ring spindles, 2552 doubling spindles, and 1122 looms, it started with full-fledged facilities for dyeing, bleaching, finishing, and mercerizing. The Arvind was very much different in this respect for, most of the companies started in the 1930s added to their processing facilities more gradually. In comparison, the Nutan was much smaller in size and had a less sophisticated machinery. It had only 20,120 spindles and 528 looms to start with.

Both the mills took longer to start production than any of Kasturbhai's mills launched earlier. But in spite of difficult times, their products were well received when they came into the market in 1933 even though they were meant for such sections of consumers which Kasturbhai's mills had never reached before. Some of the goods produced by the Arvind found ready market and the directors were confident that "other goods will also secure an equally good position" in none too distant future. Likewise, the Nutan cloth met with the approval of the buyers in 1933 and its management had no doubt that very soon it would "have a bigger hold on the market."

There were some indications in the environment to justify these hopes. The depression in the agricultural prices appeared to be losing some of its rigours in 1934 when the prices of farmer's products showed a feeble upward trend. At the same time the government continued to fortify its protective measures against foreign competition. The duty on the Japanese goods was increased in successive stages to 75 per cent by 1933. Forced by these measures Japan considered it prudent in 1934 to enter into an agreement with India under which Japanese imports were to be limited to 325 million yards, somewhat below the previous year's actual figures. At the same time the impact of the Swadeshi movement on the consumers had not yet lost its vigour.

None of these positive trends, however, proved enduring. After some recovery, the prices of agricultural products slumped again after 1935-36 and showed no sign of a real recovery well until after the outbreak of the Second World War in 1939. The result was a continued reduction in the buying power of the major group of consumers. At the same time Japan cleverly manoeuvred to import more than its quota permitted and the quantum of imports from that country always exceeded the limit till the war put an end to the trade between the two countries. To add to the hardship of the Indian producers, the duty on the British goods was reduced on the plea that imports on Japanese goods had been reduced after the introduction of the quota system. The Indo-British agreement of 1935 brought down the duty on British cloth from 25 to 20 per cent and that on yarn from 6.25 per cent to 5 per cent. The rates were again revised in March 1939 to effect a further 5 per cent cut in the import duty on cloth. In a period of slackened demand and stiff competition, the mills, ironically enough, needed more money to keep themselves going. The fall in the prices of some of the essential inputs such as raw cotton, stores, colours, and chemicals, was not as steep as in the case of the final product. It is no wonder, therefore, that the expense per loom in all the mills of Kasturbhai showed a successive increase between 1934 and 1938. Thus, all signs, barring perhaps the spirit of Swadeshi, which had generated some optimism in 1934 gradually vanished and the industry continued to remain in doldrums throughout the 1930s.

In the face of all these adverse factors, the performance of the Arvind was really gratifying. As Table IV. 2 indicates, its profits showed a continuous increase throughout this period. This was possible because its sales increased by more than 50 per cent during this period, and it could keep the expenses per loom under control. The result was that the profit as percentage of sales increased from 6 to 14 per cent. Among other mills in the group only the Raipur maintained a satisfactory level of performance. The Nutan, on the other hand, could never come up to the expectations and made no real profit until 1938. In order to be able to declare dividend the managing agents had to forego a part or the whole of their commission from the Nutan continuously for four years beginning with 1934. The condition of the Asoka was only slightly better. Even though the managing agents gave up their entire commission in 1934 and again in 1935, the company could declare no dividend at all

TABLE IV.2

Working of Kasturbhai Group of Mills: 1934-1938

Mills		*1934*	*1935*	*1936*	*1937*	*1938*
Raipur	Sales (in lakhs)	27.89	26.64	25.02	26.03	24.79
	Profit (in lakhs)	2.14	1.10	1.52	1.32	0.04
	Profit as percentage of sales (%)	7.67	4.13	6.08	5.07	0.16
	Dividends (%)	15.00	15.00	10.00	20.00	20.00
Asoka	Sales (in lakhs)	25.40	26.34	25.16	25.93	43.19
	Profit (in lakhs)	—.89[1]	—.94	0.58[2]	0.68[3]	0.51
	Profit as percentage of sales (%)	3.50	3.57	2.31	2.62	1.18
	Dividends (%)	0	0	10.00	10.00	10 00
Saraspur	Sales (in lakhs)	26.51	24.83	23.00	25.09	27.02
	Profit (in lakhs)	0.54	0.02	0.80	0.80	0.48
	Profit as percentage of sales (%)	2.04	0.08	3.48	0.04	1.78
	Dividend (%)	8.00	8.00	0	8.00	8.00
Aruna	Sales (in lakhs)	28.96	28.86	31.02	50.47	51.48
	Profit (in lakhs)	0.68	0.52	0.63	0.95	1.65
	Profit as percentage of sales (%)	2.35	1.80	2.03	1.88	3.21
	Dividend (%)	10.00	10.00	10.00	10.00	10.00
Arvind	Sales (in lakhs)	45.76	66.13	70.09	73.02	74.07
	Profit (in lakhs)	2.82	5.20	7.83	9.40	10.32
	Profit as percentage of sales (%)	6.16	7.86	11.17	12.87	13.93
	Dividend (%)	12.00	15.00	25.00	25.00	35.00
Nutan	Sales (in lakhs)	16.55	26.25	27.50	29.51	28.78
	Profit (in takhs)	—	0.11	0.01	0.26	1.43
	Profit as percentage of sales (%)	—	0.42	0.04	0.88	4.97
	Dividend (%)	6.00	7.00	7.00	7.00	8.00
Ahmedabad New Cotton	Sales (in lakhs)	—	—	—	—	22.02
	Profit (in lakhs)	—	—	—	—	4.42
	Profit as percentage of sales (%)	—	—	—	—	1.91
	Dividend (%)	—	—	—	—	0

[1] Profit after deducting commission given up by agents.

[2] Profit after deducting other receipts.

[3] Profit after deducting the amount transferred from stores adjustment account

in these years. In the next two years, the books showed slight improvement in earnings. But in analyzing the performance of the Asoka during this period it should be kept in mind that the profit figures for the year 1936 included a surplus of Rs. 7,700 realized by the sale of Ahmedabad Municipal Loan, and the figures for 1937 were inflated by the transfer of Rs. 25,000 from the stores adjustment account. Again the company's net earnings in 1938 would have been negligible had the managing agents not given up their commission. The fate of the Saraspur was no better. After earning a marginal profit in 1934, it suffered continuously for three years before registering a slight recovery in 1938. The Aruna was the only other mill in the group, besides the Arvind, whose sales and profits registered consistent rise, although its rate of profit was less steady and less impressive.

Uneven performance of the Kasturbhai mills is easily explicable. The only mill which did consistently well was the Arvind which catered to the taste of higher income groups. Depression normally affects these groups less adversely than those in the lower income groups. This is exactly what happened during the 1930s and the mills like the Arvind benefited. On the other hand the buying ability of those who patronized the coarse and medium varieties had reached its nadir. It was not surprising, therefore, that the mills which concentrated on the production of these varieties suffered.

Of course, factors peculiar to individual mills also affected their working. The Asoka remained closed for about a month and a half because of the re-erection of engine during 1934. The next year, some of its looms remained idle since the mill could not produce sufficient yarn of the desired quality and it was considered unremunerative to purchase yarn from outside. Likewise, the changeover of machinery disrupted the working of the Raipur for the major part of 1938. Also the wage bills of all the mills in the group increased that year as a result of the implementation of the interim recommendation of the Textile Labour Enquiry Committee without any corresponding change in the cloth price. Such adverse factors, however, had only marginal effect on the quantum of profits. The conspiracy of circumstances proved much more prejudicial. Kasturbhai and his associates took several steps to alleviate the situation.

One of these was to introduce a double shift in order to achieve the economy of scale in the operation and, thus, bring down the cost of production. The Arvind and the Nutan were the first to be brought under this scheme. Later, as the market situation worsened, double shifts were introduced in the Asoka, the Raipur, and the Saraspur also. The strategy, however, achieved only limited results except in the case of the Arvind. For, the second shift was stopped in other mills only after a few months.

The strategy to expand production facilities and add processing equipment, too, had only marginal effect on the immediate earnings, but their impact on the long-term working of the mills in the group was bound to be profound. As we have noted earlier, only the Arvind had been installed with the full processing facilities at the time of its birth, and a small bleaching plant had been added to the Raipur as early as 1918. But the real addition to the processing facilities in other mills took place only in the 1930s. The depressive trends in the machinery prices, visible in the beginning of the decade, became more marked as the 1930s progressed. Not only did the world economy continue to remain under pressure, the British monopoly on the export to India of these goods was successfully broken by the entry of the United States, Germany, and Japan. Taking advantage of the lower movement of prices in the machinery market, Kasturbhai added processing facilities of various description to all his mills. Bleaching and cheese dyeing plants were added to the Asoka in 1938. The same year bleaching, finishing, and dyeing plants were installed in the Aruna. A year earlier the total machinery of the Raipur had been replaced by more efficient equipments along with processing machinery. The Nutan was fitted with sprinklers and humidifying plant in 1936 and with cheese dyeing and bleaching plants in 1938. The Arvind which started off as an integrated unit continued to expand its production capacity and processing facilities. The Saraspur was the only company in the group to which no processing facilities were added during the period. Perhaps the Saraspur machinery was so worn out that it was felt that the quality produced by these equipments would improve but little by the installation of bleaching, dyeing, and finishing plants. To what extent did the new equipments push up or arrest further decline in the sales is by no means an easy question to decide. One thing is, however, certain that the addition of the processing facilities transformed the character of the group and laid a solid foundation for future growth.

In the meantime Kasturbhai had acquired another mill, the Ahmedabad New Cotton Mills Ltd. The company had been floated in 1905 by a prominent industrialist, Amratlal Damodardas Shodhan, who hailed from the Vaishnava *bania* stock. The Shodhan family had entered the field of textile manufacturing as early as 1892 and had floated several mills. During the depression, however, the old and dilapidated machinery could not stand the strains of the times. As he had done at the time of the Saraspur failure, Kasturbhai again stepped forward and brought the mill under his own management. The capital of the company then stood at Rs. 10,00,000 divided into 6,000 ordinary and 4,000 preference shares of Rs. 100 each. A new managing agency Messrs Narottam Chandulal & Co., named after the son of Kasturbhai's second sister, took over the management of the acquired company. We may recall that Chandulal had assisted Kasturbhai and his brother in managing their mill affairs when they were yet to gain maturity and experience. Chandulal was by this time dead and Kasturbhai's loyalty to his family induced him to provide for gainful employment for his children.

The transition to the new management in the case of the Ahmedabad New Cotton did not prove as smooth as it had been in relation to the Saraspur. Several persons owed money to the company and it was not easy to realize the debts. One of these was the firm of Pari Harshadlal Amritlal who owed Rs. 5,00,000 to the mill. The debtor firm procrastinated and the management had to file a suit, attach a part of its property, and eventually settle the claims out of the court at a loss of Rs. 75,000. In settling another claim of Rs. 70,000, the new management had to be content with some shares that the firm of Pari Harshadlal Amratlal had in another concern and which the company had to dispose of at below par value.

On the top of it all the machinery of the new acquisition was in a hopeless condition and needed complete reorganization if the operations were to be run efficiently. The new management, therefore, had to make strenuous efforts for two years

Ahmedabad New Cotton Mills in 1920

Arvind Mills : A View of the Spinning Section

TABLE IV.3

Growth of Kasturbhai Group of Mills: 1931-1938

Item	*1931*	*1932*	*1933*	*1934*	*1935*	*1936*	*1937*	*1938*
Paid-up capital (Rs. in lakhs)	57.86	62.83	68.11	68.11	63.25	63.25	48.25	48.25
No. of spindles	15,54,140	1,82,508	2,44,404	2,44,404	2,47,092	2,57,872	2,57,872	2,35,060
No. of looms	81,137	8,267	12,128	12,212	12,279	12,868	12,868	11,425
No. of workers	6,174	6,677	7,483	8,987	2,259	8,605	8,675	8,619

before the mill could start functioning satisfactorily. During this period, the plant and machinery were reorganized, new looms and spindles were ordered, and complete dyeing and bleaching plants were installed. Eventually, the new machinery was put to use in 1938. There was some improvement in the working, but the question of such a company turning the corner in a short time, and that too under unfavourable market conditions, did not arise. The future of the mill was still uncertain when the Second World War began.

With the expansion effected between 1931 and 1938, Kasturbhai came to occupy the position of the biggest textile magnate in the city and one of the biggest in the country. His seven mills together contained 2,35,060 spindles and 11,425 looms which respectively constituted more than 12 per cent and more than 24 per cent of total spinning and weaving capacities in Ahmedabad. Practically all his mills had new machinery and other processing facilities. A glance at Table IV.3 would reveal the progress made by the group during one of the worst periods in the history of the Indian textile industry.

By the time the Second World War began, Kasturbhai's ambition to create a textile empire had reached a saturation point. There was a justifiable basis for it in spite of the uneven performance of his mills during the depression. He had created a network of manufacturing concerns which together were capable of producing practically all varieties of goods, for which there was demand in India, and catering to various sections of the population. Himself the chairman of four of these companies, he had become the guiding spirit of all the units in the group, and the reputation of his management was unrivalled. The completion of this manufacturing infrastructure symbolized in Kasturbhai's business career the end of the first phase of what we have called entrepreneurial continuum in our conceptual scheme. The idea of expanding his textile ventures further did not excite him any more. He now looked for new pastures, new fields.

CHAPTER V

Entrepreneurial Continuum: Diversification

NO perceptive observer in the 1930s could have failed to notice that the Ahmedabad textile industry was fast approaching a plateau. The decade did not witness the establishment of a single mill after 1932. The depression had something to do with the entrepreneurs' reluctance to risk their resources, but some of them had also started wondering whether it would not be more prudent to avoid putting all their eggs in one basket. Kasturbhai was among these. As early as 1935 he had come to the conclusion that there were "many other industries where profit margin is much better." In fact it is doubtful that but for somewhat extraneous consideration, he would have acquired the Ahmedabad New Cotton with all the concomitant complications. He was more keen to diversify his business interests.

Kasturbhai, however, was not quite sure about the line in which he would like to branch off when one of his cousins, Chinubhai, came forward with the suggestion to start a factory to manufacture starch. Chinubhai was the son of Manibhai, one of the two uncles of Kasturbhai from whom he had acquired the Saraspur Mills. Ignoring the bitterness of a bygone generation, Kasturbhai had treated his uncles kindly and porvided for their personal comfort and well-being. More importantly, he had taken good care of their children's education and development. After acquiring bachelor's degree in Chemistry and Law, Chinubhai had started an insurance business in 1934. He had done so at Kasturbhai's instance, out of deference for him; he had no intrinsic interest in this line nor did his initial experience give much promise for the future. He began to fancy manufacturing ideas and finally approached his illustrious cousin again not for advice but with a proposal. He intended to take up starch production.

Whether Chinubhai knew it or not, his suggestion had a sound basis. A basic requirement for processing cloth, starch is used for producing a host of other commodities such as adhesive, cosmetics, paper, and confectionery. Since there were no starch factories in the country, India had to depend solely on imports. With the development of the cotton textile industry, demand for this product was increasing consistently, and imports jumped from about 8,000 tonnes in 1932-33 to more than 13,000 tonnes in 1934-35. Moreover the idea to manufacture a product resulting into vertical integration was consistent with the diversification strategy pursued by most of the Indian business groups in general. Starch could feed the needs of the textile mills in the group and thus the risk in producing it was minimal indeed. Also an Ahmedabad-based company would have some locational advantage because maize, the basic raw material, was grown in plenty in the Panch Mahal district of Gujarat and the adjoining regions of Panjab.

Though not unaware of these advantages, Kasturbhai chided his young cousin for having come out with a half-baked proposal. "This is no way to approach me or start an industry," said the industrialist. "Have you studied the problem? Study the markets and the costs and the problems of raw materials, profitability, and the capital and come with a report when you see me next in this connection. You will have to equip yourself thoroughly with the production aspect of the business." Chinubhai took his cousin's 'order' in all seriousness. He not only made a first-hand study of the cost and marketing aspects of the proposal but also joined the Bombay University to study chemical technology and production processes. And when he returned to Ahmedabad, he had no difficulty in convincing his older cousin of the viability of the venture. That Chinubhai was not alone in gauging the profitability of the new line is clear from the fact that in 1937 at least one starch company had already started. This was the Bharat Starch and Chemicals Ltd., Jamunanagar in Panjab founded by Karam Chand Thapar who later rose to a prominent position in Indian business.*

Thus, seen in a proper historical perspective, the Anil Starch Products Ltd., promoted by Kasturbhai in 1938, was a venture of pioneering nature. With the initial paid-up capital of Rs. 5,00,000, the company had a modest beginning, but the promoters expected it to grow fast as the authorized capital was fixed at Rs. 25,00,000. Also, though the immediate plan was to manufacture starch and its by-products alone, the company in due course was to go into the production of related commodities such as glucose, dextrine, industrial adhesives, flour starches, and cattle foods. The managing agency was vested in a new firm under the style of Kasturbhai Lalbhai & Co., in which Chinubhai's family had 50 per cent interest; the balance was equally divided among Kasturbhai, his two brothers, and the family of his other uncle.

Though some of the industrial magnates of Bombay contemptuously dubbed the starch venture as a "toy-company", Kasturbhai and his associates had little doubt about its future. They went ahead with their preparation. Using his acquaintance with an English firm, Gannon and Dunkerly & Co., Kasturbhai secured the services of a German expert who agreed to negotiate and order for the appropriate machinery. After a great deal of study and consideration, the expert placed orders with a German firm and sent the drawings to his clients in Ahmedabad. The German engineer then came to India to help the company erect the equipments. But only a part of the machinery had arrived in India when the Second World War broke out causing a complete chaos in maritime commerce. A German vessel then was on her way to Bombay with another consignment of the Anil Starch machinery worth about

*According to *Investors' Encyclopaedia, 1952-53* (p. 760) another starch company, Indian Starch Products Ltd. had been registered in 1936. But probably it started functioning after the establishment of the Anil Starch.

Rs. 1,60,000. To protect herself from the possible enemy shelling, the vessel moved to a neutral port instead of calling at Bombay. Nobody could be sure about when the machinery would be delivered or whether it would be delivered at all, and yet the commencement of production could not be allowed to be postponed indefinitely without jeopardizing the future of the infant enterprise. To add to the misfortune of the promoters, the German expert was interned and sent to Australia. Kasturbhai did not lose heart and asked Chinubhai and one Ardeshir Babycon, a Parsee engineer then with the Arvind Mills, to fabricate the machinery with the help of the drawings. It was by no means an easy job but the two 'experts' finally succeeded in putting up a working contraption by means of setting and arranging iron scraps. On Kasturbhai's representation, the Government of India secured the release of the German expert who was pleasantly surprised to see on his return to India that the company was all set to start production in spite of a large part of its machinery having gone stray. Also the loss of the consignment did not result in any financial loss to the company as the underwriters accepted and honoured the claim for compensation preferred by the company under the insurance contract, though after a long legal battle.

Production started in February 1941. Starch was the only commodity which was produced initially and that too in small quantity—about 1 tonne a day. The plant could not reach its full productive capacity until the end of 1941 and thereafter difficulties in procuring raw material hampered the working of the company. By this time the number of companies producing starch had increased to more than 40, and the demand for maize had shot up. At the same time, the shortage of food-grains in the country and the disruption of supplies from abroad, following the outbreak of the war, rendered procurement of maize for manufacturing purposes extremely difficult. The result was that the starch companies, including the Anil Starch, had to contend with the short supply of their basic raw material. Eventually the government of India interceded and prevailed upon the provincial governments to supply a larger quantity of maize for starch production. Consequently the Anil Starch's production increased and the sales figures jumped from Rs. 3,65,000 in 1941 to more than Rs. 17,57,000 in 1942. For the first time since its birth, the company made a modest profit of Rs. 1,55,650 which enabled it to distribute a dividend of 5 per cent on the preference shares and 6 per cent along with a bonus of Rs. 2 on an ordinary share.

The management felt that the problem of raw material had been permanently solved. Their optimism, however, was premature and misplaced. The very next year the problem became more acute as the food crisis deepened. After the fall of Burma in 1942, the imports were cut off altogether. At the same time famine conditions in many parts of the country caused unprecedented shortage of supplies in 1943. To meet the crisis, the government issued its Starch Control Order which prohibited the production of starch from wheat and fixed the price of various varieties of starch. The following year some restrictions were placed on the use of maize also. This created a grave crisis for the industry and most of the starch factories had to stop operations for want of raw material. The Anil Starch, however, not only survived but also succeeded in augmenting its production, sale, and profit. In 1943 the sales increased to four times and profits to more than 15 times over the previous year's figures. In the next two years, the profit declined as the Table V.1 indicates. The company's position, nevertheless, was quite sound when the war ended.

TABLE V.1

Working of the Anil Starch: 1939-1945

Year	*Total sales* (*Rs. in lakhs*)	*Profit* (*Rs. in lakhs*)	*Profit as percentage of sales* (%)	*Dividend* %
1941	3.66	0.03	0.8	0
1942	17.58	1.56	8.9	8
1943	74.02	24.53	33.1	20
1944	81.38	19.97	24.4	20
1945	57.39	14.20	24.7	20

Three factors helped the company during these crucial years. First, it had sufficient quantity of raw material in its stock when the crisis deepened in 1943. Ever since 1941 when it had its first taste of maize shortage, the company had kept an eye on the raw material stock and maintained sufficient quantity in store. The restriction imposed in 1943 and 1944, therefore, did not have any adverse effect on its fortunes. In fact, the raw material shortage indirectly benefited the company. Several less efficient units went out of production leaving only 15 companies in the field. This eased the pressure on demand for raw material on the one hand and reduced competition on the other. This was the second factor favourable to the Anil Starch. And thirdly, the profit margin throughout the war remained very high as there was total stoppage of imports while the textile companies, the principal users of starch then, needed the product in ever increasing quantity for their ever increasing production.

Ironically enough, the return of peace brought with it almost insurmountable difficulties for the starch industry in general. The wartime demand suddenly disappeared and the food crisis became so acute that the Anil Starch found it difficult to maintain its level of production. The result was that the value of its sales in 1946 declined to a meagre sum of less than Rs. 13,40,000 and profits were reduced to just a little more than Rs. 1,76,000. This naturally affected the quantum of dividends. While the company managed to pay preference shareholders at the rate of 5 per cent, the ordinary shareholders had to forego their bonus of Rs. 10 per share to which they had become accustomed during the years of prosperity.

The following year was worse still. Production of starch came to an almost dead halt as the worsening food situation prevented the government from allocating any quantity of maize to the Anil Starch. Realizing that the end of the food crisis was nowhere in sight, the company management experimented with the use of materials other than food-grains for producing starch. These experiments bore little fruit and the quantity of maize available in the company stock was too inadequate to keep the plants running. Inevitably, the starch plant remained closed for the most part of the year and the value of its starch products plummetted to less than half of the previous year's total.

The Anil Starch would have been in a deeper trouble had it not added a new item to its production line. This was sulphuric acid. The commodity was a crucial input for textile manufacturing but very little of it was indigenously produced. In view of the growing demand for the product and in the context of the overall policy of the company to diversify production, it had decided, as early as 1945, to start the manufacture of sulphuric acid. Erection of the plant took a little more than a year and production started in the beginning of 1947. A part of the plant capacity, however, remained idle because of the difficulty of railway freights. Consequently, the total value of the acid sold by the company in 1947 remained limited to a little more than Rs. 2,11,000.

The cumulative effect of all this was to make 1947 as the worst year in the short history of the company. For the first time it incurred a loss of about Rs. 1,96,000 and for the first time its ordinary shareholders had to go without dividends and its managing agents without their commission. To satisfy the claims of the preference shareholders, the company had to draw Rs. 25,000 from its dividend equalization fund. The only factor that could give some satisfaction to the management was that while more than 30 starch companies had bowed out of the scene in the face of the crisis, the Anil Starch was still able to maintain its existence; only five other units in the entire country could claim this distinction.

II

It is by no means easy to determine whether Kasturbhai would have held on to starch production had not the profits from his textile operations during these years sustained his determination. As we have seen earlier, most of his mills along with the industry as a whole were suffering under the yoke of depression when the Anil Starch started its career. The outbreak of the Second World War, however, set in motion forces which turned the tide. Though the general outlook for the industry, or for that matter for the economy as a whole, remained uncertain almost till the end of 1940, enduringly favourable trends were clearly visible as the war progressed with the resultant drastic reduction in imports. After the entry of Japan in the fray in 1942, a major source of competition was completely eliminated and imports reached a negligible figure. At the same time there was a great spurt in the internal demand because of ever increasing volume of goods required for war purposes and some improvement in the consumers' ability to buy. Also, the neighbouring countries, whose needs were met through imports from western countries and Japan before the war, came to depend increasingly on India after the traditional sources of their supply were closed. The result was that the Indian mills were now called upon to satisfy not only the internal requirements but also to supply goods to the countries in the East and South East Asia.

It was a god-sent opportunity for the Indian mills. While they prepared themselves to meet the challenges, they found that the Government was more than willing to help them. To ensure maximum production, the government offered a series of incentives to manufacturers and invoked the infamous Defence of India Rule to ban strikes and lockouts. Several provisions of the Factories Act were relaxed and efforts were made to ensure the supply of stores and raw materials necessary for uninterrupted operations. The industry somewhat resented the introduction of the Excess Profit Tax and Compulsory Deposit Scheme in 1940, but these were minor irritants compared to the encouragement given to the producers during the early years of the war.

The positive factors were, however, somewhat tempered by a few negative elements in the environment. The dazzling success of Japan on the eastern borders created panic in the market and caused an unprecedented dislocation in manufacturing and trading activities. The setback was, however, temporary and as the Japanese threat receded, the industry recovered. Likewise the impact of the Quit India Movement in 1942 had only a limited impact even though the workers struck work for prolonged periods at every manufacturing centre to express their solidarity with the national cause. Ahmedabad mills experienced the longest strike—of three and half months' duration—and surprisingly enough Kasturbhai himself, as we shall see later, played a crucial, though clandestine role, in bringing it about. As a result of the fall in production caused by these developments coupled with the virtual cessation of imports the supply lagged far behind the demand. The prices of textile goods, consequently, skyrocketted. In the case of some varieties, the rise was as high as 400 per cent. Under these conditions, beginning with 1942 the mills all over the country set off on a course of unprecedented profit and prosperity.

Kasturbhai must have congratulated himself on his wisdom to have reorganized and updated the machinery of all but one of his mills before the war began. He did not have to lose time in improving his production facilities when the profitable trends set in. As the demand situation improved and production increased, all his mills were placed on double shift beginning with 1941. As Table V.2 indicates, a definite upward movement in the earnings of the group began the same year. All the companies were the beneficiaries of this trend. So favourable was the market situation that even the Saraspur and the Ahemdabad New Cotton which were in dire straits before 1939 manifested unmistakable signs of recovery. Kasturbhai and his associates were still unsure about the future but the results of 1942 set all their doubts at rest. For, the cumulative earnings of the mills in the group increased by more than 50 per cent though the production had been badly hit by a long labour strike following the arrest of the nationalist leaders in August 1942. As is obvious from Table V.2 the increase in the profits was due more to the rising prices of the finished goods than to the increase in sales.

TABLE V.2

Consolidated Performance of the Kasturbhai Group of Mills: 1939-1945

Item	*1939*	*1940*	*1941*	*1942*	*1943*	*1944*	*1945*
Paid-up capital (in lakhs)	33.0	43.50	43.50	43.50	43.50	43.50	43.50
Sales (in lakhs)	210.99	328.73	433.69	453.39	1115.29	1085.50	851.05
Profit (in lakhs)	2.51	13.79	58.26	89.06	433.65	304.04	154.17
Profit as percentage of sales	1.19	4.19	13.43	19.64	38.79	28.01	18.12
Dividend (%)	10.48	12.83	22.09	19.66	23.77	24.11	24.11
No. of workers	8734	8873	9129	9039	8728	9132	9040

The sale-profit ratio, however, declined in 1944. This was due to change in the policy of the Government which abandoned the 'hands-off' attitude and clamped a number of controls to protect consumers' interests. A scheme to require the textile mills to produce what came to be known as the "standard cloth", though devised earlier, was enforced in 1942 and the task of distribution was entrusted to the provincial governments. What, however, affected the earnings of the textile manufacturers most was the promulgation of the Cotton Cloth and Yarn (Control) Order of 1943 under which the government fixed the ceiling price of different varieties of goods. The prices fixed were somewhat lower than those ruling in the market even though there was no reduction in the cost of production. The earnings of 1945 were further slashed as a result of a drastic cut in the government requirements after the termination of the hostilities.

One of the notable features of the working of Kasturbhai's mills during the war was that percentage rise in the earnings of the Arvind and the Raipur, which had so successfully weathered the storm during the worst days of depression, was much l ss in comparison to the increase in the profits of other mills. The reasons are not far to seek. These two mills produced only fine and superfine varieties for which there was little demand from the Government, and the Government was the major consumer during the war. Consequently, the other five factories which produced coarse or medium varieties did much better business. The agriculturist, with marketable surplus at his disposal consequent on the high prices of food-grains, also patronized these varieties.

The profits earned during the war enabled the Kasturbhai mills to pay increased and regular dividends to the shareholders. The management's enthusiasm to provide cash benefits to shareholders was, however, not allowed to go beyond a limit. A part of the earnings was used to build reserve or increase the capital. The paid-up capital of the Arvind, for instance, went up to Rs. 26,25,000 between 1940 and 1945 through capitalization of a part of reserve and issuance of bonus shares to the existing shareholders. The same method was adopted to increase the paid-up capital of the Raipur and the Aruna in 1942. Though the capital structure of the other mills in the group remained unaltered, their reserves went up. There is no doubt that the war helped Kasturbhai to consolidate his textile ventures. If he did not take any steps to expand his manufacturing facilities, it was only because most of his mills had already undergone reorganization before the war. He would have certainly liked to change the machinery of the Saraspur but import difficulties during the war forced him to postpone the much needed modernization of the oldest mill in the group.

Perhaps the most significant aspect of Kasturbhai's wartime business was the manner in which the profits were earned. As S.D. Mehta has rightly remarked, during the war years "the actions of large sections of the industry were anti-social in character, even if they were not positively illegal."[41] At the time when a larger number of millowners succumbed to the irresistible temptation to resort to underhand practices, particularly before the controls were imposed, Kasturbhai was among a small minority who did not swerve from upright business principles. He did not hold back stocks in the hope of realizing higher prices later, nor did he alter his production schedules to realize higher quantum of profits. It is significant that a committee of the Government of India set up to enquire into the wartime business practices of the Indian groups gave a clean chit to Kasturbhai's concerns.

The sales of the mills naturally shrank after the war ended in the middle of 1945 as the military requirements declined. At the same time increased dearness allowance to the workers and the rising cost of essential inputs such as coal, fuel, oil, and cotton resulted in the rising cost of production. Profits consequently declined and the trend continued into 1946 when the communal riots which rocked the country on the eve of its independence hit production. At the same time, the implementation of the new wage awards increased the salary bills. Fortunately for Kasturbhai, Ahmedabad mills were relatively free from labour unrest which affected the working of mills in Bombay and other manufacturing centres after the war ended. The result was that the consolidated profits of his mills were better as compared to the national average. While the earning of the industry, as a whole, in 1945 and 1946 was about 4 times that of 1939, Kasturbhai's mills had a ratio of 1:5 and in 1947 it jumped to more than 9 times the 1939 figures.

III

The wartime profits from his mills and starch company undoubtedly boosted Kasturbhai's confidence and resources but left him with a nagging sense of discontent. His achievements essentially were no different from a number of textile manufacturers in Ahmedabad and other centres in the country. He could as yet boast of but little accomplishment in any other line of business. The Anil Starch was too modest a venture and too closely related to the textile industry to prove anything. Kasturbhai's search for exploitable opportunities in fields other than textile had been only suspended during the war. The improved state of resources after the war intensified this search.

Several possibilities were considered and given up during the first two years after peace. For some time in 1945 Kasturbhai toyed with the idea of manufacturing telephones in the country. There was no indigenous production of the equipment. The attitude of the government was encouraging and the British Telephone Company, London, was willing to participate in the proposed venture. The negotiations were still at a preliminary stage when Kasturbhai realized the full implications of the new scheme. Telephone being a Government monopoly, the Government was going to be the sole buyer of the product. The Government also insisted on the right to fix the price. Resenting the idea of being at the perpetual dictates of a single buyer, Kasturbhai retraced his steps. At about the same time, the Greaves Cotton offered Kasturbhai the agency for distributing their products in India but the industrialist had no interest in being a distributor. Another proposal which fell through came from the Burmah Shell which wanted the Sheth to join them in a refinery venture in Bombay. But he was reluctant to be bound by a price structure determined by the international partner. He, therefore, remained aloof from the slippery world of oil.

The textile magnate eventually settled on the production of synthetic dyestuffs which the textile industry required in large quantities. The development of the industry was important for the overall economic health of the country as the experience of industrially advanced countries had proved. Apart from supplying colouring materials for textile and non-textile industries, it could form, as it had done elsewhere, a nucleus for the development of a whole range of chemicals. As the Indian Tariff Commission was to remark later:

> Its progress is linked up with the development of essential chemical industry and coal tar industry on one hand and fine chemical and pharmaceutical industry, explosives, synthetic plastics, and solvent industries on the other. The products of this industry contribute to the strength of the national economy in times of peace and the industry can be readily converted to the production of defence materials in times of crisis.[42]

And yet, the dyestuff industry in India, the land which had a virtual monopoly on indigo supply in the world till the discovery of synthetic dyes in the mid-19th century, was yet to be born when the Second World War began. Since there was no restriction on imports, the needs of the country were met through imports. Germany, then the most important exporter of dyestuffs in the world, was the major supplier to India before 1939 with the well known firm, I.G. Farben, holding a near monopoly position in the Indian market. It is doubtful whether the government of the times had a comprehensive vision of the value of the dyestuff industry for the nation's economy or realized the danger inherent in India's dependence on imports, but the difficulties in importing the commodity after the outbreak of hostilities stirred the official machinery into appointing a working group under the chairmanship of K. Venkataraman, the Director of the Department of Chemical Technology in the University of Bombay, to suggest measures to promote indigenous production. Its report suggested a phased programme which was to culminate in the production of all the dyes in the country so as to meet a substantial part of internal demand within 15 to 20 years. The Associated Research Laboratories at Bhatghar near Poona, which had started production in 1940, was then the only company in the field. Its output, however, was too small, and range of production too limited to meet the requirements of the country. Little progress was made towards implementing the recommendations of the Venkataraman report during the war. A few small units sprang up during the war to manufacture what is known as Stabilized Azoics but their total production made little material difference in the situation. Consequently, when the war ended, the country's dependence on imports for its dyestuff requirement was as great as ever before.

The government in the meantime had appointed another committee in 1941 under the chairmanship of Sir Ardeshir Dalal, then a director in the Tata Sons, to review the recommendations of the Venkataraman group and study the problem more deeply. The Dyestuff Exploratory Committee, as it came to be known, took a long time to complete its deliberations and could not submit its report until after the end of the Second World War. By this time John Matthai, a well-known economist of his times, had replaced Dalal as the Chairman of the Committee consequent to the latter's appointment as a member of the Viceregal Council. The Matthai report outlined a scheme under which the range of dyes recommended by the earlier group could be indigenously produced within a period of five years, and stressed its belief that it was feasible to "manufacture all the dyes in substantial demand together with all the necessary intermediates in the country within 15 to 20 years."[43]

Even though Sir Ardeshir had dissociated from the Dyestuff Exploratory Committee, his interest in promoting the production of synthetic dyes in the country had not declined. Sometime after the war ended, he invited a number of experts from abroad to suggest ways and means to develop chemical industry in the country. One of those who visited India in 1945 on his invitation was Malcolm Cressey, a representative of the American Cyanamid Company, New York. After a visit to a number of industrial plants in the country, including the Anil Starch, he expressed his strong conviction that the future for the dye industry in India was extremely bright.

The American company was among the major producers of certain varieties of dyes. Its dyestuff products were distributed in India through a subsidiary in Bombay known as the Ameer Trading Corporation Ltd. in which the family of Bhulabhai Desai, an outstanding advocate of his times, had some interests. In the course of his conversation at Bombay with Bhulabhai's son, Dhirajlal Desai popularly known as Dhirubhai, Cressey again referred to the excellent business opportunity in the field of dye production in India and hinted at his willingness to collaborate with a reputable Indian party in promoting a suitable venture. Dhirubhai suggested the name of Kasturbhai.

Seeking a non-textile opening for himself Kasturbhai jumped at Dhirubhai's suggestion. Kasturbhai himself went to New York to finalize the terms of collaboration. The American company agreed to design the plant and provide technical know-how on an annual royalty of 2.5 per cent on sales for 10 years. The Cyanamid's demand for low royalty surprised Kasturbhai and his associates, but the Americans were more concerned with a long-term association than in the short-term gains. "By the time your firm is firmly established," said Sid Moody, the Vice President of the Cyanamid, "you will not need us, but you will be so much involved in chemicals that, one time or the other, you will have to come to our door." Kasturbhai also extracted an unusual promise. The American Cyanamid agreed to have 10 per cent interest in the proposed company. The American firm had never made a direct investment in a developing country but Kasturbhai insisted on this provision because he wanted the collaborating firm to have a financial stake in his venture instead of remaining a mere supplier of technical expertise from afar. Significantly enough, right at this time the house of the Tatas was negotiating with the Imperial Chemical Industries a proposal for manufacturing dyes in India in collaboration with the renowned British leader in the field. Kasturbhai had no knowledge of the Tatas' move but had he taken longer to make up his mind, the Tatas most probably would have forestalled him. In fact the Tatas tried to dissuade him from going into the new line, but their plea made little impact on Kasturbhai's resolve.

As it turned out, the Tata-ICI negotiations bore no fruit, while the Kasturbhai-Cyanamid plan culminated in the registration of the Atul Products Limited on the 5th September 1947. The birth of the new company, in the words of a competent observer, was "the beginning of the full-fledged dyestuff industry in the country."[41] But the promoters, by no means, wanted to remain confined to dyes alone. The object clause in the company's memorandum of association clearly emphasized their intention to "produce . . . chemical products of every nature and description, and components, intermediates, derivatives and by-products thereof and products to be made therefrom. . . ." That this was not a hollow declaration is clear from the fact that the authorized capital was fixed at Rs. 5,00,00,000 divided into 5,00,000 shares of Rs. 100 each. Only one-fifth of this capital, however, was issued and subscribed initially.

The management of the company was entrusted to a new managing agency firm, the Lalbhai Sons and Company. As a gesture of appreciation to his services, Dhirubhai was allotted nearly 8 per cent share in the managing agency. Kasturbhai was appointed the chairman and a representative of the American Cyanamid Company, Herbert Edward Lorenz who was then its export manager in India, was given a place of honour on the board of directors. Soon after its registration the new company formalized the agreement with the Cyanamid Company under which the latter was to provide technical know-how for 18 Direct and Acid Azo dyes and also for the manufacture of another dye known as Sulphur Black. It also agreed to supply the know-how for any other chemicals which it was manufacturing and which the Atul might need for a wider and integrated development of the proposed venture.

B.K. Muzumdar was appointed the General Manager of the new company. But he was much more than a general manager. In fact the development of the Atul is as intimately linked with Muzumdar's name as with Kasturbhai's. Born in 1902 in Surat in a family of modest means, Muzumdar had a brilliant academic career which culminated in a master's degree in economics from the Benares Hindu University (1926) and a bachelor's degree in commerce from the London School of Economics (1930). Having had a brief stint at teaching economics at his Indian *alma mater*, Muzumdar was persuaded by Kasturbhai to join the Arvind Mills in 1931 when the young lecturer accompanied his Vice-Chancellor, Pandit Madan Mohan Malaviya, to Ahmedabad to collect funds for his university. Muzumdar's brilliance was visible in his new job as much as it had been in the academic field, and he soon won the confidence of the Sheth. With an unostentatious and rather innocuous designation as "Secretary in English Office," he did a great deal to modernize the working of the mills in the group by adopting new statistical and cost control methods. The mills, however, were denied of his services for most of the war years because of Muzumdar's participation in the nationalist movement. A staunch nationalist with very close links with the then Socialist leaders, particularly Jayaprakash Narayan, he actively participated in the '42 movement, remained underground for two years, and then in jail up to 1945. After his release, he returned to the Arvind Mills and served the mill until he was asked by Kasturbhai to take charge of the Atul project in 1948.

The first task before the promoters of the new company was to decide about the location of its production facilities. It was clear to them from the very beginning that Ahmedabad was hardly the place for a huge chemical complex of their dreams. They needed a large area of land, abundance of water, and outlet for effluent disposal. Even if the land was not as scarce and expensive near the big city then, Ahmedabad could hardly satisfy the other two basic conditions. Two sites were explored in what is now the State of Maharashtra. One of them near Ulhasnagar in Thana district was rejected because of bad contours and another near the present location of the Hindustan Organic Chemicals (HOC) in the vicinity of Panvel was given up because there was no direct rail link, and the effluent facilities were considered inadequate. Eventually Dhirubhai, who hailed from a village near Valsad, suggested a site near Valsad railway station about 300 kilometres to the south of Ahmedabad. The site selected was in a rural area and was virtually fallow land which grew nothing but natural grass and wild flowers, and housed none but snakes and lizards, squirrels and monkeys, birds and butterflies, and mosquitoes and flies. Most of the land was uneven and stony with marshy patches at places. And, situated as it was in the tribal region, the social life in the surrounding localities was not free from strain. Because of these ostensibly negative elements, Kasturbhai was able to strike an extremely favourable bargain and acquire through government help a huge piece of about 900 acres at a price far below what he would have paid for a similar area in or near an urban centre. He would later add about 250 acres to this property through purchase from private parties.

Cheapness of land was only one of the factors which attracted the Atul promoters to the Valsad region. There were several other more important considerations. The site was only 11 kilometres from the railway station; the Western Railway ran to the west of the site. Very soon Kasturbhai would have the railways extended to his plants and Atul itself would become a railway station. The eastern side of the location was flanked by a national highway running between Bombay and Ahmedabad and the river Par flowed in the south. From a distance of only three kilometres the roaring sound of the Arabian sea broke the silence of wilderness. The river would be the major source of water supply and the sea would absorb the effluents of the chemical company reducing the fear of pollution. An added advantage was that the nation's two major textile centres, the principal consumers of the product, were almost equidistant and easily accessible from the proposed site. Even the tribal location promising a relatively cheap labour supply was a blessing in disguise. The site selected for the factory, thus, was almost as ideal as a textbook would recommend.

The selection of the site was very much influenced by the stipulations of Sid Moody, the Vice-President of the American Cyanamid, who saw no limit to expansion of dyes and chemical industry in India. It was Muzumdar's job to develop the complex. To give his entire attention to the project he decided to reside in Valsad, leaving behind in Ahmedabad his various social and political activities. There were three major tasks before the General Manager: to survey and acquire the land, to develop the site and physical infrastructure, and to put up the plant and machinery. Perhaps the last was the easiest to achieve with the help of the American collaborators, but the first two demanded a great deal of patience, tact, and foresight.

Surveying and acquiring a huge property in rural India has always been a complicated matter because of conflicting claims to the title and consequent legal intricacies attending on such transactions. To make the matter worse, the Atul property fell under the territorial jurisdiction of three different villages. Negotiations had to be conducted not with one but several title-holders and boundary divisions were not always clear, as is normally the case with regard to rural fallow lands. The mishandling of even a simple situation could result into litigation and consequent delay in starting production. With an instinctive insight, due perhaps to his own rural background, Muzumdar dealt with the villagers with great tact and perseverance. Finally all formalities of acquisition were completed by September 1949, somewhat later than the promoters had expected. Muzumdar consolidated the property into a new village, which was named Atul so that all factory land fell under a single administrative unit. This was an act of great foresight, for when the village panchayat system was introduced in Gujarat in the late 1960s, the company property came under the jurisdiction of a single panchayat instead of three different village panchayats.

After the site had been cleared and levelled up, Muzumdar got down to developing production facilities. In addition to the factory buildings, the new company was going to need a large quantity of water for its manufacturing activities. To ensure self-sufficiency in this respect, a weir, 800 feet long was constructed across the river with the approval of the Government of the erstwhile Bombay State. The weir would form a large reservoir with a storage capacity of about 300 million gallons of water. Another weir, about 15 kilometres upstream, was planned to be constructed later to form another reservoir with a capacity of 700 million gallons. The weir would also prevent the water of the sea from entering the reservoir during the high tides. The plan also included arrangements for purifying river water through calorification and flocculation, and the construction of another reservoir big enough to hold more than 1,00,000 gallons of water. Work on the factory buildings in the southern part of the property simultaneously continued.

The development plan incorporated much more than mere production needs, for the Kasturbhai-Muzumdar scheme envisaged more than a factory. The promoters dreamt of a modern industrial township on the lines of Jamshedpur developed by the Tatas in Bihar. It was going to be extremely difficult, if not impossible, to attract a competent work force to a place like Valsad unless satisfactory housing along with proper educational, medical, and recreational facilities were provided to the employees. The Atul construction plan, therefore, aimed at developing a residential colony with all modern amenities. This was to be situated in the eastern and northern portions of the village. With an old historic fort overlooking on it, and the river flowing alongside, the residential complex would develop in the idyllic surroundings away from the factory sites. The colony was to be divided into four sectors consisting of nearly 1,150 tenement-type houses with roads or avenues between two rows. Located centrally in the township and accessible from all sides were the sites for amenities and welfare activities with a club, a sports complex with facilities for various kinds of games, a full-fledged medical centre, and educational buildings. Provisions were also made for a police outpost, banks, post and telegraph office, a swimming pool, and places of worship for all major communities. The plan envisaged the conversion of a shallow pit in the ground into a bowl-type theatre with a seating capacity for 5,000 persons. The theatre was to have a beautiful green room and a large screen for films and a permanent scaffolding to set up a stage for dramatic performances at short notice. It was decided to plant about 1,00,000 trees of 200 different varieties which, besides providing shade, served as a bulwark against pollution. The completion of these schemes converted the barren area into one of the most pleasant and well planned industrial townships in the country.

While these plans were in progress, the manufacturing complex was developing more or less satisfactorily. The hope that production would start in the middle of 1950 proved illusive because of the delay in acquiring land and completing the factory buildings. The delay gave some time to Kasturbhai to review his production plan. Under the initial arrangements, the Atul was to produce initially a few dyes only. This was dangerous in view of the prospects of stiff competition from the European manufacturers which were firmly entrenched in the Indian market. As a safeguard against possible losses in the dye line, Kasturbhai needed to include in the production plan a few other items which faced less competition. He explained his problem to his American collaborators. The Cyanamid Company had been distributing some of their pharmaceutical products in India through their subsidiary, Lederle Laboratories (India) Ltd., since 1947. On Kasturbhai's suggestion, his collaborators agreed to provide penultimate materials which the Atul would bring to the final stage to produce such items as Aureomycin and Sulfadiazine in bulk. To cement his relations with the American company, Kasturbhai agreed to lease a small area of land on the Atul site to the Cyanamid Company to start its manufacturing operations in India. The Atul also agreed to subscribe for 35 per cent of the share capital of the

Cyanamid India Ltd. The remaining 65 per cent was held by the American company itself.

A few months after the 1950 agreement was signed, a large part of the machinery purchased and despatched under the overall supervision of the American Cyanamid reached India. Fortunately for the Atul, about two-thirds of the price of the entire order had already been paid before the rupee fell from about 30 cents to a dollar to 21 cents as a result of the devaluation of 1949, and thus the incidence of devaluation on the company's capital expenditure was only marginal. The installation of the machinery, however, took longer than expected, and the company could not be ready to go in for production before the beginning of 1952, frustrating the management's hope to commence manufacturing somewhat earlier.

The beginning of the Atul's production was the consummation of a dream, and Kasturbhai did not want the event to go unnoticed. He planned for a gala opening of his chemical-pharmaceutical complex, and invited Jawaharlal Nehru, the Prime Minister, to inaugurate the company. Whatever differences Kasturbhai may have had with Nehru's economic philosophy, he rightly looked upon him as a symbol of modern India. And Nehru, who normally avoided associating himself with the opening of a private sector company, could not refuse Kasturbhai's invitation. The Prime Minister's long association with the industrialist's family (Nehru's sister Krishna was married to Kasturbhai's third sister's son, Gunottam Hutheesing) and his personal regard for Kasturbhai, whose activities in social and educational spheres had attracted considerable notice, might have been a factor in Nehru's acceptance of Kasturbhai's invitation. But what influenced his decision most, he confided to his audience in his inaugural speech on 17 March 1952. "I have come here to join your rejoicings," Nehru declared in his characteristic halting style but sonorous voice, "because Sheth Kasturbhai has set up a basic industrial unit which will go a long way towards our industrial progress. The dyestuffs and chemical industry has a special significance in our total economy. I view this project in a broader national perspective, the advantage it would bring to the nation, and not in terms of profits to an individual or a company set up by an individual."[45] More than a lakh of people attended the inaugural function.

Among them were prominent political and industrial leaders including Morarji Desai, then the Home Minister of undivided Bombay State, G.V. Mavalankar, the Speaker of the Lok Sabha, Jivraj Mehta, who was to be the first Chief Minister of Gujarat, and Ghanshyamdas Birla, the premier industrialist. Sid Moody, the Vice President of the American Cyanamid, had flown all the way from his American headquarters in order to be present on this auspicious occasion.

The inauguration of the Atul marked the end of another and probably the most significant aspect of Kasturbhai's entrepreneurial continuum. In future his entrepreneurial and managerial abilities would find expression in expanding and consolidating the major manufacturing lines already initiated rather than entering new fields. After 1952, only two companies were established to exploit opportunities which had no direct connection with the manufacture of textile, starch, or chemical goods. The Anup Engineering Pvt. Ltd. produces certain kinds of textile machinery, and the Anup Containers makes paper drums. Established in 1962 and 1963 respectively, these two companies were and continue to be small ventures initiated and nurtured by younger members of the family. The patriarch obviously blessed the establishment of these ventures but he took little direct interest in developing them. In fact, technically these companies have no affiliation with the Kasturbhai group of industries.

CHAPTER VI

The Ordeal of the Older Lines

MUCH water had flown down the river between the year of the Atul's incorporation and the one in which it started production. India, as an independent country, was less than three weeks old when the Atul was born. There was a great deal of uncertainty about the future course of industrial development and the basic framework within which it would be attempted. The alien British Government with its commitment to a policy either of *laissez faire* or least possible regulation had given considerable freedom to the private enterprises to participate in the process of industrialization. And yet the Indian industrialists, by and large, welcomed the eclipse of the British power in India. They had as much instinctive love for self-rule as any other section of the nation, and they also knew that the end of an imperialist regime would considerably reduce foreign economic presence in the country and open up new vistas for industrial undertakings. What they were not at all sure about was how much of the cake of the new opportunities they would be allowed to bite, and how much of their freedom of action would be curbed by the new national government.

The uncertainty about the basic economic philosophy of the

new Government arose because the Indian National Congress, which embodied the nation's aspirations for freedom, had failed to evolve a clear-cut policy for economic reconstruction before it assumed power on 15 August 1947. True, the economic policy resolution adopted by the Karachi session of the Congress in 1931 contained some ingredients of a development framework and the appointment of the National Planning Committee under the chairmanship of Jawaharlal Nehru in 1938 was a pointer of some significance to future directions. The Karachi resolution as well as the deliberations of the Nehru Committee had hinted at the possibility of public ownership of basic industries and greater regulation of the economy. Also, an influential section of the Congress leadership, including Nehru himself, professed socialism of one variety or the other. An equally influential group, however, was opposed to any kind of socialism as the basic creed of economic reconstruction. The fact is that the Congress, constituted as it was in 1947, was incapable of advocating a coherent economic philosophy. It was a motley assortment of conflicting interest groups whose only ground for unity had been their common concern for freedom from an alien rule.

The apprehensions of the private enterprise about its future role in the nation's life receded into the background as the broad features of the policies and the programmes of the new government gradually crystallized between 1948 and 1951. First was the Industrial Policy Resolution of 1948. While emphasizing the need for progressively greater participation of the state in the economic activity, the resolution recognized the role played by the private capital in the industrial development of the country in the past, and assured it of a significant place in the future industrial endeavours, though within a framework of regulation and control. Under the provision of the resolution, the state was to have an exclusive right to establish new undertakings in certain fields, but the private sector was left free to operate in the remaining spheres. Admittedly, the resolution did contemplate progressively increased participation of the state in the residual fields as well, but in view of the fact that the task of developing the economy was stupendous and the resources of the state limited, it was thought best that the state marshalled its resources primarily to develop those industries in which the private enterprise was unable or unwilling to invest. The First Five Year Plan (1951-56) underscored the principles embodied in the Industrial Policy Resolution.

The system of industrial licensing introduced in 1951, was another major instrument through which the Government hoped to achieve its objectives. Under the new policy, the existing undertakings in the scheduled industries had to be registered, and no undertaking could be established nor any substantial expansion of existing plants effected without prior license from the Government. The criteria were not clearly defined and elaborate bureaucratic procedures delayed, sometimes inordinately, action on applications for licences. The system of licensing, nevertheless, was only a minor irritant to the private sector. Liberalization of imports of capital goods beginning with 1950, on the other hand, argued well for the private investors. Likewise, the tariff policy emphasized the need to protect embryonic industries from foreign competition—the industries which required heavy capital outlay or involved high degree of specialization in personnel, plant, and equipment.

These features ofthe Government's approach to industrial development taken together removed much of the misgivings about the place of the private sector in the efforts for industrial development of the country. Of course, occasional pronouncements of radical nature emanating from responsible quarters still created some degree of apprehension, but no discerning observer in the private sector could miss the point that the private enterprise had now a whole range of new industrial opportunities open to it. While a large number of foreign houses were winding up their businesses in India, the number of those willing to enter into collaboration with Indian business was on the rise. These factors aided by a more sympathetic Government created for the Indian enterprise a much wider and more promising horizon for investment and profit. In later years, the private sector would come under greater surveillance and control, but the general economic thinking of the Government in the immediate post-independence era posed little threat to private industrialists.

II

As an industrial leader with nationalist sympathies, Kasturbhai rejoiced over the advent of India's freedom, but freedom did not come without problems for Kasturbhai's oldest and till then the major manufacturing line. For one thing, the partition of the country reduced considerably the number of effective consumers of textile goods in the country. Also the creation of Pakistan meant the loss of some of the finest cotton growing tracts in the subcontinent. These regions grew as much as 30 per cent of the total Indian crop between 1941 and 1947 and supplied cotton of longer staple required for manufacturing finer goods. This factor along with only marginal increase in the Indian cotton crops between 1947 and 1951 led to the successive rise of imports from abroad particularly of the varieties which Kasturbhai's mills required. Naturally the cost of the basic raw materials went up to which the devaluation of the rupee in 1949 made its own contribution. The prices of other inputs such as coal and stores and the wage bill also showed an upward trend. The cumulative effect of all this was a rise in the cost of production.

And yet the performance of Indian cotton mills was not too discouraging thanks to a progressive rise in commodity prices aided by the boom that followed the outbreak of the Korean War in June 1950. Kasturbhai's mills reaped the benefits of the national trends. But what is significant is that his group as a whole showed better results than the average performance in the industry as Table VI.1 indicates.[46]

TABLE VI.1

Index Number of Industrial Profits of Kasturbhai Group of Mills as Compared to That of the Industry as a Whole : 1947-1951

(1939=100)

Year	*Index no. for industry in general*	*Index no. for Kasturbhai group of mills*
1939	100.0	100.0
1947	317.7	509.0
1948	548.1	1076.9
1949	292.0	331.8
1950	356.6	440.5
1951	551.1	682.0

The increase in the earnings of the group, it must be noted, was not due to the performance of one or two companies alone; each and every textile unit contributed to the group's prosperity. The profits earned by each company in the group as compared to the figures before the outbreak of the war given in Table VI.2, bear this out. It is clear that except the Saraspur, Nutan, and the Ahmedabad New Cotton, all other mills increased their earnings as compared to the profits earned in 1947. Comparison with the 1948 figures is unrealistic as the fortunes of the industry, and those of Kasturbhai mills that year were aided by the temporary removal of all controls on cloth and yarn prices. No sooner was the decontrol announced, the prices rose by 50 to 75 per cent above the controlled levels. The government reimposed controls only after four months, but the period was long enough for the textile manufacturers to take the fullest advantage of the Government's folly. Though the earnings naturally declined after the 1948 aberration, the companies in the group continued to register steady and significant increase in the profits as the comparisons between the figures for 1949 and 1951 indicate.

TABLE VI.2

Profits of Companies in the Kasturbhai Group of Mills as Compared to the 1939 Figures

Name	*1939**	*1947*	*1948*	*1949*	*1950*	*1951*
Raipur	0.50	22.15	55.04	14.59	17.54	27.32
Asoka	0.59	17.48	46.73	12.62	15.19	23.03
Saraspur	0.40	19.41	38.30	11.37	6.11	18.21
Aruna	1.48	16.44	43.80	11.13	12.78	21.85
Nutan	2.93	11.77	13.58	4.89	7.33	8.00
Arvind	8.59	43.25	85.80	26.47	36.87	54.98
Ahmedabad New Cotton	0.75	10.18	N.A.	2.37	N.A.	7.76

*While looking at the 1939 profits, it should be noted that figures for the Saraspur and the Asoka include 0.47 lakhs and 0.58 lakhs of the commissions respectively given up by the Managing Agents. The figures for the Ahmedabad New Cotton include 0.75 lakhs which the company had written off as bad debts that year.

An indication that the performance of the textile companies

in the group augmented the confidence of the management is that between 1948 and 1951 the authorized capital as well as the paid-up capital of all the companies were increased, as Table VI.3 indicates. The management did not have to go to the general public for additional investment. Over the last several years, the companies had built substantial reserves thanks to Kasturbhai's policy of moderate dividends. Parts of these reserves were capitalized to issue bonus preference shares to existing ordinary shareholders in certain proportions. It is significant that before 1948, the paid-up capital of these companies coincided with the authorized capital. Thereafter, the management's decision to steeply increase the authorized capital of these companies without intending to issue the entire capital immediately was indicative of the confident optimism with which they looked into the future.

There were, however, ominous signs in the atmosphere which should have made Kasturbhai more cautious. The boom in commodity prices had started receding in June 1951 when a truce in Korea was proposed but the downward trend was so gradual that it had little impact on the fortunes of the profits. But what happened later proved that the future of the textile industry was not as secure as many might have thought in 1951. In March 1952 there was a virtual crash in the market and the general price index dropped lower than the pre-Korean war level. The fall in the commodity prices meant a fall in the internal demand for consumer goods including textile products. This along with a steep decline in exports resulted in a huge accumulation of stocks causing a fall in the price of textile goods by 15 to 25 per cent below the ceiling fixed by the Tariff Board. Consequently, the sales of the Kasturbhai group in 1952 were down by more than Rs. 100 lakhs. What was more serious, however, was that the total profits touched a low figure of Rs. 32 lakhs and the sale-profit ratio that year was the lowest in the history of the group. This happened because there was a rise of about 10 per cent in the variable cost, principally because a part of the raw materials and stores used in production that year had been acquired when the prices were still high. In a year in which a large number of mills in the country suffered severe strains and even incurred losses, Kasturbhai must have felt lucky that the working of his textile empire

TABLE VI.3

Kasturbhai Group of Mills—Capital Structure: 1947–1951

Name of the Company	*1947*	*1948*	*1949*	*1950*	*1951*
Raipur					
Authorized capital (in lakhs)	10.00	50.00	50.00	50.00	100.00
Paid-up capital (in lakhs)	10.00	15.00	20.00	20.00	20.00
No. of ordinary shares	5,000	5,000	10,000	10,000	10,000
No. of preference shares	5,000	10,000	10,000	10,000	10,000
Asoka					
Authorized capital (in lakhs)	12.00	60.00	60.00	60.00	100.00
Paid-up capital (in lakhs)	12.08	18.08	24.08	24.08	24.08
No. of ordinary shares	6,000	6,000	12,000	12,000	12,000
No. of preference shares	6,000	12,000	12,000	12,000	12,000
Saraspur					
Authorized capital (in lakhs)	6.00	60.00	60.00	60.00	100.00
Paid-up capital (in lakhs)	6.00	12.00	18.00	18.00	18.00
No. of ordinary shares	6,000	6,000	12,000	12,000	12,000
No. of preference shares	Nil	6,000	6,000	6,000	6,000
Aruna Mills					
Authorized capital (in lakhs)	10.00	50.00	50.00	50.00	100.00
Paid-up capital (in lakhs)	10.00	15.00	20.00	20.00	20.00
No. of ordinary shares	5,000	5,000	10,000	10,000	10,000
No. of preference shares	5,000	10,000	10,000	10,000	10,000
Arvind					
Authorized capital (in lakhs)	26.65	105.00	105.00	105.00	210.00
Paid-up capital (in lakhs)	26.25	36.75	47.25	47.25	47.25
No. of ordinary shares	10,500	10,500	21,000	21,000	21,000
No. of preference shares	15,750	26,250	26,250	26,250	26,250
Nutan Mills					
Authorized capital (in lakhs)	5.00	30.00	30.00	30.00	100.00
Paid-up capital (in lakhs)	5.00	10.00	10.00	10.00	10.00
No. of ordinary shares	5,000	5,000	5,000	5,000	5,000
No. of preference shares	Nil	5,000	5,000	5,000	5,000
Ahmedabad New Cotton					
Authorized capital (in lakhs)	10.00	30.00	30.00	30.00	100.00
Paid-up capital (in lakhs)	10.00	16.00	16.00	16.00	16.00
No. of ordinary shares	6,000	6,000	6,000	6,000	6,000
No. of preference shares	4,000	10,000	10,000	10,000	10,000

ended up in a profit, howsoever small.

Never was the Kasturbhai management caught napping again with regard to the management of raw material inventories because the prices remained more or less stable in the rest of the decade; at least they did not register sudden fluctuations. But the slump of 1952 established beyond doubt a significant change in the character of the textile industry; the seller's market which the industry had enjoyed throughout the 1940s had disappeared. Finer varieties had been affected even earlier, but the 1952 slump affected the coarse and medium goods as well. The law of supply and demand, the buyer's preference, and his purchasing power would henceforward shape the fortunes of the textile industry to a much greater degree than ever before. The government's decision to abolish all controls on cotton cloth and yarn was an explicit recognition of the new trend in the largest organized industry in the country.

But the question of any industry remaining entirely free from control in a planned economy did not arise. The decision of the government to impose a ceiling on the production of cloth in the organized sector was a serious curb on the textile industry. This was done to encourage production in the unorganized sectors, such as handloom and *khadi*. With the same end in view limitation was placed on the production of *dhotis* in 1952. Within a year, a special cess of 3 pies per yard was levied on the production of fine and superfine varieties. Increase in the excise duties in 1956 served to further depress the markets for these varieties. Even though slight relief was granted on occasions, the net effect of these and other measures adversely affected the demands for these products. The situation would have been better if the general price movements were favourable to the industry. But the commodity prices remained low throughout the First Plan period. In fact, they declined slightly in the last year of the Plan and there was only marginal improvement in the situation during the Second Plan period.

It is no surprise, under these conditions, that the sales of Kasturbhai's mills remained low throughout the decade after the 1952 slump as Table VI.4 indicates. Sales, of course, fluctuated in response to market forces and demand situations, but there were greater fluctuations in profits as compared to sales. It was so because of fluctuations in the cost of inputs like labour, energy, raw materials, and stores. To be specific, the profits of 1953, when the price situation was slightly favourable, would have been higher, if the labour cost had not gone up, thanks to the introduction of a provident fund scheme as required by an act passed by the Union Government in the closing months of the previous year. In the subsequent years, the profit margin showed some improvement, thanks to the decline in the price of raw materials, till a statutory gratuity scheme introduced in 1957 resulted in a steep rise in the wage

TABLE VI.4

Kasturbhai Group of Mills: Sales and Profits: 1951-1960

Year	*Sales*	*Profits* (*Rs. in lakhs*)	*Profit as percentage of sales* (%)
1951	1507.21	166.93	11.08
1952	1405.46	32.06	2.29
1953	1323.08	86.01	6.50
1954	1270.61	78.54	6.19
1955	1348.20	144.09	10.69
1956	1365.95	208.36	15.26
1957	1285.51	68.40	5.32
1958	1393.49	128.68	9.24
1959	1472.33	97.10	6.59
1960	1353.95	204.74	15.12

bill. The scheme had been suggested by the Textile Labour Association and accepted by the Bombay Industrial Tribunal. Significantly enough, while some of the Ahmedabad millowners decided to appeal against the Industrial Tribunal award, Kasturbhai preferred to implement the scheme even though it meant considerable strain on the financial position of his mills. The labour cost again rose in 1959 because of higher dearness allowance, and in 1960 owing to the implementation of the recommendation of the Central Wage Board.

The improvement in the working of the mills as reflected in the profits of 1960, both in absolute and relative terms, could not be sustained for long. In fact the new decade heralded an era of higher sales but relatively lower profits as is clear from the following Table. It must be stressed, however, that the trading conditions were not as unfavourable during the first year of the decade as they became subsequently. In fact, more than 7 per cent rise in the commodity prices on one hand and the reduction in cloth prices consequent to the adoption of a voluntary price control in September 1960 by the Indian mills gave considerable spurt to demand for textile products in 1961.

TABLE VI.5

Kasturbhai Group of Mills: Sales and Profits: 1961-1976

Year	*Sales*	*Profits*	*Profit as percentage of sales* (%)
	(*Rs. in lakhs*)		
1961	1774.68	241.50	13.53
1962	1731.23	155.49	8.98
1963	1836.69	163.55	8.90
1964	2006.09	140.89	7.02
1965	2057.43	128.76	6.26
1966	2405.25	223.24	9.28
1967	2633.66	175.26	6.65
1968	2907.34	46.41	1.60
1969	3299.95	260.48	7.89
1970	3773.26	363.45	9.63
1971	4198.66	338.93	8.07
1972	4513.31	295.10	6.54
1973	5234.52	424.57	8.88
1974	6715.54	428.85	6.39
1975	7573.82	390.47	5.16
1976	7676.86	359.81	4.69

The rise in dearness allowance and a slight increase in prices of other inputs somewhat pushed up the production cost and thus reduced the group's earnings in comparison with the quantum of sales. And yet the results of 1961 in no way reflected the future trials and tribulations which were in store for Kasturbhai's textile companies.

As the table above clearly shows, in no year after 1961 did the profit as percentage of sales exceed 10%. Though the sales figures continued to maintain consistently upward trend, except in 1962 when the dislocation in the cloth trade following the Chinese invasion caused a slight reduction, the profits remained relatively low. The basic factor behind this phenomenon was a serious inflationary pressure from which the Indian economy suffered almost throughout the 1960s. The causes of the inflation were complex and can be traced back to the deficit financing resorted to during the Second Plan period. The economy was already under strain when crop failures for four years in a row after 1962, the Sino-Indian conflict of 1962, and the war with Pakistan in 1965 imposed still heavier burden on an already overburdened economy. The result was a runaway increase in prices throughout the 1960s and even later.

The development benefited the agriculturists whose purchasing power improved with the rise in the prices of agricultural products. But the inflationary pressure resulted in a steep rise in the cost of living index of the industrial worker and with that the dearness allowance payable to them. In addition, various welfare measures enforced by the government added to the labour cost. The cost of stores, dyes, chemicals, and other inputs also went up simultaneously particularly after the devaluation of the rupee in June 1966. The price of raw cotton had been going up ever since the onset of the 1960s because of the failure of Indian crops. The devaluation made the imported cotton more expensive creating difficulties for the mills which used, for the most part, the imported staple. On occasions, the unavailability of raw material forced the mills to stop production and lay-off their workers. The Arvind, the Aruna, and the Raipur, for instance, were closed for a number of extra days in 1966 and 1967. The only way the mills could offset the impact of the rising production cost was to increase the price of their product. But this was not possible in view of the fact that the mills were operating on the basis of a voluntary price control up to October 1964 which became statutory thereafter.

The crisis deepened further in 1968 and created unprecedented suffering for the textile industry. A total of 85 mills, unable to bear the strain, stopped production and others made losses or only marginal profits. The government tried to come to the rescue of the industry by removing the price control on certain varieties of goods. But the relief was too meagre and came too late. The Kasturbhai mills could not escape the onslaught of the adversity and four of the seven companies in the group—the Ahmedabad New Cotton, the Saraspur, the Nutan, and the Asoka—incurred losses of varying amounts. If the group as a whole was able to avoid losses, it was because of the performance of the other three mills—the Arvind, the Raipur, and the Aruna—whose products were better suited for exports and which were also better entrenched in the Indian markets.

Though the industry, and with that all the mills in the Kasturbhai group, recovered in 1969 in spite of the tragic communal riots that year in Ahmedabad dislocating production for more than a month, the factors which had caused the crisis in 1968 by no means disappeared. The labour cost continued to rise and so did the cost of other inputs. The price of raw cotton continued to be high except in 1975 when a better crop reduced the price of Indian staple. To meet the difficulties of raw material, the mills in the group reduced the use of foreign cotton and increased the intake of improved Indian varieties. Also efforts were made to use larger quantities of man-made fibre. These measures proved helpful only to a degree because the steep rise in the price of crude, an essential commodity for manufacturing polyester, created an acute shortage of DMT after 1973. Also, the Indo-Pakistan war of 1971 created difficulty in the movement of goods in the closing months of the year affecting the sales and profits for the following year.

The strain on the industry became unbearable again in 1976 when the number of mills which had to close down during the year reached the staggering figure of 41. None of the Kasturbhai mills stopped production but three of them—the Ahmedabad New Cotton, the Saraspur, and the Nutan—were in the red. The group as a whole ended up in a marginal profit thanks to somewhat better performance of the more established companies. Things improved in the following year, but the experience of the post-independence period clearly stressed the need for much greater vigilance and foresight in managing a textile mill than in the earlier period characterized by a stagnant economy.

III

It was Kasturbhai's foresight and vigilance that enabled his mills to face successfully the crisis that became an almost inseparable feature of the textile industry after the beginning of the First Five-Year Plan. As we have seen before, he had always been very particular about the quality of his manufacturing apparatus. It was because of the reorganisation effected in his mills during the worst days of depression that his companies had done so well during the war and later. But by the middle of the 1950s, he realized that most of his equipment was at least twenty years old and needed replacement. The Working Party for the Cotton Textile Industry, which submitted its report to the Union Government in April 1952, had also emphasized the need for modernization. Modernization was necessary not only to improve output and reduce cost, but also to produce a variety of goods of better design and quality. That the Indian consumer was developing taste for much better fabrics was obvious. Also the government had decided to permit expansion of capacity to produce export quality goods. The products of most of the existing equipment would have had a competitive disadvantage in international market.

What, perhaps, made Kasturbhai give a practical shape to his desire to modernize his textile units was the decision of the Government of India to grant development rebate to industrial units on amount spent on new plant and machinery. Within a few months after the official announcement to this effect Kasturbhai launched a vigorous programme of reorganization and renovation. Beginning with 1956, every year some equipment was retired to make room for new and sophisticated one and every year new equipment and buildings were added. Ordinary spinning frames were replaced by high draft frames, ordinary looms yielded place to automatic looms, new and more modern plants for bleaching, dyeing, mercerizing, printing, and sizing were installed. No area of production facility escaped the attention of the management. As a result of the reorganization, and modernization, the Kasturbhai mills gradually became among the most sophisticated and modern in the country. The result was that whereas most of them were producing coarse goods before the beginning of the 1950s, all of them were now equipped to produce finer stuff.

The programme of modernization and renovation cost the group a total amount of nearly Rs. 40 crores over a period of two decades. Much of it came from the reserve and depreciation fund which the mills had built up over the years. Kasturbhai all along had pursued a policy of more or less constant, though relatively low, dividend. This had helped him build substantial reserve which he could use for modernizing his mills. It is significant that between 1956 and 1966, a large part of the amount spent for this purpose came from internal sources. Only a small part was borrowed from the Industrial Credit and Investment Corporation of India Ltd. (ICICI) for the purposes of financing imports.

The modernization programme enabled the Kasturbhai mills to put new products into the market consistent with the changing taste of the consumer. Practically all the mills in the group brought about significant modification in their production pattern in order to reduce cost and also to cater to demands for goods of better quality and pattern. These changes enabled the companies to claim a significant share of internal market and consistently increase their exports. It is noteworthy that while the aggregate value of their export was only Rs. 85 lakhs in 1968, it increased to about Rs. 205 lakhs by the end of 1976.

Kasturbhai's steps to capture an increasingly larger share of exports was an act of great foresight. This will be clear if we bear in mind that while the internal market for textile products since the beginning of the First Five-Year Plan remained dangerously uncertain, the exports registered a consistent increase. Following the foreign exchange crisis of 1957-58, the government offered a series of incentives to the textile manufacturers for producing export quality goods. It is no surprise, therefore, that Kasturbhai decided in 1966 to set up a separate company to streamline his export operations. Floated jointly by all the mills in the group with a paid-up capital of Rs. 1,00,700 and formally registered in 1967, the Lalbhai Exports Ltd. became the sole export agents for Kasturbhai's textile products. Perhaps this was a slightly premature step as the textile companies seldom provided enough business to the Lalbhai Exports to break even, and it had to undertake the exports of other items, such as light engineering and hosiery goods, in order to boost its sales. But the company achieved important breakthrough for the group's products in the African, East Asian, and American markets by its sales promotion activities.

Kasturbhai's mills were not alone in their attempts to claim a large share of the external market. The industry in general looked upon export as a partial solution to the problems created by a sluggish home market. But in the field of research and development, Kasturbhai was among the first to take some concrete steps. Indian industrialists have not been known for their enthusiasm to develop new processes and products. Textile manufacturers did not have to worry about research and development during the years of stable prosperity. But even after the halcyon phase was over never to return, few textile producers turned their attention to this crucial area. Kasturbhai, on the other hand, initiated his efforts in this direction as early as the middle of the 1950s. The Arvind, the largest and the most prestigious unit in the group, took the lead. One of the early discoveries of the mill was a method of cotton mixing, perfected in 1959, which resulted in substantial saving without affecting the quality.

By the beginning of the 1970s, however, Kasturbhai had come to the firm conclusion that there was no escape from increasing investment in research and development, if he wished to retain his position in the frontline of nation's textile producers. To systematize the group's efforts, therefore, he started a Research and Development Department in 1972. It was to be a part of the Arvind Mills, but its benefits were to be available to all the mills in the group. The department made a rapid progress towards developing new products. The device to produce 100% cotton stretch yarn and fabric won the Independence Day award from the Union Government in 1973. This pace-setting contribution also received the Indian Merchants Chamber's award for invention and a cash prize from the National Research and Development Corporation of India. No R & D department of any textile manufacturing concern in India had ever won such honours. The progress of the Arvind's department was so fast that barely three years after its inception, the Union Government granted it national recognition. The Arvind was the second mill in the country to claim this signal honour. A tangible effect of the government recognition was that the company would be able to develop the department at less cost because a recognized R & D department was entitled to tax deduction on capital expenditure. By 1976, the department came to have its own buildings, fully furnished with modern equipments. Named after Kasturbhai's younger brother and one of the past directors of the Arvind Mills, the Narottam Lalbhai Research Centre has undertaken a series of research projects covering the whole spectrum from textile manufacturing to wet processing. Its most significant contributions include the development of a process to impart permanent press property to bed sheets and other cotton fabrics with comparative lower strength loss, and discover ways and means to minimise the adverse effects of low quality cotton on textile manufactures. The products made by this process are superior to similar goods produced not only in India but also elsewhere. On these achievements the Arvind's research scientists were given the prestigious Hari Om Ashram Award by the Ahmedabad Textile Industry Research Association in 1976.

With a view to alleviating the rigours of the crisis in the industry after 1966, some of the mills in the group attempted to undertake production of non-textile goods. The Raipur, for instance, set up a separate division in the closing years of the 1960s for manufacturing fine china crockery. Kasturbhai had secured a licence to produce high tension and low tension porcelain insulators and glazed tiles in 1965. To implement the new project, he decided to set up a new company, the Arvind Ceramic Ltd. He was not quite sure, however, about the future of the new undertaking in view of the increase in the price of industrial raw material, labour, and rising import duty on machinery. Rather than surrender the licence, he considered it expedient to transfer it to the Raipur Mills. His request, however, did not find favour with government but the Raipur was issued a letter of intent to manufacture 1,800 tonnes of fine china crockery per year. The company entered into an agreement with a reputed Swiss firm, M/s Porzellanfahnik Langenthal AG, for this purpose. While the company's application for an industrial licence was still pending before the government, Kasturbhai concluded that the rise in the cost of fuel, raw materials, and wages had considerably reduced the potential of the project. Accordingly, it was all but given up in 1971 when the management decided to "defer the decision of implementing the project".

The Arvind's effort to undertake the production of low density polyethelene met with a similar fate. The move was tied up with the government effort to promote the production of petrochemicals in Gujarat in the middle of the 1960s. The company applied for a letter of intent in 1967, but the government took two years to act on it. By the time the Arvind secured the letter of intent the terms of collaboration with the National Distillers and Chemical Corporation of New York had been settled. As required by law, the Government of India agreed to the collaboration arrangement. In the meantime, however, serious political differences had arisen between the Government of India and the United States, following the Bangla Desh crisis of 1971. Under these conditions, the American Company decided to withdraw from the commitment precisely when the Arvind was about to secure the necessary industrial licence. The matter rested there since the government was not willing to let the Arvind find another collaborator on the same terms and conditions.

Another abortive project was promoted on behalf of the Asoka Mills. This was to produce 5,000 tonnes of PVC through extrusion process. The letter of intent issued in 1967 stipulated that the plant must be located in the State of Maharashtra. The project seemed profitable, but Kasturbhai was unwilling to go out of Gujarat. A fresh application was submitted in 1968 for processing slightly different materials in Gujarat. The government agreed to this proposal and issued a letter of intent in 1969 for the manufacture of heavy duty PVC sacks and laminated jute bags. These were becoming very popular after the discovery of synthetic jute. Even though the company fulfilled all conditions for an industrial licence by 1971, the government did not issue the necessary industrial licence and the group lost interest in the project.

Unlike the above schemes, the move to start the production of art silk met with partial success. The proposed line was directly related to the textiles, and there were reasons to believe that demand for art silk product would increase. It was decided in 1968, therefore, to acquire a going concern, the Artex Private Ltd., by purchasing all the equity shares of this mill at their face value amounting to Rs. 11,55,400. After the completion of necessary formalities, the art silk unit with 176 looms was amalgamated with the Asoka Mills in 1970 and became the latter's silk division. Difficulty in procuring art silk yarn and rising cost of production beset the operations of the new unit, and it took several years to stabilize itself. It was only after 1973 that the division was able to show steady improvement.

In spite of the failures or only partial success of these minor projects and uneven progress during the three stormy decades after freedom, Kasturbhai's textile empire was, on the whole, in a sound shape at the time of his retirement from active management. His seven mills together had 3,56,104 spindles and 6,852 looms, out of a total of 26,33,000 and 47,078 possessed by the Ahmedabad textile industry as a whole. Their paid-up capital had increased from Rs. 1,55,25,000 in 1951 to Rs. 7,64,00,000 in 1977, as the capital was increased several times through issuing bonus or right shares. During the same period the reserves and surpluses went up from Rs. 5,92,65,684 to Rs. 20,28,22,747, total net fixed assets from Rs. 77,59,147 to Rs. 21,60,29,045 and the number of employees from 8,687 to 17,616. In quantitative terms it was an impressive progress by any reckoning. But what gave satisfaction to Kasturbhai on the eve of his retirement from active leadership was that his mills had built up a solid reputation for quality. It had been a major factor, according to him, in the success of his textile operations.

IV

Like the textile companies, Kasturbhai's other older concern, the Anil Starch, experienced severe ups and downs in its fortunes after independence. As we have seen before, the company was virtually tottering on its feet in 1947 in the face of intensified foreign competition after the war on one hand, and the bottleneck in production as a result of acute shortage of the basic raw material on the other. The following year brought a glimmer of hope as the Government of India decided to grant protection to the starch industry, and allot a quota of deteriorated maize. Consequently, the company made sufficient profits in 1948 to wipe off the losses incurred in the previous year. Though the supply position of maize became more precarious or remained uncertain, the next three years witnessed considerable improvement in the working of the Anil Starch so that its profits in absolute terms increased from Rs. 1.59 lakhs in 1948 to Rs. 6.23 lakhs in 1951.

Diversification of product lines was largely responsible for this welcome development. Superphosphate was a new addition. The country, suffering from acute food shortage, needed this chemical fertilizer badly. Indigenous manufacture of the commodity on modern lines was barely two years old and there were only a couple of companies in the field when Kasturbhai's unit started producing it in 1948. He did not have to worry about the demand as the distribution of fertilizer products was channelled through a fertilizer pool, operated by the Government of India, which bought off the entire quantity from the producers. The new item not only provided a cushion against the uncertain trends in the starch side of the business, but also provided additional market for the sulphuric acid which the company had started producing earlier. Sulphuric acid is an indispensable input for manufacturing superphosphate.

That this was a move in the right direction became clear during the very next year when the government allotted very little maize to the starch companies. In the face of continued food crisis, internal supply of maize was painfully inadequate, and the government was unwilling to bear additional financial burden in importing the commodity which the devaluation of the rupee in 1949 necessarily entailed. The starch producers were, therefore, put to great hardship. The Anil Starch had some stocks left from the previous year and did not have to shut down its starch plant entirely, but its production of starch went down considerably. Consequently, the company's proceeds from the sale of starch products in 1949 fell down to nearly 2/3rd of the previous year's level. The situation remained almost unchanged in 1950. And yet if the Anil Starch made an overall profit of Rs. 2.66 lakhs and Rs. 1.49 lakhs in these two years respectively, it was mainly because of the increased sale of sulphuric acid and superphosphate. The production plants for these commodities worked to the full capacity throughout these two years and the sale of the company's products from these units together was more than four times the 1948 figures. There is no doubt that the strategy of spreading the risk had paid off.

Kasturbhai, however, could not afford to leave his starch plant idle. He joined hands with other starch manufacturers to jointly represent to the government to grant them licence to import maize for industrial purpose. After initial hesitation, the government agreed to their suggestion in September 1950.

The starch manufacturers formed a pool for the purpose of importing the commodity. The first shipments arrived in April 1951 and the future of starch manufacturing appeared to have become more secure. This was reflected in the working of the Anil Starch for the year 1951. The company that year sold starch worth more than three times the previous year's proceeds from the sale of this product. At the same time the sale of acids and fertilizers also registered an increase of about 100 per cent. The cumulative effect of all these developments was that profits of the Anil Starch jumped to more than Rs. 6.24 lakhs at the end of 1951. This was the highest profit in absolute terms which the company had earned since the end of the Second World War. The shareholders felt happy that for the first time after the good old affluent years they received 20 per cent dividend on their shares. Kasturbhai and his associates rejoiced over the fact that at long last their starch company seemed to have come out of the woods.

This optimism, however, was short-lived. The crisis that gripped the textile industry after March 1952 crippled the ability of the principal users of starch to buy this commodity. Consequently the Anil Starch's sales of this product went down from nearly Rs. 57 lakhs in 1951 to less than Rs. 33 lakhs in 1952. The crash in commodity prices also reduced the demand for fertilizer and the state governments refused to take further supplies. Consequently, the union government dissolved its fertilizer pool—the principal distribution channel for this product. This affected not only the sales of the superphosphate but also that of the sulphuric acid as the latter was an indispensable input for fertilizer production. The drastic reduction in the sales of these products from nearly Rs. 22 lakhs in 1951 to less than half of this figure was the inevitable consequence. Once again the Anil Starch found itself in the red though by a small amount of Rs. 1.7 lakhs.

The company had no serious difficulty in procuring the basic raw material for its starch plant for several years to come. The food situation showed improvement in 1953 and remained more or less satisfactory during the rest of the decade, thanks to the increase in food production in the country and the decision of the government to permit imports from the United States under the PL-480 agreement. Demand for the product also picked up as the textile mills recovered from the agonies of 1952. The production as well as the quantity of starch sold increased consistently. And yet the Anil Starch made only a moderate profit in 1953 and incurred a substantial loss during the next year.

The crisis was the starch producers' own making. After the improvement in the supply of raw material and demand situation, a host of new companies emerged creating a glut in the market. In order to dispose of their stocks, these companies, including the Anil Starch, indulged in the self-defeating policy of price cutting. As the unwholesome impact of their imprudence became evident, three of the four biggest starch producers—the Anil Starch of Kasturbhai Lalbhai, the Maize Products of Vadilal Lallubhai, and the Bharat Starch of the Thapars—started negotiation to cooperate with one another to enable the industry to earn reasonable returns. Their deliberations were yet to conclude when the Birlas, the fourth big producer, decided to unload nearly 1,000 tonnes of stocks lying in their stores. Incensed by the unfounded rumours that it was in a financial crisis, the premier Marwari house decided to dispose of its stock at whatever price was available and scrap the starch unit which, in any case, was a small part of its total operations. All efforts on the part of other principal starch producers to dissuade the Birlas from their proposed course of action failed. And when the Birlas stocks were unloaded, the prices crashed resulting into huge losses for other producers.

The 1954 crisis revealed to the starch manufacturers the folly of cutting each other's throat. They decided to observe an informal code of conduct and maintain a uniform price. The All India Starch Manufacturers' Association proved a helpful instrument to achieve this kind of cooperation. The Association had been formed in the early years of the 1940s by relatively small producers; it was only after the war that bigger companies joined it. Sometime after the crisis of 1954, Chinubhai was elected the President of the Association. He concluded that the root of the price cutting approach was the mutual distrust among the manufacturers. He, therefore, evolved a system under which the representatives of all major companies in the field met for informal discussion once in a month. This helped the starch producers to know each other better and develop a sense of community of interests. The decision to charge a uniform price and avoid penetration into each other's market evolved out of these monthly meetings.

The Anil Starch, in the meantime, had taken up the production of glucose and dextrose. The move was in line with the strategy pursued by most of the starch producers as starch is the basic ingredient for the production of glucose and related items. The initiative to start production of glucose had been first taken as early as 1946 when during a visit to the United States Kasturbhai broached the idea of collaboration with a large starch manufacturer. The American company, however, showed little enthusiasm as the Indian market was too small. Kasturbhai, continued his search for companies or individuals who could provide him with technical know-how. Eventually one James Warsh, whose name Kasturbhai's friends in the United States had suggested, agreed to help the industrialist. Warsh had just retired as a research director in a reputed starch producing concern in the United States. The dextrose line of the American firm, in fact, had been developed by him. Chinubhai then went to the United States. He worked with Warsh for three months to design the whole plant under his guidance, and spent another three months visiting a number of glucose producers. On his return to India, he prepared a feasibility report for the consideration of his illustrious cousin. With Kasturbhai's approval Chinubhai again went to Europe in 1954 to purchase the machinery. The production eventually started in 1955.

There were only two companies in India then which produced glucose items. These were the Maize Products, Ahmedabad, and the Glucose and Foods, Bombay. It is surprising that in spite of the tariff protection having been granted to the industry, the starch producers had virtually ignored the opportunity. Even the two companies mentioned above produced only glucose, and that too in small quantities; they were yet to take up the production of dextrose which is the purest form of glucose. The Anil Starch started producing these items under the brand names of Glucanil and Dextranil. At the initial stages Glucanil came only in liquid form. Used in confectionery, jams, fermentation, and also in paper, textile, and leather industries, the product, according to the estimates of the Tariff Commission, was expected to have a much larger demand than the powder glucose. From the very beginning the Glucanil and Dextranil compared favourably "in quality with the best of imported products". Kasturbhai's company did not have to bother about marketing these products as the Glaxo, a well-known pharmaceutical firm, agreed to pack and market the Anil Starch's total production under its own popular brand name, Glaxose-D.

In the meantime the company had decided to expand the capacity of its starch plant as the Planning Commission estimated a hundred per cent rise in the demand for starch products during the Second Plan period. The policy of expansion and diversification was pursued with greater vigour in the years that followed. The capacity for producing sulphuric acid was expanded in 1959 and again in 1960 by the installation of new plants. Significantly enough, the new equipments were designed by the company's own technical staff, and manufactured locally. The decision to increase the production of the acid had been taken because the company's existing acid plant was not in a position to supply this essential input to the fertilizer section, hampering the production of superphosphate. Now that this bottleneck had been removed, it was decided to raise the production of fertilizer from about 10 to 15 tonnes a day to 100 tonnes. All indications suggested that the demand for this product would increase. A composite unit was installed in 1961 to facilitate the production of powder glucose along with the liquid variety. In its bid to reduce its dependence on the textile industry, the company also undertook the production of chemicals like alum and a few more acids between 1960 and 1965. But these constituted a very small part of its operations.

A significant step to update the production process of dextrose was taken in 1967. Till then the basic method employed by the company to convert starch into dextrose was to boil the raw material with sulphuric acid. In the meantime a more sophisticated and economical system of manufacturing had been developed in the United States and Japan. The new method involved the production of a special kind of enzyme to convert starch into dextrose. On careful examination, the Anil Starch management found the Japanese system better and cheaper as the Japanese parties were expecting lower fee for supplying the know-how. The company, therefore, entered into an agreement with a famous Japanese firm, the Nagase & Co., so that an important input for dextrose could be produced in its own factory. The Japanese company had a partnership with the CIBA, Switzerland, which as we shall see latter, had already entered into collaboration with the Atul. The Nagase & Co. and the Kasturbhai starch company were, thus, no strangers to each other. It is noteworthy that the Anil Starch was among the first companies to bring the enzyme process of dextrose production to India.

The contact with the Nagase inspired the Anil Starch management to start a new line of operations. One of the several lines in which the Japanese company had interest was forging. An impressed Chinubhai thought of going into this line. A few years before Chinubhai's trip to Japan to negotiate the enzyme agreement, his nephew Arunbhai, had started the Anup Engineering for manufacturing textile machinery. He, therefore, thought that going into the forging line would help the company to diversify into metal industries and feed the Anup Engineering. The idea was sound but the process of implementation was not so easy. The most difficult problem was to secure a licence; being the part of a big group, the Anil Starch could not hope to get it. To get around this difficulty Chinubhai and Shrenikbhai, Kasturbhai's younger son, secured a licence in their own names, floated a company under the style of Amul Spanners Ltd., and later on amalgamated the new company with the Anil Starch with the approval of the Gujarat High Court. This was the beginning of the forging division of Kasturbhai's starch company. The court's approval signified that the circuitous process through which the new division came into being was perfectly legal.

Another product that the Anil Starch started producing in the latter half of the 1960s was activated carbon used for decolourization of products like glucose and dextrose. At the first stage the company tried to enter into collaboration with the Atlas Power Company, one of the biggest producers of the product in the United States, but the negotiations dragged on for a long time owing to delay in obtaining the government approval for the terms. The American Company. therefore, withdrew from the negotiation. But the Anil Starch was not to give in so easily. Chinubhai secured the services of an Indian who knew the process of manufacturing activated carbon but had failed in his attempt to make an industrial application of it. After a couple of years the new employee succeeded in developing a new process to produce activated carbon from rice husk which was available in plenty near Ahemdabad. The company's next logical step to produce sodium silicate from the by-products did not succeed, as the commodity was among the items reserved for small-scale sector under the Government policy.

The efforts of the company to produce a few other items also failed. One of these was insomerase syrup—a starch-based product made through enzyme process. The process had been developed by the Japan Industrial Technology Association and the technical know-how was owned by the Government of Japan which was not willing to let the company benefit by it unless the agreement conformed to the Japanese laws—a condition which was impossible to fulfil. An accident thwarted another scheme of the Anil Starch. The company planned to make a commercial success of an enzyme used in producing detergent for washing synthetic fibres. The process had been developed in Holland, but only two companies in Europe were making the enzyme in question. The price of the product was naturally high. The Anil Starch tried to develop its own process to produce the desired enzyme and had nearly succeeded when it was discovered in the United States that the clothes washed with the detergent caused rashes on infants' skin. The market for the product, thus, suddenly disappeared and with that crumbled the Anil Starch's well-conceived scheme. If the factors beyond the company's control militated against the implementation of its syrup and enzyme ideas, bureaucratic bottlenecks frustrated the production of a more sophisticated kind of starch known as speciality starch. A well known American firm—the National Starch and Chemical Corporation—had agreed to collaborate with the Anil Starch in the venture but the Government refused to grant necessary permission in spite of the unanimous recommendation of the Monopolies and Restrictive Trade Practices Commission.

While the strategy of diversification and expansion enabled the company to spread its risks and utilize its production capacity more efficiently, the decision to shift the superphosphate plants from Ahemdabad to Bhavnagar had great locational advantage. Bhavnagar was the principal city of the Saurashtra region of Gujarat which had emerged as a major market for the Anil Starch's fertilizer product after the dissolution of the fertilizer pool in 1952. Following the bifurcation of the bilingual Bombay State in 1960, the first Chief Minister of Gujarat, Jivraj Mehta, was very keen to develop sea ports in the new state. Bhavnagar caught his attention as it was already a natural port. The new Government brought about several improvements at the port site and offered various inducements to industrialists to set up their manufacturing operations in the city. The Chief Minister pointed out to Kasturbhai that after the construction of a lock gate at the port, transport facilities to that place had greatly improved and it was easier to import raw materials such as sulphur and rock phosphate required for the fertilizer production. He assured the industrialist that the government would provide all help to facilitate the transfer of his fertilizer manufacturing infrastructure to the port town. An added attraction of the suggested location was the availability of plenty of land at a cheap rate. These considerations led the Anil Starch to shift its fertilizer division to Bhavnagar in 1962.

Concern for expansion and diversification did not relegate to the background the need for modernization to which Kasturbhai always paid great attention. Starch plant was the oldest equipment in the company and by 1963 it had clearly become obsolete. In the next two years, therefore, the entire plant was reorganized on more modern lines in a new building and with a new lay-out.

These strategic decisions enabled the company to finally stabilize its position and obviate the possibility of the re-emergence of the kind of instability it had experienced before 1955. As Table VI 6 shows, after the Anil Starch launched its programme of expansion and diversification, rarely was the upward trend in the sales interrupted, and the company incurred losses only once. It was difficult to maintain the tempo of sales from 1969 to 1971 when the country faced one of the worst industrial recessions in recent history. The loss in 1970 was due to the fact that the recession was particularly severe that year. Recessionary conditions were again responsible for the decline of sales and profits in 1975. Except these particularly bad years, the rigours of which very few industrial units escaped, the Anil Starch maintained a reasonably satisfactory level of sales and profits. It was largely due to its product-mix policy

TABLE VI.6

Working of the Anil Starch: 1955-76

Year	*Sales*	*Profits*	*Profit as percentage of sales (%)*
	(Rs in lakhs)		
1955	99.43	4.20	4.22
1956	145.51	4.71	3.24
1957	191.17	8.40	4.39
1958	195.39	7.59	3.88
1959	230.22	22.11	9.60
1960	267.70	31.98	11.95
1961	280.32	29.68	10.59
1962	327.74	33.53	10.23
1963	342.42	32.48	9.49
1964	410.09	20.20	4.84
1965	418.60	39.33	9.40
1966	508.90	55.92	10.99
1967	674.43	51.42	7.62
1968	758.72	50.63	6.67
1969	713.06	30.34	4.25
1970	743.24	—7.79	−1.05
1971	748.85	29.17	3.90
1972	919.08	56.14	6.11
1973	938.40	59.51	6.34
1974	1283.60	67.57	5.26
1975	1118.38	19.46	1.74
1976	1160.37	58.64	5.05

that unfavourable performance of one division in a given year was counterbalanced by better results in the others.

Expansion and stability of operations naturally led to the growth in the size of the firm. While the paid-up capital of the Anil Starch in 1955 was limited to Rs 10.84 lakhs, it rose to Rs 105.00 lakhs in 1977 and its net fixed assets during the same period increased from Rs 42.71 lakhs to Rs 272.28 lakhs. A company which Kasturbhai had started somewhat half-heartedly and which had maintained a precarious existence during the first 15 years of its career had risen to be one of the largest and most diversified companies in its field before its founder handed over the leadership to the next generation.

CHAPTER VII

The March of the Incomparable

THE euphoria that marked the Atul's inauguration had a justifiable basis, but soon it yielded place to a more sombre mood. The hope that the company would start regular production immediately after the formal launching vanished as some of the machines refused to start owing to mechanical trouble. It was not till the end of May 1952 that these defects were removed and the preliminary working of the plant started. Teething technical difficulties held up the commencement of regular production for another three months and the progress was slow even after that.

The company planned to manufacture 20 different dyes initially. All these belonged to the Direct and Acid Azo or Sulphur Black groups. The dyes in both these groups were used in producing coarse and inexpensive textile goods. Since a majority of the Indian mills still concentrated on the manufacture of coarse materials, there was a sizable demand for these varieties of dyes. Also, the cost of their production was not too high nor the manufacturing process too complex. Obviously the Atul wished to enter the market cautiously and gradually with products involving not more than moderate risk.

Even though these dyes fell into two major groups, each dyestuff by the very nature of the process was a separate chemical. The manufacturing processes varied greatly and the production of each dye required a separate process by itself. In spite of these difficulties, the company succeeded in putting 12 different Azo dyes and Sulphur Black in the market by the end of 1952. Some sulpha drugs and aureomycin were produced on the pharmaceutical side to be formulated, packaged, and marketed by the Cyanamid Company under its own brand name in accordance with the agreement reached earlier. Kasturbhai had no doubt that the production would pick up in due course. And it did in the very next year to enable the company to increase its sales from Rs. 17.85 lakhs to Rs. 75.39 lakhs. Also, its products now numbered 29 dyes which included, in addition to Sulphur Black, a larger range of Direct and Acid Azo dyes. These together catered to the dyeing needs of not only cotton but also wool and silk fabrics.

The company's product had good reception in the market "in the matter of standard, quality, and strength". And yet the Atul's ability to withstand competition was in serious doubt. As we have seen earlier, at the time of company's birth, the dye market in India was virtually controlled by foreign suppliers. It was by no means easy to displace them from their deeply entrenched position. The tariff structure greatly enhanced their competitive ability for, the import duties on some of the specific intermediates used by the Atul were as much as 38. 2 per cent *ad valorem*, whereas the varieties manufactured by the company were subject to a duty of only 12 per cent. The result was that the cost of production of the Atul's dyes was higher than the landed cost of the imported dyes, lower labour cost in India notwithstanding. This was a serious handicap particularly because the size of the Atul's operations was still limited and the company had yet to diversify its product lines.

With the foresight characteristic of them, Kasturbhai and Muzumdar had brought the matter to the attention of the Government of India almost two years before the Atul started actual production. The Sheth again approached the Ministry of Commerce and Industry in May 1952 and presented convincing statistics to bring home to the authorities the great threat to the young dyestuffs industry of India posed by the ill-conceived tariff policy. Even though the Government was satisfied about the need to review the tariff structure, with its slow moving machinery there was little it could do immediately to help the Atul. Under these conditions the need to diversify product lines was inescapable. As early as 1953, therefore, Kasturbhai and his associates decided that the range of their products must be "substantially expanded so that the company is able to enter a large field of supply". The strategy to achieve the objective was to be a judicious blending of horizontal expansion and vertical integration. This implied that the company would, on one hand, place in the market a larger number of items produced from imported intermediates; on the other hand, it would gradually move into producing the intermediates and other inputs to reduce its dependence on foreign suppliers.

The policy of horizontal expansion was to receive priority at the first phase so that the campany could build a strong base for the next logical step. But the Atul's financial position was far from satisfactory; its shares were quoted at 60 per cent of their original value in the stock market. In fact, it was a substantial loan from the family *pedhi* of Kasturbhai that enabled his chemical operations to continue unhampered in 1953. To expand production without mobilizing more resources, under these conditions, was well-nigh impossible.

The visit of T.T. Krishnamachari to the Atul site at this time led to a partial solution of its resource problems. Greatly impressed by what he saw, the Commerce Minister in the Union Government enquired why the production facilities were not expanded. Kasturbhai's reply was candid and direct; he had no finance. Krishnamachari put him in touch with the Finance Minister, C.D. Deshmukh, who, as we shall see later, was no stranger to the Sheth. On Deshmukh's enquiry, Kasturbhai indicated that he required Rs 30 million for the Atul's expansion. It was a conservative estimate and the Government readily agreed to sanction the amount on an annual interest of 4.5 per cent. Kasturbhai later regretted that he had not asked for more and wondered what would have been the Atul's course of development if the Government had not been unusually generous.

The Government assistance helped the Atul to set up production plants in 1956 for manufacturing Naphthol, one of the most important groups of fast dyes. Plants were also set up for production of stabilized Azoic dyestuffs popularly known by their German names of Rapid Fasts and Rapidogens. For the production of the latter two groups, the Atul entered into a technical collaboration with the Ciba of Basle, Switzerland, which possessed special competence in this field. On the pharmaceutical side, the company started making active constituents of well-known drugs "Vioform" and "Coramine" in collaboration with the reputed Swiss firm. The new groups of dyes added substantially to the Atul's range of production as they were much faster than the Direct Azo varieties which the company had been making till then.

In the meantime, a "wide and dependable sales organization" had emerged. The first step towards creating an efficient marketing channel had been taken as early as 1950 when the Atul management acquired the Ameer Trading Corporation Ltd., Bombay. The Ameer had been the sole distributors in India for the Atul's American collaborator's products such as dyestuffs, pigments, and intermediates and was reputed to have a network which, in the judgement of the management, could "eventually be used as a competent medium of distribution for the products of our company." The management, however, soon realized that the Ameer, which had efficiently organized the country-wide sale of the relatively small quantity of goods of the American manufacturers, was too modest an organization to be the sole distributor of a large concern such as the Atul. Appointment of a number of selling agents in various parts of the country was considered more expedient.

It was not at all difficult for Kasturbhai to find reliable parties for this purpose. His textile companies had, throughout these years, sold their products through selling agents who had come to rely on the quality of his products. These agents had close relations with textile companies which were the main users of the dyestuffs produced by the Atul. In most of the cases, either the agents handling the sale of the mill products or their affiliates were granted the franchise for the Atul's products. By the end of 1955, the company had appointed as many as 11 selling agents in different parts of the country to bring practically all segments of national market within the Atul's reach. These networks were further strengthened in subsequent years and distribution through selling agencies remained the cornerstone of the Atul's marketing strategy.

Governmental action helped the company's efforts to consolidate its position. Heeding Kasturbhai's pleas, the Tariff Commission had imposed certain restrictions in 1954 on the imports of dyes which the Atul was engaged in manufacturing. The same year, the Commission instituted a thorough enquiry into the demand of Indian dye manufacturers, led by Kasturbhai, for protection and decided in their favour. On its recommendation, the import duties on the intermediate products, used as raw materials by the Atul and other dye manufacturers, were reduced to 10 per cent *ad valorem* and the duties on the imports of finished dyes were raised to 20 per cent—the maximum permissible rate under the provisions of the General Agreement on Tariffs and Trade.

The measures mentioned above provided great relief to the Atul and led to an all-round improvement in its working. Statistics clearly bear this out. The account books show that the annual sales of the company in 1953 were limited to Rs. 75.4 lakhs, and the overall profits to less than Rs. 1.22 lakhs. But the operations that year had actually resulted in considerable loss if we keep in view that profit figures do not account for depreciation, and include about Rs. 1.75 lakhs earned from sources other than the sale of manufactured items. The working results for the next year following the grant of limited relief by the government were much better. The profits before depreciation against the total sales of Rs. 115.80 lakhs amounted to Rs. 12.44 lakhs while the earnings from other sources were limited to Rs. 1.84 lakhs only. In 1955, the year in which the industry came under protection the Atul's total earnings, subject to depreciation, increased to Rs. 20.62 lakhs against the sale of Rs. 130.53 lakhs with income from other sources being only 3.19 lakhs. But what is more significant is that the percentage of profit increased from 1.6 in 1953, to 8.5 in 1954 and jumped to 15.4 in 1955. More importantly, it was in 1955 that for the first time the Atul earned a distributable surplus after providing for depreciation, and declared a dividend of 5.25 per cent.

Even though Kasturbhai's chemical company had consolidated its position to a considerable extent, its production lines touched only a fringe of its expansion plans. The Atul still produced only inexpensive varieties of dyes which possessed relatively lower degree of fastness. In fact more sophisticated dyes with greater endurance properties were not manufactured in India at all and the country's needs were met entirely through imports. The production of more expensive varieties would at once help the company to diversify its product lines and reduce the nation's dependence on foreign supply. The production of these dyes, however, required entirely different equipments, technical know-how, and processes from those employed in manufacturing the kinds of products the Atul was making or its American collaborators could help it make. Essentially, Kasturbhai needed a new party with whom to set sail in a new direction.

He did not have to wait for long for a new collaborator. The Imperial Chemical Industries (ICI) of the United Kingdom, who had made an abortive attempt to start a joint venture with the Tatas in the late 1940s, were watching the progress of the Atul with great interest. The ICI enjoyed world leadership in the production of a certain group of dyes, called Vat dyes, and had several outstanding discoveries to its credit in this line. Known for their superior fastness, the Vat dyes are insoluble in water and must be applied in a strongly alkaline solution of sodium hydrosulphite, popularly called "Vat". One of the top executives of the English company had attended the opening ceremony of the Atul. So impressed was the Englishman by Kasturbhai's complex that he suggested to him to permit the ICI to hold some interests in his company. Even though there was no direct competition between the ICI and the Atul's American collaborator, as each of these companies specialized in distinctly separate lines of products, Kasturbhai considered it inappropriate to agree to the ICI's proposal. Sometime later, Sir Alexander Fleck, the Chairman of the English firm, met Sid Moody of the American Cyanamid in London to impress on him the advantages of the ICI-Atul tie-up but the latter's position remained unchanged.

In 1954, the ICI offered to Kasturbhai to float a company

in partnership with the Atul to manufacture the range of dyes for which the English firm was known. Since there was no fear of any conflict of interest arising out of this arrangement, the American Cyanamid raised no objection. This cleared a great hurdle and the Atic Industries Ltd. was born with the Atul and the ICI holding equal financial interest in the new company. With an authorized capital of Rs. 5,00,00,000 out of which Rs. 50,00,000 were initially subscribed, the new associate company was registered on 8 September 1955. The ICI agreed to provide the technical know-how and the manufacturing facilities were to be located at the Atul site. Almost a year after its registration, the Atic commissioned its first plant which turned out Vat Jade Green, one of the fastest dyes known to man, which the ICI had discovered in 1920. It was the most popular dye in India in the Vat range. The same year the company obtained licences to manufacture a number of other Vat dyes from the imported intermediates. The management decided to increase the paid-up capital of the company to Rs. 1,98,00,000 to enable it to carry out its production plans.

The policy of horizontal expansion and vigorous sales promotion aided by the change in tariff structure and gradual recovery in the textile industry after 1954 had a positive impact on the fortunes of the Atul. As shown in Table VII.1, both its sales and profits registered sharp increase between 1956 and 1960. Clearly, the company had successfully come out of the crisis that it faced during the initial years of its operations.

TABLE VII.1

The Working of the Atul: 1956-1960

Year	*Sales*	*Profit*	*Profit as percentage of sales* (%)
	(Rs. in lakhs)		
1956	183.42	18.27	9.96
1957	271.86	34.51	12.69
1958	289.52	34.46	12.25
1959	353.82	81.84	23.13
1960	418.95	117.87	28.13

II

Nothing much was done during these years to move towards vertical integration even though the Atul management had sensed the need for it quite early. This lay in the logic of the industry because it was necessary for the company to build a strong horizontal base before moving vertically. Also in spite of occasional bureaucratic delays in receiving necessary licences, importing penultimate products did not pose much difficulty during the first five years of the Atul's manufacturing career. Converting the imported intermediates into ultimate products involved much less risk but selling the finished goods under the Atul's name provided an excellent opportunity for the company to build a solid foundation of goodwill. Concentration on the manufacture of ultimate products rather than intermediate goods, thus, was both a sound business policy and consistent with the economic environment in the country.

Depletion in India's foreign exchange reserves changed the situation radically. The signs of the crisis had been visible on the horizon as early as 1956 but it assumed alarming proportions in 1957 when the nation's holdings of foreign currency touched the rock-bottom. The government responded by restricting imports. In fact a large number of import licences already issued to some business establishments were cancelled. The Atul did not suffer this fate but it did not miss the writing on the wall. After 1957, therefore, it started taking more vigorous steps towards producing penultimate products on its own site. The policy of vertical integration henceforward received much greater attention than in the past, though the need for horizontal growth continued to be duly recognized in the company's developmental plans. Significantly enough, the Atul's thinking coincided with the government policy which stressed the need for greater attention to the production of intermediates.

Conforming to the new attitude to production, the Atul started manufacturing phosphorous trichloride in 1959 and sulphuric acid and oleums in 1960. In the meantime, the American Cyanamid came forward to help the Atul in implementing the policy of vertical integration by giving know-how for intermediates like Sodium Naphthionate and Sulphuric Acid. The plants for these were commissioned in 1961. These, however, were small steps towards self-sufficiency. A more significant move in this direction was a scheme drawn up in 1958, envisaging the production of Beta Oxy Naphthoic (BON) Acid and intermediates based on Fast Colour Bases and Naphthalene. BON Acid was important intermediate for making Naphthols, Fast Colour Bases were required for the application of Naphthols, and the Naphthalene-based intermediates were needed to produce a number of products. And yet indigenous production of these ingredients was woefully small.

The scheme was given a more practical shape during several visits to Europe by Muzumdar and Siddhartha Kasturbhai. The elder of the two sons of the Sheth, after completing his education in the United States, had started taking active part in managing the affairs of the Atul. Know-how for the Naphthalene-based intermediates was secured from the Ciba and for Fast Colour Bases and BON Acid from another reputed Swiss firm, The Rohner Limited. Even though the plants were to cost about 70 millions—more than seven times the informal estimates of the Atul's executives—and the manufacture of the intermediates did not appear to be very lucrative at that time, Kasturbhai decided to go ahead with his plans. His commitment to the policy of vertical integration was so strong that when at one stage, Siddharthabhai and his associates, not sure whether the Sheth would agree to so high a price, decided to check with him before finalising the deal, they were rebuked for their undue caution and hesitation.

The Government of India approved of these schemes in principle. The company also secured the industrial licence for the entire scheme, but the Government took a long time to grant permission to import plants and machinery necessary for implementing the projects. Meanwhile the foreign exchange crisis became worse and import difficulties impeded the operations of even the existing plants. Production in the Azo and Sulphur Black Plants had to be curtailed and on occasions the company was forced to close down some of its plants for brief periods.

Under these conditions it was not possible to obtain import licences entailing sizable foreign exchange investment unless the company could make its own arrangements for foreign currency to the full satisfaction of the Government. The estimated foreign exchange component of the Naphthalene and Fast

Colour Bases projects alone amounted to Rs. 85,00,000. The Industrial Credit and Investment Corporation of India (ICICI) agreed to provide Rs. 75,00,000, sufficient to cover the free-on-board value of the equipment. Kasturbhai persuaded the Scindia Steamship Company to accept the freight, and the New India Assurance Company the insurance charges, in rupees. A loan from the Commonwealth Development Finance Company of London provided for the balance of the needed resources. The company secured the import licences in November 1962 and the plants were commissioned in 1965. In the meantime, the Atul had further expanded the production of a number of chemicals required for its manufacturing processes including caustic soda and chlorine. These would satisfy the needs of dyestuff and other plants. In the same plant the production of sodium sulphide, an important ingredient for Sulphur Black, was also envisaged. At a later stage the company would produce dicalcium phosphate from the chlorine coming out of its caustic soda plant and the same consideration would lead to the production of a number of chlorinated items including pesticides.

The equipment installed in 1965 would enable the company to produce about 70 products, each containing four to a dozen chemical steps. The technology acquired and developed to run the plants would form the backbone of the company's technical and economic strength in the years to come. How wise was the Sheth's decision in taking what appeared to be an undue risk then became clear at the end of the 1960s when the prices of all intermediates in foreign countries began to rise abnormally.

While the Atul's plans were being implemented, its associate, the Atic Industries, was going ahead with its own schemes of horizontal expansion and vertical integration The first step in this direction was taken in 1959 when the company placed a large range of Vat dyes in the market. The next logical step was to undertake the manufacture of Betamine and Benzanthrone which were essential raw materials for the range of dyes produced by the company. There was little difficulty in procuring the necessary licenses. But because of the difference of opinion between the company and the Government of India on the quantum of design costs to be paid to the Imperial Chemical Industries, action on the Atic's application for import licence was unduly delayed. The British firm was not willing to charge anything less than £108,500 (Rs. 14,50,000) and the Government of India would not agree to the payment of more than £37,250 (Rs. 5,00,000). The Atic overcame this difficulty by carrying out a part of the design work in India with the help of the technical data supplied by the consultants. The import licence was finally granted in November 1962. The attitude of the Government, however, delayed the commencement of the project by at least 17 months. How shortsighted the Government's approach was, is clear from the fact that the completion of the Atic's project was to result in a foreign exchange saving worth Rs. 25,00,000 per year. After the import licence had been granted, the Atic took the least possible time to implement its scheme to produce Betamine and Benzanthrone and succeeded in putting these products in the market by the beginning of 1965.

The beginning of the 1960s also witnessed rigorous and effective efforts on the part of Kasturbhai and his associates to produce pharmaceutical intermediates. A major step in this direction was taken in 1960 when it was decided to float a new company jointly by the Atul and the Ciba to produce Sulpha drug intermediates. The Atul was to hold 65 per cent of the share capital of the new company and the remaining 35 per cent was allotted to the collaborating firm. The Cibatul, the name of the new concern, represented a combination of the names of the collaborating firms as had been done in the case of the Atic. Along with the production of Sulpha drug intermediates the Cibatul was to go in for the production of two plastic adhesives, Urea Formaldehyde (UF) and Melamine Formaldehyde (MF) resins. The UF resins found an industrial application as wood-bonding agent for building furniture, and sports goods industries as well as in manufacturing plywood and chipboard. Some special varieties of this category were also used as textile auxiliaries. The MF resins were extensively used to make decorative and industrial laminated sheets for furniture, building, and electrical industries.

Foreign exchange difficulties, however, impeded the progress of these projects. Implementation of these schemes required a huge outlay in foreign currency. The question of securing any part of this large sum through regular Governmental sources did not arise. The Government also turned down the Cibatul's application for a loan of Rs. 75,00,000 from the Indo-Swiss Credit Arrangement. Under these conditions, the excellent relations that Kasturbhai had built with the Ciba proved invaluable. The Swiss company agreed to grant a large loan sufficient to meet the entire foreign exchange cost of these projects. Eventually, the import licence for the Sulpha drug project was issued in September 1961, and that for the resin scheme more than a year later in January 1963.

III

With the implementation of the Atul-Atic expansion plans and the launching of the Cibatul, Kasturbhai's chemical-pharmaceutical complex became one of the most diversified in the country. However, the complex was yet to become fully integrated as there were significant gaps in the range of products manufactured by the Atul and its subsidiaries or associates. Another expansion plan was launched in 1967 to fill up these gaps. There were three principal features of the new expansion scheme: (i) undertaking manufacture of new items which served as intermediate or raw material for the final products of any of the companies, (ii) addition of new final products, and (iii) expansion of the existing production facilities.

Supplementing Kasturbhai's determination to move forward in the new direction were the needs of the nation. The production of Phosgene was undertaken in response to a suggestion from the Government which needed this product very badly for defence purposes. The Atul was already using Phosgene and phosgenated products for making intermediates and dyes and therefore possessed experience in an extremely intricate technology. The production of Phosgene started in 1970. Four years later the company took the next logical step by producing carbamite, a pharmaceutical intermediate, for which Phosgene was an essential input. While these developments were in progress, the Atul also took up the production of additional intermediates such as Betanaphthol and Micheler's Ketone.

The installation of the Betanaphthol plant in 1976 was an event of unusual significance. The product was an extremely important primary intermediate required for manufacturing other intermediates and a number of dyes. To meet its need of about 1200 tonnes a year, the Atul used to import or purchase it from other sources. The decision to produce the item on the site was, thus, in line with the company's expansion plans and its will to be self-sufficient. The American Cyanamid provided some preliminary information but it is a measure of the competence and the confidence that the Atul's technologists had gained by this time that the plant was designed, installed, and commissioned entirely by its own staff without the involvement of any consultant.

The company in the meantime continued to expand horizontally and increase the capacity of its existing plants. A full range of Azo Disperse dyes in granular form began to be produced in 1974. And the plants whose existing capacity was expanded included those for Naphathalene intermediates, Caustic Soda and Chlorine, Phosgene, and Chlorosulphuric Acid.

The Atic expansion proceeded on similar lines. Between 1967 and 1970, it introduced a whole range of new Vat dyes—the yellow, orange, brown, red, and grey—to complete the spectrum. In 1970 the manufacture of anthraquinone, a basic intermediate required for the production of almost all dyestuffs, was taken up. Significantly enough, the plant for the new product was based entirely on design and process technology developed by the Atic engineers. The most important development, however, was the introduction of the Procion dyes in India. Named after Procyon, a bright star over the northern hemisphere, the Procion dyes are noted for their brilliance. Hues not obtainable with conventional dyes are found in Procion dyes which are versatile, easy to apply, and possess a high wet fastness. Since these dyes enter into a chemical bond with the fabric instead of being fixed physically on it, they fall in the category of reactive dyes. First developed by the ICI in 1956, the Procion dyes opened up infinite possibilities to the fashion designers. In 1969, the Atic installed and commissioned a new plant to manufacture a full range of Procion dyes, and thus became the first Indian company to introduce this product in the Indian markets.

When the Atic started manufacturing reactive dyes, man-made fibres were making significant inroads into the Indian textile industry. Kasturbhai's own mills were gearing themselves to the production of synthetic fibres. Reactive dyes could not be useful for the new products which required what are known as disperse dyes. It was as early as 1968, that the company decided to undertake the production of a variety of synthetic dyes. However, because of the inevitable bureaucratic delay, it could not secure an industrial licence before 1971, and the final stage of the project could not be completed before the second quarter of 1974. As in the case of the parent company the Atic, while adding new items to its product lines, expanded the capacity of its existing plants.

At the time of the commencement of the second expansion, both the Atul and the Atic had achieved a good measure of financial stability, and, thus, were in a position to finance their expansions largely through their internal sources. The Cibatul, in 1967 had not yet reached that happy position. The company was yet to come out of its infancy and yet to declare dividends. In fact during the first five years after registration, it had accumulated a loss of about Rs. 72,000. This was understandable because the company had not yet started production, but there was no sign of the reversal of the trend even after its manufacturing plants were commissioned. On the contrary, the quantum of accumulated losses increased to Rs. 26.42 lakhs in 1966, the first year of production, and jumped to Rs. 97.56 lakhs by 1969.

One of the reasons for the unsatisfactory performance of the young company was that its plants worked much below the capacity because of difficulties in securing raw materials. The Sulpha drug intermediate plant did not yield desired results because it could not get all the imported raw materials in time, and difficulties in procuring formaldehyde, an essential raw material for producing resin, created idle capacity in the plastic department. More important, the company had to buy this essential raw material from outside sources at uneconomical prices which affected the profitability of this operation. It was decided, therefore, as early as 1966 to undertake the production of formaldehyde. But the Government of India rejected the company's application for an industrial licence and all efforts for the revision of this decision failed till the licensing policy was relaxed in 1970. The formaldehyde plant, therefore, could not be commissioned until June 1973.

In the meantime, the Cibatul had undertaken the production of Epoxy resins. This was a case of horizontal expansion. Epoxy resins, first developed by the Ciba-Geigy of Switzerland, possessed excellent adhesive properties. They could be applied to different materials including metals. Their insulating qualities made them useful for electrical industry and, because of their toughness and resistance, to chemical attack and moisture, they could provide excellent surface coating. They could also be used in making tools and foundry patterns as they could be easily cast into structures of great strength and resilience.

These qualities of the product notwithstanding, it was not an easy decision for the Cibatul management to go in for the production of Epoxy resins. In 1965 when the company first dreamt of moving into the new line, demand for the product in India was negligible. Kasturbhai and his associates, however, could foresee considerable rise in demand in the near future because of its possible application in a number of vital industries and projects such as the production of defence equipments, manufacture of electrical goods for indigenous and export market, fabrication of rockets for space research, erection of atomic power plant, construction of dams for irrigation and power projects, protection of floors in steel plants, and as surface coating agent in steel structures to prevent them from being chemically eroded.

The company had little difficulty in securing an industrial licence for the manufacture of Epoxy resin. The entire project was to cost about Rs. 50 lakhs including Rs. 16.78 lakhs in foreign exchange. The Government of India agreed to the Cibatul's request for an Italian credit for Rs. 12.48 lakhs and U.K. credit for Rs. 430 lakhs to enable it to place orders for the entire imported machinery with a reputed Italian firm. The remaining amount was sought to be arranged through the increase of Ciba's share capital in the company from 35% to 50%. This proposal which the Swiss collaborators unhesitatingly accepted would have pushed up the Ciba's investment in the company by Rs. 60 lakhs but the Government did not agree to the proposal. The Epoxy resin project was finally financed through loans from the Bank of Baroda and the United Commercial Bank. The plant was commissioned in 1968 and soon the production increased to 50% of the licensed capacity.

The performance of the Epoxy resin plant would have been still better if there would have been less difficulty in obtaining necessary raw materials. Irregular supply of Bisphenol-A, one of the essential inputs, caused the greatest concern. In 1970, the operation of the plant was seriously handicapped because of the difficulty in securing this chemical in "required quantity and of the desired quality". In keeping with its policy of vertical integration, therefore, the Cibatul decided to manufacture this product in its own factory. Production of Bisphenol-A at the company's site involved little extra investment as what was required was nothing more than the "installation of some balancing equipment of a very minor nature". As soon as the Government permission was received, manufacturing operations commenced in October 1970. As a result within the next two years, the production of the resin plant jumped to 85% of the installed capacity as compared to only 50% in 1968. To place its Bisphenol-A production, and, thus, the production of Epoxy resin, on a more sound footing, the Cibatul set up for this purpose a separate plant "wholly designed by the chemists and engineers of the company" in 1974.

The pharmaceutical side of the Cibatul also underwent expansion. As has been noted earlier, the company had started production of various Sulpha drug intermediates, including sodium salts, in 1968. The manufacture of almost all Sulpha drugs require two chemical components—Acetyl Sulphanilyd Chloride (ASC) and an amino base. The chemical reaction of ASC with the appropriate base produces a Sulpha drug. The Cibatul was the only unit in the country equipped to produce its own ASC from the most basic chemical, Aniline. At the first phase, it started producing two very important bases—Aminothiazole and Cyanmethine. In 1971 it obtained the licence to produce a third important amino base known as Pyrazole. A foreign exchange loan from the ICICI enabled the company to import the requisite plant and machinery. With the installation of the Pyrazole plant in 1973, the Cibatul equipped itself to produce all the three amino bases it needed for manufacturing a whole range of Sulpha drugs.

IV

The expansion helped the Atul group of companies to

TABLE VII.2

Atul Products: Sales, Profits, and Dividends 1961-1976

Year	*Sales*	*Profits*	*Profit as percentage of sales (%)*
	(Rs. in lakhs)		
1961	474.81	102.41	21.57
1962	414.83	90.41	21.79
1963	427.86	53.68	12.55
1964	602.56	56.17	9.32
1965	629.83	42.50	6.75
1966	745.93	56.75	7.61
1967	727.72	1.97	0.27
1968	959.58	35.08	3.66
1969	1154.13	94.22	8.16
1970	1364.38	155.75	11.42
1971	1432.91	133.96	9.29
1972	2045.58	200.23	9.29
1973	2218.11	314.16	14.16
1974	3016.83	492.03	16.31
1975	3864.97	599.74	15.52
1976	4795.11	730.23	15.23

stabilize their position. Even the Cibatul, which made consistent losses till 1969, made sufficient profit during the next two years to wipe off all accumulated deficits, and declare its maiden dividend in 1973. Likewise the Atic Industries, which had stopped contributing to the revenue of the parent companies after 1965 because of ploughing back its profits to implement its expansion plans, resumed the payment of dividends in 1970. The contributions from these companies along with its own improved performance enhanced the profitability of the Atul as Table VII. 2 indicates. Admittedly, the company passed through a period of lean profitability between 1965 and 1969. This was due to the difficulties in securing raw material, and higher cost of inputs and labour. Several times during this period, one or the other plants had to be shut down for varying periods of time because raw materials in sufficient quantity could not be secured on time. Also the Atic and the Cibatul, in which the company had substantial investment, were making no contribution to its revenue. As mentioned earlier, the former's expansion scheme prevented it from declaring dividends, and the latter was yet to come out of the gestation period.

Expansion both horizontal and vertical—of all the three companies in the group after 1968 eased the raw material situation to a considerable degree. But the problem was not entirely solved. In fact, the last quarter of 1973 witnessed "the beginning of a period of unprecedented scarcity of raw materials." The Government of India decided that the imports of some of the materials used by the Atul and the other two companies associated with it would be canalized through the State Trading Corporation which did not always keep enough stocks or order the materials sufficiently in advance. While the scarcity remained unabated during the next two years, the price of some of the raw materials registered phenomenal rise in 1974. Some items became as much as 400 per cent more expensive than in the previous year. The recession in the textile industry that year also affected the sales of the company products. If in spite of these adverse factors, the Atul could maintain a reasonable level of profitability, it was largely due to the diversified nature of its own product lines and those of the Atic and the Cibatul. Table VII.3 presents a consolidated picture of the product-mix of the Atul group of companies as compared to the situation at the time of the company's inception in 1952.

The expanding activities of the Atul and its associates enabled them to retain a pre-eminent position among the chemical and pharmaceutical producers in the country. When Kasturbhai's chemical complex started production in 1952, competition was negligible. In the wake of protection and other inducements offered by the Government to the industry, several new companies came into existence and the halycon days of non-competition were over. And yet, the Atul group continued throughout to hold a preponderant share in the nation's total production of most of the major items it produced.

When the Atul started production in 1952, the country's dependence on imports for its dyestuffs needs was total. By 1976, the nation had almost become self-sufficient in the field. The Atul's contribution to this welcome development cannot be underestimated. In addition, the company and its associates helped the country to earn a large amount of foreign exchange. The group made its debut in the foreign market in 1965 with a small quantity of the Atic products. The value of

TABLE VII.3

Atul and Associated Companies : Product mix—1952 and 1976

Class of Goods	*Varieties Produced*	
	1952	*1976*
Dyes	Direct Dyes, Acid Dyes and Sulphur Black	Direct dyes, Acid dyes, Sulphur dyes, Naphthols, Bases, Disperse dyes, Pigments, Vat dyes, Solubilised Vat dyes, Reactive dyes, Optical brighteners.
Dyes Intermediates	—	H Acid, Gama Acid, Chicago Acid, Betanaphthol, Anthraquinone, Benzanthrone, Betamine and a large number of other intermediates.
Pharmaceuticals and Drugs	Sulfadiazine and Sulfathiazole	Sulfas, Tetracyclines, Quiniodochlor, Nikethamide, Menadion, Saccharin, etc.
Pharmaceutical Intermediates	—	OTSA, PTSA, Methyl, Dichloro Acetate, Acetyl & Sodium Salts of Sulfas, etc.
Pesticide	—	2-4-D, Malathion, Thimet, etc.
Basic Inorganic Chemicals	—	Sulfuric Acid, Oleums, Chlorosulfonic Acid, Caustic Soda, Caustic Potash, Sodium Sulfide, Chlorine, Hydrochloric Acid, Phosphorous Trichloride, etc.
Resins	—	UF/MF/PF Resins, Epoxy Resins, Hardeners & Ancillaries.

exports continued to rise in the next three years and the Government of India accorded priority status to the company because of its export performance during the period from 1 April 1967 to 3 March 1968. The progress of the Atic in this sphere in subsequent years is clear from the fact that the value of its exports went up from Rs. 37 lakhs in 1968 to Rs. 99 lakhs in 1976. In the meantime, the Atul itself launched its own export drive in 1969 by placing goods worth Rs. 16.44 lakhs in the international market. By 1976 the value of its exports had reached an impressive figure of Rs. 346 lakhs. The export performance of the Cibatul, which was the last to enter the international market, was less impressive, but even this company increased its exports from Rs. 3 lakhs in 1971, when it despatched its first consignment abroad, to Rs. 7 lakhs in 1976. In the context of India's total exports of dyestuffs the share of the Atul and the associated companies in 1976 amounted to about 15 per cent.

Significantly, the products of the Atul group of companies found ready markets not only in the developing countries but also in advanced nations such as the United States, the United Kingdom, Japan, and Switzerland. Two major factors helped the Kasturbhai's concerns to increase the exports to developed countries. First, in the wake of growing automization, large chemical companies in advanced countries lost interest in batch process of production in which the Atul group specialized. Consequently, these countries increased their imports of products made through the batch processes from the developing countries. And secondly, excessive fear of pollution resulting from the concentration of industries led to the dropping of several products from the manufacturing lists of major companies in the industrially developed world. The third world countries with relatively less incidence of pollution were in a happy position to increase their exports of these items. The Atul and its associated concerns with their developed and sophisticated manufacturing facilities reaped the benefit of these developments. The success of these companies in widening their export base won for them several concessions the Government of India usually granted to the companies with such accomplishments. And these concessions helped the Atul to boost its export drive still further.

A large part of the Atul's success during the first twenty-five years of its existence can be attributed to its choice of collaborators. Each one of them was a world leader in some specific field and Kasturbhai's companies could draw on their collaborator's technical knowhow and the reputation of their products. At a very early stage, however—much earlier than many other managements—Kasturbhai and his associates foresaw the need to undertake research and development activities. As early as 1962, the Atul joined the Ciba Ltd., in establishing a Research Laboratory at Goregaon in Bombay with the object of promoting basic research in some chemical fields. A special section for research in dyes and their application was added to this laboratory. A more concrete step towards promoting research and development was taken in 1975 when a scheme to establish full-fledged R and D laboratories on the Atul site at a cost of Rs. 30 lakhs was taken up. A substantial part of the laboratories was ready when Kasturbhai announced his retirement. The associated companies, in the meantime, had established their own R and D laboratories. Noting the progress achieved by the Atic and Cibatul laboratories, the Government of India's Department of Science and Technology accorded recognition to them in 1975 and 1976 respectively.

V

On the basis of this broad survey of the growth of Kasturbhai's chemical complex it can be safely maintained that the Atul and its subsidiaries present a veritable saga of developing one of the most critical industries necessary for India's economic progress. Starting literally from scratch, the Atul in less than a quarter of a century became the largest company of its kind in India. The capital employed in Kasturbhai's chemical-pharmaceutical concerns exceeded Rs. 1332.29 lakhs in 1976 as against Rs. 100 lakhs in 1952; the gross value of its products during the same period increased from Rs. 24.63 lakhs to Rs. 8147.7 lakhs. In the first year of its production the Atul's sales were limited to Rs. 17.84 lakhs and gross assets to Rs. 160.45 lakhs only; twenty-five years later these figures including those of the Atic and the Cibatul had crossed Rs. 9931 lakhs and Rs. 5145 lakhs respectively and the number of employees increased from 337 to 5386. There is no doubt that when Kasturbhai decided to step down from the leadership role, his chemical complex had come of age.

It is important to remember that the success of the Atul's manufacturing activities was inseparably linked with its success in training and developing a large number of technical and managerial staff. When the company started production, it hardly had a qualified staff to boast of. Most of the technical and executive personnel were raw graduates with little experience in manning the intricate technology that the processes of producing dyes, pharmaceuticals, and intermediates needed. As the company and its associates expanded their operations, the employees gained in confidence and technical skill. And this helped the companies to utilize their plants and resources to the optimum extent. Some of these employees even contributed to the development of other chemical enterprises which emerged later. Also significant is the fact that the rise of a number of dye manufacturers in the country was directly or indirectly inspired by the Atul experiment. A senior executive of a principal Indian firm in the field unhesitatingly conceded to an Atul manager on the occasion of the latter's silver jubilee: "Since you could so successfully do it, all of us felt that we could do it likewise."

The full significance of the Atul experiment, however, cannot be appreciated in business terms alone. In fact, some of its competitors in recent years have shown better business results. But none of these—indeed very few industrial undertakings in the country—can claim to have created as much impact on the society as the Atul has done. Situatedin a backward rural region, inhabited largely by tribals and people of backward sections, the Atul operations have unfolded great employment opportunities for the population around it. In fact more than 35 per cent of its total workforce belongs to the scheduled castes and tribes—15 per cent above the Government of India stipulations. Various ancillary industries and services that have grown around Kasturbhai's chemical complex have benefited the region further. Both men and women work in these companies to better their economic prospects. A large number of these employees live on the Atul complex in the houses provided by the company on nominal rent. As such, the employees partake of the cultural and recreational facilities that the campus provides, and their children benefit by the educational opportunities available on the campus. As a result of the prosperity and the glimpse of a new life that the Atul has brought, the quality of social life around the region has considerably improved. The multiplier effect of all this, though not easy to measure, is not difficult to judge.

On the eve of his retirement from the Atul chairmanship in January 1977, Kasturbhai rightly claimed that the Atul had transformed a "waste land into a land of prosperity" and has brought about "a great social transformation." The conversion of the tiny village of Sakchi into Jamshedpur as a result of J.N. Tata's decision to locate his steel mill there is perhaps the only parallel example of this kind in the entire industrial history of India. The literal meaning of the Atul's Sanskrit name is "incomparable". And the company has lived up to its name in more than one sense.

CHAPTER VIII

On Structure and Strategies

THE growth of a business enterprise depends, to a large extent, on the strategies it adopts to exploit the perceivable opportunities and the structure it designs to mobilize its human resources. The preceding chapters have dwelt at considerable length upon the growth of the Kasturbhai group of industries. How far was its success due to its ability to match its structure with its objectives and adopt strategies capable of achieving optimum results? In answering this question, it must be remembered that an organization is not entirely free to choose its structure and strategies. The long experience of and the prevailing managerial practices in the society in which the organization has to operate condition and influence the choice to a considerable degree.

When Kasturbhai's father led the family into industrial field by establishing the Saraspur Mills, the most commonly accepted form of corporate management in India was the managing agency system. Born sometime in the early part of the 19th century, this type of organizational design was unique to India under which the promotion and management of one or several companies, though legally independent, were controlled by a single firm, and the controlling firm, in turn, was usually controlled by a single family. The modus operandi was simple. A family with considerable financial strength would launch a company and allot to its own members or near relatives sufficient number of shares necessary to control the new concern. Simultaneously, those holding the controlling interests in the new company joined to form a managing agency firm to which the management of the new company was entrusted under an agreement stipulating the terms and conditions. Technically speaking, thus, the managing agents did not own the company; they only managed the company for which they were remunerated. But in practice, all critical and strategic decisions about the company in question were taken by the managing firm.

The managing agency structure was nothing but the adaptation to industrial management of the joint family system which in the 19th century was the most dominant feature of the Indian society. The head of the family controlled the purse, exercised authority over the junior members, and had a dominant, almost decisive, voice in matters affecting the family. Prior to the emergence of industrial organizations in India there was little qualitative difference between the role played by the heads of commercial families and those of the non-business families in managing their respective affairs. In other words, the business management structure was conterminous with the family management structure. The commercial families, therefore, found it easy to adopt the managing agency framework for managing their industrial undertakings as it entailed little change in their mangerial attitudes and practices.

Under these conditions, it was perhaps most logical for Lalbhai to weave the administrative structure of his two mills around the managing agency system. The system had been an article of faith for all the business magnates who had preceded him in establishing textile mills and other industrial ventures in Ahmedabad and elsewhere in India. The trading and banking businesses of his family had long been managed under the joint family framework, and the managing agency structure offered little threat to the authority and freedom of decision-making that he, as the head of the family, had enjoyed in the matters affecting the family. He must have noticed that when his first mill came into being, the managing agencies were under heavy attack in the Ahmedabad and Bombay press for various real and imaginary abuses. But nobody had come out with an alternative system, and there was no real danger to the continuance of the system. In fact, the prevailing legal framework in the country favoured the growth of this system, as the Indian Company Law of 1882 required neither the constitution of an elected board of directors for a company nor the appointment of managing directors.

The Lalbhai Dalpatbhai and Company, the managing agency which Lalbhai established for the Saraspur Manufacturing Company, was a partnership firm, as most of the managing agencies were, in which he and his brothers, Manibhai and Jagabhai, had equal shares. Between them and their close relatives, the brothers contributed the entire initial paid-up capital of the company. As the head of the managing agency firm and the family that floated the mill, Lalbhai could have become its chairman without any difficulty. He, however, invited Manibhai Premabhai to occupy this office. As a scion of the Nagarsheth family Manibhai enjoyed a great deal of social standing in the city. The business glory of the illustrious family, though now past, was still a part of popular imagination. Perhaps Lalbhai derived some degree of psychological satisfaction from this symbolic identification of his young concern with his old heritage. Among others who joined the board of directors, which every joint stock company was required by law to have, were, besides Lalbhai himself, Veerchand Deepchand and Hirachand Pitambardas. The former enjoyed some reputation in the business and industrial circles of Bombay and had earned the title of the C.I.E. from the British Government. The latter was a well-known lawyer of Ahemdabad. After the death of Manibhai Premabhai at the young age of 37 in 1900, Lalbhai himself assumed the Chairmanship of the company. The same year, one of his two brothers, Manibhai Dalpatbhai, was inducted into the board. In 1904, Manilal Mohanlal, who had come in contact with Lalbhai as a yarn broker, was offered a seat on the board, and Lalbhai Hirachand occupied the seat caused vacant by the death of his father.

In associating persons with professional and business standing with his board, Lalbhai was conforming to a common practice followed by the founders of the industrial establishments those days. But the composition of the board had little effect on the unlimited powers of Lalbhai in deciding crucial matters affecting the company, since the board did nothing more than ratify the decisions of the managing agents whose financial control over the mill was almost total. This form of management was replicated when the Raipur Mills came into being. In fact not only the managing agents but even the members of the Raipur board were the same as those of the Saraspur Mills.

The size and the complexity of the undertakings were such that Lalbhai, assisted by his brothers, exercised a close personal supervision over his industrial enterprises. In a sense, there was no qualitative difference between his style of managing the mills and that of managing the banking business. The family's banking operations had given him a keen insight into financial matters and he did not have to worry about marketing his goods as these were sold through the local wholesalers. Labour front posed little problem as the trade unionism in the country was still in its infancy. Under such a situation, there was no need for an elaborate organization to manage the mills, and none emerged. The mills had only two key officials: a secretary to deal with the shareholders and the board; and an accountant to help in financial matters. A senior employee was named manager for the purposes of legal matters but possessed no intrinsic powers. All authority was centred in Lalbhai. Nothing escaped the attention of the hardworking millowner who attended his mills daily and spent several hours there. For all practical purposes Lalbhai's was a one-man management, as was the case with practically all the textile mills then in Ahmedabad.

II

A few months before his untimely death, Lalbhai had become the sole owner of his managing agency firm as a result of the division in the family. His three children—Chimanbhai, Kasturbhai, and Narottambhai—who came to own the Lalbhai Dalpatbhai and Company jointly along with other assets and liabilities of the family introduced no change in the basic management structure of the Raipur Mills except some minor ones forced by the Indian Companies Amendment Act of 1914.

These changes, however, in no way affected the powers of the managing agents in managing their concerns. One of the provisions of the amended act, for instance, required a majority of the company directors to be elected independently of the managing agents. But because of the controlling interests in their companies, the managing agents had absolutely no difficulty in ensuring the "election" of handpicked candidates. In fact so ineffective was this provision that its implementation brought about no change in the composition of the Raipur board; those who were the members of the board before the enforcement of the election requirements continued to be on it. More significantly, the membership of the Raipur and the Saraspur boards continued to remain common even though the latter was managed by a separate managing agency formed by Lalbhai's brothers after the family division.

Lalbhai's three sons had little experience of business affairs when he died. Chimanbhai, the eldest, was the only one who had attained adulthood. Even though he had been inducted into the business during the life-time of his father, his insights into business matters were limited indeed. This is why Lalbhai's widow persuaded her second son, Kasturbhai, to discontinue his education and look after the business much to the latter's chagrin. Lalbhai's second son-in-law, Chandulal Jhaveri, guided the children in managing their affairs at the initial stages. From the very beginning Kasturbhai showed his mettle as a potential manager. After his induction into the Raipur board in 1914 he gradually assumed the position of the chief decision-maker in the family. Everyone, including his elder brother who remained the formal head of the family, recognized his superiority. His reputation as a person of unfailing business judgment soon transcended the narrow circles of his relatives, friends, and associates; the Ahmedabad business circles in general took notice of his keen insights into business matters. It is no surprise, therefore, that in all future expansion of the family's industrial ventures beginning with the floating of the Asoka Mills, it was Kasturbhai Lalbhai, rather than Chimanbhai who played a key and decisive role. By sheer merit, he earned for himself an enviable reputation for right judgment so that not only the members of his family but also his relatives and business associates considered it advantageous to submit to his decisions almost blindly. As Chinubhai Manibhai, his cousin only a few years his junior, put it: "If Kasturbhai asked me to jump down out of the window, I would do so without any thought for the consequences because it was *his* business to think about what would happen to me if I jumped!"

Chinubhai is not alone with this sense of loyalty to Kasturbhai. Others in the family express similar sentiments, though in somewhat less exaggerated terms. It was his sense of fair-play and utter impartiality in dealing with people that earned him this position. Himself a product of a joint family, he had an unwavering faith in the virtues of the system. He could easily perceive that the *sine qua non* for the continuance of the system was the faith on the part of all the members of the family that the interest of each one of them was safe in the hands of the principal member. In managing the business, he kept this aspect constantly in view and treated all members alike. Pointing to this trait of his father, Shrenikbhai, the younger son of the Sheth, claims with full justification that in dealing with the family members, Kasturbhai would err on the right side, that is, against his own kith and kin. In keeping with the joint family tradition the millowner believed firmly that even if a person did not work, the rest of the family had a duty by him and he had a claim over the family. And for Kasturbhai, the family meant not only the children of Lalbhai, but also the latter's daughters and brothers and their families.

The way he divided the shares in his managing agency firms clearly demonstrate his concern for his extended family and the desire that everyone was adequately provided for. The Raipur Mills which he inherited from his father was under the management of the Lalbhai Dalpatbhai and Company, the ownership of which was equally divided among the three brothers. Later when the Asoka Mills was launched, its management could have easily been entrusted to the ancestral firm. Instead of doing so, Kasturbhai formed a new managing agency partnership in which the family of his second sister, Manekben, was given a small share. We may recall that Manekben's husband, Chandulal Zaveri, had given a helping hand to Lalbhai's children during the first few years after the latter's premature demise. By inducting Chandulal's family into his managing agency firm Kasturbhai at once repaid a moral debt and discharged what he considered his obligation to one of his blood relations. Likewise, when he acquired the Saraspur Mills, he considered it necessary to form a new managing agency partnership in which each of his two uncles was given 12.5 per cent shares even though they had given ample proof of their incapacity to manage a textile mill. The family of his first sister, Dahiben, was invited to join the new managing agency firm with a small share of 3.12 per cent. If the family of his third sister was not given any share in these agency firms, it was only because they were doing relatively well as stock brokers and did not need Kasturbhai's help.

The families of Kasturbhai's three sisters decided at a later date to expand their interests in textile manufacturing. The floating of the Aruna and the Nutan and the acquisition of the Ahmedabad New Cotton was, to some extent, due to their keenness to invest in industrial ventures. Kasturbhai was actively involved in promoting these ventures because of his sense of commitment to his sisters' families. In the managing agency firms entrusted with the management of these companies—P.M. Hutheesing and Sons, Jagabhai Bhogilal Nanavaty and Company and Narottamlal Chandulal and Brothers respectively— his sisters' families had substantial shares. In the Kasturbhai Lalbhai and Company the managing agents of the Anil Starch, Chinubhai, the initiator of the venture, was given 50 per cent share.

To constitute a separate managing agency for each of the companies controlled by the same family was somewhat unusual in India. In most cases, a managing agency managed more than one company with a view to achieving administrative integration and the advantages of the economy of scale. Kasturbhai's decision to deviate from the common practice was influenced by the need to take in different partners in each firm. He and his two brothers who held shares in all the managing agency firms were the common links between them. Even though the quantum and nature of their contribution to management differed from one another, they held exactly equal shares in every managing agency firm. This method brought all the managing agencies under a common umbrella. Another common link was the personality of Kasturbhai Lalbhai himself who evoked complete loyalty from all those who constituted the apex of his management structure. Because of these links the companies in the group pursued common policies in all crucial fields and came to be identified with the Lalbhai group of industries.

Kasturbhai's reputation as a competent manager, who valued integrity, honesty, and fair-play as much as business success, drew the attention of the the investing public. The way he tackled the crisis which overtook the Asoka Mills at its very infancy won laurels for him, and his action in protecting the interests of the shareholders, when he took over the Saraspur Manufacturing Company from his uncles, brought forth the finer qualities of his managerial approach. The image that he acquired as a result of these events and his business behaviour in general helped Kasturbhai in floating his future companies with relatively small investment from the group; the market response to the opportunity to invest in his companies rendered very high investment on the part of the group unnecessary. It is significant that whereas the group controlled as much as 53 per cent of the share capital of the Raipur initially, in none of the companies floated after the First World War, the group investment exceeded 35 per cent in the Saraspur it was as low as 16 to 17 per cent. The Arvind was the only exception as it was the Raipur's gift to its own shareholders. It is also noteworthy that the group holdings in the Arvind as well as in the Raipur were substantially diluted after the depression. In the middle of the 1950s, by which time all the major companies in the group had been formed, the family did not have more than 40 per cent voting power in any of the companies and in the Atul it was as low as 15 per cent. Also the role of the inter-corporate investment in these companies has been negligible, and the group has always enjoyed wide public participation and support. In other words, Kasturbhai and his associates avoided recourse to the methods which the promoters of industrial concerns in India usually employed to control their companies. It was the reputation of the management that largely helped the group to control its industrial undertakings.

III

As long as the size of the group remained small and level

of operations limited, there was no need for an elaborate organization. During the initial years, therefore, Kasturbhai with the help of his two brothers supervised practically all aspects of business. In fact the three brothers made a perfect team. Temperamentally withdrawn and non-interfering, Chimanbhai played the role of a titular head who preferred to leave the actual decision-making and implementation to his two younger brothers endowed with more active and agile minds and greater capacity for hard work. Kasturbhai was extrovert, aggressive, and daring by temperament. Narottambhai, the youngest of the three on the other hand, was an introvert and extremely meticulous in his method of working. While Kasturbhai possessed keen insights in financial intricacies and used his skill and personality to deal with the business and government circles, the strength of his younger brother lay in production and marketing fields. Starting his career in the Asoka Mills in 1921 after graduating with a science degree from the University of Bombay, Narottambhai soon mastered various aspects of textile operations. Though uneasy in social limelight, the youngest of Lalbhai's sons was a great asset to the textile side of the group's business from behind the scene.

With the brothers and the nephews sharing most of the managerial responsibilities, the mills did not need more than a skeleton of professional staff well up to the end of the 1920s. For most of the time during the day, the members of the managing agency firms were present at the mill premises. After the establishment of the Arvind, however, the Lalbhai textile complex had grown too big to be managed by the simplistic organization that prevailed till then. Kasturbhai, then, felt the need to bring in more professional talents into the operating system. Looking for competent and trustworthy people with a sense of values, he happened to spot B.K. Muzumdar and appointed him in the Arvind Mills. It is doubtful, however, that the mill magnate had any clear idea of how he was going to utilize Muzumdar's services. With an ambiguous and somewhat unimpressive designation, Muzumdar's ostensible duty initially was to help Kasturbhai in carrying on correspondence in English language with various parties.

Proximity to the chief decision-maker in the group coupled with his abilities to deal with people enabled Muzumdar to learn various aspects of business. He also impressed Kasturbhai by his remarkable talents for organization. Consequently within a few years after joining the Arvind, he became the principal adviser and confidant of the millowner. It is indicative of the informal approach of the Sheth towards organization structure that even though Muzumdar's position in the field of textile operations in the 1940s was next only to Kasturbhai's and Narottambhai's, he continued to have the same innocuous designation till his appointment as the General Manager of the Atul Products in 1947. The industrialist apparently did not believe in designations as much as responsibilities and duties. With a similar attitude, Muzumdar established such an excellent rapport with his master that he put forward his views without fear or favour and more often than not carried the principal decision-maker with him. From such a vantage position, he was instrumental in introducing a number of modern managerial techniques in the areas of accounting and marketing with the active support and help from Narottambhai.

Muzumdar possessed not only exceptional managerial abilities but also a rare sense of social responsibility. Having risen from a poor background, with close links with Indian Socialist leaders including Jayaprakash Narayan, he possessed genuine sympathy for the workers. Committed to the belief that the contentment of the workforce was an essential prerequisite for furthering the interests of business and that the workers had a right to share the profits of an undertaking, he introduced a series of welfare measures much before they became statutory requirements. A system of bonus on profits earned, for instance, was introduced in 1940 and voluntary provident fund scheme came in force a year later for low-paid employees. Central legislations making these measures obligatory for industrial undertakings did not come till after India attained its independence.

Even though Muzumdar was most active in managing the Arvind Mills, the policies and procedures introduced by him influenced the working of other mills also, and to some extent, of the Anil Starch as well. For, the individual companies in the group functioned within the broad framework of the policies determined by the group as a whole consisting of the members of the family who constituted the different managing agency firms. The presiding spirit of the group, of course, was Kasturbhai largely because of the force of his personality and the reputation for shrewd judgment. Through his influence on the principal decision-maker, Muzumdar could influence the general direction of the management of the group as a whole. But Kasturbhai remained in close touch with the affairs of the business and himself spent some time every week at each establishment. During these visits, he practised an open door policy and even the most junior member of the staff could meet him without prior appointment.

Muzumdar's appointment as the first General Manager of the Atul facilitated the evolution of its managerial structure on the same lines as in the case of the textile and starch companies. His vacancy in the textile operations was filled up by an equally competent and forceful executive, Chandraprasad Desai. Having joined the Arvind in 1933 he had caught the attention of the Sheth because of his hard work and commitment to the organization. As the first formal General Manager of the Arvind, Desai carried forward the work that Muzumdar had initiated. One of his special contributions was the creation of the Group Division in 1948 which was the central pool of essential data about all the mills in the group. His access to these crucial data coupled with a forceful personality and great sense of purpose made Desai the most trusted and powerful executive in the textile side of the business.

Notwithstanding the contribution of these salaried executives in the management of the group, the basic feature of the Kasturbhai management remained essentially informal woven around a paternalistic and individualized leadership. Only the managerial structure of the Atic developed on a somewhat different lines because of the impact of the British partner. In contrast to the Atul and its subsidiary Cibatul, in which the Atul had a controlling share, the Atic evolved a more professionalized and formal approach to management. Kasturbhai seldom attempted to cast the structure of the Atic management in the same mould which characterized the management of his other major concerns. His impact on its management, however, was in no way less than on that of other companies in the group. The ICI executives looked upon him as a person "with whom, once a relationship of confidence has been established, business can be done quickly and satisfactorily using the utmost economy of words." And it was largely due to the feeling of respect that the ICI management had for "Kasturbhai's ability and foresight"[47] that he exercised a great deal of influence on the decision-making process of the Atic.

IV

Convinced though Kasturbhai was of the role of professionally competent salaried executives in running his business affairs, he had no intention of reducing the hold of the family or families, that constituted the group, on the top management structure. Because of the keen understanding of the business affairs that he himself and other principal members of the family had come to possess, there was no fear that the professional executives could ever dominate the decision-making processes as long as he himself or other senior members of the family, who had worked closely with him, were at the helm. He, however, could easily realize that the character of his business had become too complex to be managed successfully by intuitive judgment alone. If the succeeding generations of family members were to communicate effectively with the professional executives and draw the best out of them without surrendering their own sense of judgment, it was necessary to train the second line of leadership. Indian business world was still nowhere near achieving complete separation of management and control. The only way to ensure a happy blending of family control and professionalism in managing an enterprise was to develop a professional orientation among those who controlled it.

To accomplish such a blending, the younger members of the family were given high professional and technical education. Kasturbhai's two sons—Siddhartha and Shrenik—went to the United States for education. The former was trained as a chemical engineer at the prestigious Brooklyn Polytechnique and the latter received a Master's degree in business administration from the world-famous Harvard Business School. Chinubhai was to proceed to Germany for higher education after his B.Sc., but was prevented because of his father's illness. The children of Chimanbhai and Narottambhai and the descendants of Kasturbhai's three nephews, likewise, received higher education. Having been denied the benefits of higher education himself, Kasturbhai did not want the future leadership of his enterprises to have the same sense of regret which he himself had throughout his career. He believed that "we cannot run the various enterprises with old-fashioned people and outlook."

The theoretical education of the younger members of the family was supplemented through a system of apprenticeship. After completing their formal education they were gradually inducted in the family business. At the first stage, they worked closely with various departmental managers without any power for decision-making. This helped them comprehend various intricacies of the business before they were entrusted with positions of responsibility. Shrenikbhai, for instance, attended to the government investigation into the operations of the companies in the group for about five years before he was assigned any decision-making role. Likewise, Siddharthabhai worked closely with B.K. Muzumdar in developing the Atul complex for several years, and Chinubhai Manibhai worked under the direct supervision of Kasturbhai himself in the Anil Starch. Even after the sons had developed adequate insights into the intricate art of management, it was only gradually that their decision-making responsibilities were expanded. At the first stage, they were given some charge in smaller companies or subsidiary firms. It was only later that they were called upon to assume more onerous responsibilities.

As the junior members of the family displayed greater maturity in dealing with people and problems, the senior members loosened their hold on the decision-making processes and permitted the younger members to assume more and more independence. The most revealing example is of Chinubhai Manibhai. Almost up to 1952, it was Kasturbhai who took all major decisions about the Anil Starch. But when it became clear that Chinubhai did not need close supervision, his role in the decision-making became more and more prominent. In fact there were occasions when Kasturbhai had to submit to Chinubhai's judgment. Two examples would suffice to illustrate his point.

Sometime in the 1950s, Chinubhai suggested to the Sheth to issue promotional literature to advertise the Anil Starch's products. Kasturbhai opposed the idea. He felt that the expenditure involved in advertising the products which only a limited number of companies required was not justified. Chinubhai persuaded him to give him a chance to prove the advisability of the step. The advertising literature brought out by him attracted the attention of the customers much more effectively than ever before and Kasturbhai received several messages complimenting him on the success of his starch operations. The Sheth candidly confessed to his cousin that he was wrong in opposing the advertising proposal. On another occasion, Chinubhai and Kasturbhai agreed to import certain machinery and Chinubhai requested the Sheth to negotiate the purchase during one of his visits to England. After Kasturbhai's negotiations with the foreign manufacturers had already reached an advanced stage, he received a cable from Chinubhai that he had decided to fabricate the machinery locally at a much reduced cost. Kasturbhai fretted and fumed but submitted to the judgment of the man on the spot. On returning home he realized that Chinubhai's decision was right.

As he advanced in age, Kasturbhai brought about a significant change in the procedure for taking critical decisions. As has been pointed out earlier, almost up to the end of the 1950s it was Kasturbhai who used to take most of the important business decisions, even though in doing so he was guided by the opinion and views of his executives. Unduly dependent on the ability of one person, however, the method could not have provided for stability and continuity. In the middle of the 1960s, therefore, Kasturbhai took the first step towards introducing a more participative system of management under which major problems affecting a company were submitted to a committee consisting of senior executives and principal decision-makers representing the family. In due course this became the predominant method of decision-making in the companies of the group. The committee system of management in no way reduced Kasturbhai's role—or for that matter that of the core managerial group consisting of the prominent members of the family and a few trusted executives—but the professional managerial cadre felt a greater sense of involvement in the decision-making processes than had been the case before. As the younger members of the family became more active in running the enterprises, the influence of the professional executives also increased. For one thing, younger members had undergone their apprenticeship with, if not under, the senior executives before assuming challenging responsibilities. This had reduced considerably the distance between these two groups and facilitated a more relaxed communication between them.

Also the development of management education in the country made available to the companies in the group a number of professionally trained employees who brought to bear on the managerial cadre a more professionalized approach. The process of professionalization went one step further when Manubhai Shah, who succeeded Chandraprasad Desai as the General Manager of the Arvind Mills in 1969, accepted a visiting professorship at the Indian Institute of Management, Ahmedabad, with a direct link with those who believed in and advocated the efficacy of professional management. Manubhai introduced a series of more modern and sophisticated practices without, of course, disturbing the basic administrative framework of the enterprises.

The process of change that started towards the end of 1950s reached a culminating point when the managing agency system was abolished in 1970. The abolition of the age-old structure, however, did not bring about any material difference in the structure of the Kasturbhai management, except that the managing agents were replaced by salaried chairmen and managing directors. But under the impact of the legal changes, the simple and informal structure that existed up to the 1950s became more formal and complex. A glance at the present organization structures of the Arvind, the most representative textile company in the group, and the Atul respectively, clearly bear this out.

In bringing about or acquiescing in these changes Kasturbhai, it appears in retrospect, had a clear purpose in mind. Almost unnoticed by anyone else, he was gradually weaning himself away from the day-to-day and routine affairs of his enterprises. In his long and eventful business career, he had come in close touch with many prominent personalities. Some of them had continued to remain deeply involved in their business affairs even after their declining physical strength had reduced the utility of such involvement. Kasturbhai abhored the very idea of suffering this kind of fate. The examples of some of his ancestors like Shantidas Zaveri, who had dissociated himself from active business career a few years before his death, also inspired him to seek retirement from active management of his enterprises before it was too late. He knew, however, that a sudden break would create a void and confusion. He, therefore, drew up a retirement plan in his mind under which he consciously and gradually left the major decision-making about various concerns to his successors. He finally stepped aside from the active management of all his concerns in early 1977 when he announced his retirement from the chairmanship of the Atul. While implementing his retirement plan, he had no fear of dislocation in the affairs of his concerns as a viable and stable structure and a competent leadership had already emerged. And, in any case, he continued to be available for consultation and counselling on major issues and problems up to the end of his life.

V

The major business strategies of Kasturbhai, like his management structure, ran on conventional lines. His group's expansion and diversification, for instance, remained confined to related lines when several well-known textile producers like Shri Ram and Sarabhai displayed much greater aggressiveness in this sphere. His strategy involved relatively much less risk, as one line could provide market for the other. The textile companies, for instance, could meet all their starch requirements from the Anil Starch and buy their dyes from the Atul group of companies. To ensure however, that the input-producing companies did not become self-complacent because of a captive market, at least in part, the mills were given full freedom to buy their requirements from out of the group. It is significant that for several years the Arvind refused to buy a whitening agent produced by the Atul and patronized a competitor's product on the ground that the Atul's product was not up to the textile company's specification.

The financial strategy of the group was cautious and conservative. The family resources of the managing agents played a prominent role in financing Kasturbhai's textile and starch ventures, and a substantial part of the working capital was raised through public deposits. Institutional financing in sizeable degree was resorted to only in the case of the Atul. Some features of Kasturbhai's financial approach, however, were much less common. First, he seldom attempted to launch a sole proprietary concern as did a large number of his contemporaries in Ahmedabad and outside. All the major companies in the group were floated as public limited companies. Kasturbhai believed that it was a much greater challenge to manage a public company than a closely held concern. He did not have much difficulty in facing the challenge but his policy of moderate dividend sometimes created difficulties. His conviction in building substantial reserves was a basically sound policy as it helped his companies modernize their plants and machinery without much difficulty or raise their capital without going to the public. The shareholders, however, did not always appreciate Kasturbhai's logic in the face of rising profits. In 1972, the shareholders of the Atul, in fact, staged an organized revolt to force the hand of the management to reverse its approach. But Kasturbhai weathered the storm successfully.

Another distinctive feature of his financing strategy was his utter lack of enthusiasm for inter-corporate investment. It was a common practice on the part of a large number of managing agents in the country to control a series of companies not through direct investment in them but through a small number of concerns in which they had controlling voting power. It is these concerns which had controlling shares in other companies. Kasturbhai considered this approach unethical. It is no surprise, therefore, that practically all his major companies developed as independent units under separate managing agencies. Admittedly, the Atul controlled the Cibatul and shared the ownership of the Atic with ICI, but there were special and understandable reasons behind it.

Transition from the simple to the sophisticated has been the most distinctive feature of Kasturbhai's approach to production. Before the establishment of the Arvind, all his textile companies produced only coarse goods but by the end of the 1950s all had equipped themselves to produce goods of higher counts. The result was that product differentiation, which characterized the production strategy of the group earlier, became exceedingly blurred and no attempt was made to curb the spirit of competition that naturally arose among the group's textile companies. Whether this was a healthy development is a matter of judgment and the rationale behind it is not very clear. Like the textile companies, Kasturbhai's starch company and the Atul also started their production with relatively less sophisticated goods but entered more complicated areas as they gained in strength and experience.

In contrast to its investment and production strategies, the group's approach to marketing was truly innovative. Even though a few sales agents had been appointed for Kasturbhai's textile goods as early as 1923, his textile companies, like all the mills in the city, used to market their goods through the wholesalers till the beginning of the 1930s. The difficulty arose when the Arvind came into being. The management of the Calico Mills did not countenance with equanimity the emergence of a competitor which threatened the former's monopoly on the production of fine and superfine goods in the city. Faced with the choice between the Calico goods and the Arvind production, the wholesalers naturally preferred to remain with the more established company. They would have been happy if they could have served both the mills, but placed as they were, this soft option was not open to them. Kasturbhai, therefore, had to make a hard choice. He decided to promote upcountry sales directly.

To achieve this objective a large number of indenting agents were appointed in various parts of the country. The task of these agents was to canvass orders for the goods, recommend the names of parties who would be interested in marketing the goods of the companies, and undertake the responsibility for payment. Under this system of marketing perfected by Narottambhai and Muzumdar, the consignments were sent to the selling merchants directly who were allowed to take delivery only after depositing the value of the goods with banks specified by the management. Adopted in the case of the Arvind at the first stage, this method became the principal marketing strategy of the group as a whole. The strategy was quite popular in England then, but Kasturbhai's companies were among the first to introduce it in India. The method proved so effective that he adopted it to market the products of the

Anil Starch and the Atul group of companies as well. While Kasturbhai's marketing device was being perfected, Lala Shri Ram was promoting a number of company-owned retail shops to market the goods of his textile companies. But the Ahmedabad industrialist considered it unwise to invest his resources in building up an elaborate retailing network.

The above survey suggests little innovation on the part of Kasturbhai in the field of organization structure and strategy. For the major part of his career the form of his management conformed to the system in vogue in most of the family-dominated concerns. As his operations became more complex, he realized the need to bring about some changes and took some steps in that direction. The leadership of his group, however, was yet to be institutionalized when he decided to retire from active management. But, then, very few Indian enterprises in the private sector have succeeded in creating institutionalized leadership. If Kasturbhai failed in moving ahead of his times, he had a large number of private industrialists in the country to keep him company. His distinctiveness, however, lay in his success in blending higher business ethics with conventional management structure—an achievement not many of his contemporaries could truthfully claim.

CHAPTER IX

Beyond the Chimneys

PETER F. Drucker has rightly emphasized that business enterprises, like any other institution, exist for the sake of society and within a community. Their managers, therefore, "have to take social responsibility, have to think through . . . the commitments of their society, and have to assume leadership responsibility beyond the discharge of the specific and limited mission of their institutions."[48] Kasturbhai could justifiably claim that he lived up to this expectation.

He had inherited his social concerns from his forefathers. But the nature of his participation in non-business activities was different. By the time he won for himself a prominent position in the management of the family and family business, the political horizon of India had undergone a sea change as the urge for freedom had become much more general and assumed a much greater intensity. Also, the demand from educational, social, and religious quarters for support had become much more varied. The nature and level of Kasturbhai's participation in and support for non-business causes reflected the demands of his age and his response to them as an enlightened business leader.

The beginning of his participation in public causes was more a result of an accident rather than any deliberate initiative on his part And it is something of an irony that the incident which revealed his potentialities for handling intricate problems, not directly connected with the management of his enterprises, brought him into an open conflict with a person whom he had come to hold in highest esteem—Mohandas Karamchand Gandhi.

Soon after returning from South Africa, Gandhi had settled down in Ahmedabad in 1915. By this time, Ahmedabad had come to have about 50 mills with more than 35,000 workers. The workers had no organization, though Anusuya Sarabhai, the sister of Ambalal Sarabhai, had started some work for their social and educational uplift. The millowners, on the other hand, had organized themselves into the Ahmedabad Millowners Association founded in 1891. Except in 1895 when there was a major conflict between the mill workers and the millowners, the industrial relations in Ahmedabad had been, by and large, peaceful. Most of the millowners were a political, and Gandhi had yet to become the symbol of nationalism. The mill magnates, thus, had little to fear from Gandhi's presence in the city. In fact his stress on non-violence, frugality, honesty, integrity, self-reliance, and peace seemed to conform to their own ethos.

Kasturbhai found Gandhi's charm irresistible. So did several others including Ambalal Sarabhai and Mangaldas Girdhardas who were the acknowledged leaders of the Ahmedabad industry then. They met Gandhi frequently, attended his public meetings, and treated him and his advice with deference. Ambalal went to the extent of donating a substantial amount to Gandhi when his ashram was in dire financial straits. The strike of the textile workers of Ahmedabad in 1917, however, found Gandhi and the millowners on opposite sides. The story of this historic conflict is too well-known to deserve repetition. It would not be inappropriate, however, to reproduce Kasturbhai's own view of his role in this event.

> There was plague in Ahmedabad in 1917 and many workers had left the mills for their villages. War was on and the profits were quite good. My mill was competing with others

for getting workers at higher wages. By the end of 1917, the workers' wages had increased to 90 per cent from the wage rates prevailing before the war. In the beginning of 1918, the demand for our goods began to slacken. The millowners, under the leadership of Ambalal, decided to reduce the wages. As our residence at Pankor Naka had a central location, millowners used to meet there. All of us decided to reduce the wage increase from 90 per cent to 20 per cent. Mahatma Gandhi came to know of our decision. So he sent word from his Ashram that it would be wrong on our part to reduce the wages thus and suggested wage increase be fixed at 35 per cent. We replied that outsiders should not meddle in industrial disputes. Gandhiji thereupon organized the workers. As no agreement could be reached in spite of several meetings with Gandhiji, he asked the workers to go on strike. Once the strike was on, we started persuading the workers to resume work. We made it perfectly clear to the workers that our decision of wage reduction was final and therefore, there was no chance of their getting higher wage-rates. The strike lasted for several weeks. The workers were hard-pressed and did not want to prolong the strike. Quite a few of them started pouring into the mills. Gandhiji saw that he was on the verge of losing the battle. So he adopted a coercive measure. He went on fast. The fast lasted for a few days when Mrs. Annie Besant, then the President of the Congress, sent a telegram to Ambalal. The telegram said that Gandhiji's life was too valuable to be sacrificed for such a small matter. We had great respect for Mahatmaji but in this case we had strong differences with him. But on the receipt of Mrs. Besant's telegram, Ambalal Sarabhai, my uncle [Jagabhai] and I went to Anusuyaben Sarabhai's house at Mirzapur Road where Gandhiji was then staying. We told Gandhiji that we had won the fight and he was coercing us into an agreement by fasting. Gandhiji replied that he was sorry that his fast was putting us in an embarrassing situation. But he made it plain that we should not accept his proposal unless we saw the justice of the workers' cause. His basic proposal was that whenever there were differences between the workers and the millowners, neither side should take a unilateral action, but should submit the issue to an impartial arbitrator whose verdict should be accepted by both the parties. As none of us wanted to risk the life of Gandhiji, we finally accepted his proposals. Gandhiji broke his fast. It was decided to appoint Anandshankar Dhruv the sole arbitrator between us and the workers. He gave an award that for the first day we shall pay 20 per cent increase, for the second day we shall pay 35 per cent increase, and thereafter 27 per cent increase. Thus came to an end one of the most historic strikes in India.

Kasturbhai's role in the strike revealed to the leaders of the Ahmedabad mill industry a hidden facet of his personality. Particularly impressed was Ambalal Sarabhai, the President of the Ahmedabad Millowners Association. He appointed Kasturbhai as a member of its managing committee. This, according to Kasturbhai, was the beginning of his "public career."

The year that witnessed the strike also found Kasturbhai involved in famine relief operation. The monsoons had failed in 1918 resulting in a famine and influenza epidemic in Kheda and Panch Mahal districts and later in North Gujarat. The Gujarat Sabha wasted little time in undertaking relief operations. A Famine Relief Committee was formed under the chairmanship of Kasturbhai Manibhai of the Nagarsheth family. Kasturbhai Lalbhai was named as one of its secretaries along with Vallabhbhai Patel, G.V. Mavalankar, Indulal Yagnik, and Krishnalal Dalal. Before the Committee could start work, however, two of its secretaries, Kasturbhai and Yagnik, came into headlong collision. The latter had prepared a report on famine operations, describing the plight of people in the famine affected areas and criticising the Government policies and administrative machinery. Yagnik wanted to publish the report and distribute the copies at a forthcoming political conference. Kasturbhai opposed the idea on the ground that the publication of the report would alienate the Government support and, thus, disrupt the relief operations. Even though Yagnik's proposal had the powerful backing of Patel, Kasturbhai refused to budge from his position. It was ultimately decided not to publish the report. The more prominent members of the Committee did not fail to notice the courage of conviction on the part of the least experienced member and perhaps the least political of them all.

The responsibility of the young millowner was to collect funds and arrange for supplies. He plunged in the task with his entire strength. Every day he would go out to collect donations from the millowners and rich *mahajans* of the city. Every pie was accounted for and the accounts were scrupulously maintained. With his innate business instincts, he arranged for supplies of relief articles from places where the prices were favourable. For instance wheat was bought in Panjab and grass and fodder near Valsad. His commitment to relief work was so total that in those days he often neglected the affairs of his mills.

His participation in relief operations provided an excellent opportunity to Kasturbhai to study the Indian people from close quarters. More than half a century later he recalled the value of this experience: "I came to know more about the people and their views and attitudes. This was my first experience to contact people for a public cause. This was to stand me in good stead, for several times in future I was called upon to collect money for public purposes." A significant outcome of his work in the relief committee was that he came in close contact with Vallabhbhai Patel and G.V. Mavalankar who in due course rose to great prominence in national life. It is because of his association with these leaders that Kasturbhai attended the Ahmedabad session of the Indian National Congress in December 1921 with "some enthusiasm". Motilal Nehru, the President of the session, was his guest, and his elder brother along with Mangaldas Girdhardas served on the reception committee.

By this time the political climate of the country had become extremely hot. The non-cooperation movement launched by Gandhi was in full swing. The Congress had already shed off its earlier hue of a welfare association to assume the character of a mass movement against the alien rule. The proceedings of the Ahmedabad session reflected this change. The Congress endorsed Gandhi's radical stance and resolved to continue the non-cooperation movement with greater vigour. Under these conditions, anyone considered too close to the Congress and its leader, Gandhi, was naturally a suspect in the eyes of the Government.

II

Kasturbhai was yet to be close to the nationalist leaders when the Swaraj Party came into being in 1923. Organized by a group of Congress leaders led by C.R. Das, Motilal Nehru, and Vithalbhai Patel, the party decided to put up candidates for elections to the Central Legislative Council constituted under the Montague-Chelmsford Reforms Act of 1919. The Ahmedabad Millowners Association was authorized to elect one member to the 144-member legislature. The most logical candidate for this seat should have been Sheth Mangaldas. More than sixty years of age, he was a senior and respected member of the Association. He, however, decided not to risk defeat when a younger man, Maneklal Mansukhbhai, announced his intention to contest. Maneklal's known softness for the British Government, was his worst liability. Vallabhbhai Patel contemptuously looked upon the Swarajist move to enter the Assembly as a mere adventure but he could not countenance the idea of a pro-government man representing the industrialists of the city which was the centre of his political activities. He, therefore, suggested to Kasturbhai, then 29 years old, to enter the fray. Maneklal was the son of one of the founders of the Millowners Association, and his family was still among the most powerful in the Ahmedabad industry. He was by no means an easy candidate to beat. Kasturbhai naturally hesitated but finally agreed to contest. The election result astonished many, including Kasturbhai's own mother. He won the seat, though by a narrow margin.

The Assembly membership was a new experience for the young industrialist. He had managed the mills but was a novice in the political field. His only asset was the sincerity of purpose which characterized his approach to the tasks assigned to him. Before proceeding to Delhi, he carefully prepared himself to meet the new challenge. He even brought about a change in his dress perhaps to remind himself and others that the legislator and the mill agent were two different beings. Or perhaps he did not want his individuality to be merged in the crowd. Whatever the reason, in Delhi he always wore a traditional Ahmedabadi turban (*pagadi*) of red colour in place of a Gandhi cap which he usually donned in Ahmedabad with his Gujarati dress of *dhoti* and long coat. He attended the Assembly regularly and followed the proceedings studiously. For some time, however, he felt too nervous or self-conscious to participate in the debate. This was natural as the Assembly was graced by a galaxy of prominent Indians including Bipin Chandra Pal, Sir Purshotamdas Thakurdas, Motilal Nehru, Mohammad Ali Jinnah, Pandit Madan Mohan Malaviya, Vithalbhai Patel, M.R. Jayakar, and Sir Hari Singh Gour. Kasturbhai, however, was keen to learn the legislative procedures. He would often visit Vithalbhai Patel—the *Chanakya Shiromani* of Indian politics as Indulal Yagnik called him—at his residence to gain insights into the working of the Assembly. Patel had been elected as the speaker, defeating a pro-government candidate, with the Swarajist support. Kasturbhai himself had actively campaigned for him.

The representative of the Ahmedabad millowners was highly sensitive to the interests he represented. He did not join any faction but his sympathies were with the Swarajists whom he invariably supported. He attended most of the private meetings of the Swarajists held usually at Motilal Nehru's or Vithalbhai's house. Sir Purshotamdas Thakurdas who represented the Indian Merchants' Chamber and was an expert on financial and commercial matters became a close friend of Kasturbhai, even though the former had no particular sympathies for the Swarajists. They drew still closer to each other after both were elected to the Standing Committee for the Department of Industries and Labour in 1924.

A few weeks after his election to this prestigious committee, Kasturbhai made his maiden speech in the Assembly on 5 March 1924. Participating in the budget discussions he congratulated Sir Basil Blackett, the finance Member of the Viceroy's Council, for presenting a balanced budget and relieving the country from the "nightmare of deficit budgets."[49] He pleaded for setting up nautical colleges and schools for the training of Indian sea-men and officers with the help of the revenue realized from the merchant marine. He asked the Government to start special engineering courses to train Indians in the field of naval engineering. He also emphasized that the Government should purchase its requirements for the Indian armed forces in India itself. Stressing the need for insulating the Indian match manufacturers against certain fraudulent practices resorted to by foreign suppliers with a view to evading import duties, "The imports of dummy match boxes and splints have shown us, . . . , how foreign suppliers are on the alert to dump their goods in the Indian market through various devices." With a candour characteristic of him, he asked Sir Basil: "What steps do Government propose to safeguard . . . the indigenous match industry adversely affected by the evasion of the import duty on matches by splints, veneers, and dummy match boxes imported into India in place of finished articles?"[50] Kasturbhai also pleaded for granting protection and assistance to the Indian steel industry, at a time when the Tata Steel was passing through an extremely difficult position. In another speech, he opposed the proposal to reduce import duties on saccharine on the ground that it would hurt the sugar industry which was yet to come under the protective umbrella.

The Railway board in the meantime had increased the freight on coal. As Kasturbhai pointed out in his speech on the floor on 26 February 1925, the freight on coal between Central Provinces and Ahmedabad had gone up by 20 per cent and that between the Jhariah coal mines and Ahmedabad by as much as 28 per cent. The cost of transporting coal by water, however, remained unchanged and somewhat lower than the railway rates. The young industrialist failed to understand why the Government was anxious to favour Bombay and other coast towns at the cost of inland industrial centres like Ahmedabad, and suspected that the Government wanted to help the British shipping interests entrenched in the Indian waters. "Be that as it may", Kasturbhai argued, "but why make Ahmedabad and other centrally situated places without any sea outlet the scapegoat of this policy and make them pay abnormally increased railway freight ?"[51] Sir Charles Innes, the Railway Member, rightly pointed out that Kasturbhai was "so eloquent" because of his anxiety "for the interests of the mill industry at Ahmedabad".[52]

The question of countervailing excise duty on Indian textile production drew the best from the young member. These duties had been imposed in 1892 to counterbalance the import duties on foreign goods. This blatantly imperialist measure had come under persistent public attack. For Kasturbhai the need for abolishing these obnoxious cesses was not an academic question; the duties had an adverse effect on the interest he represented. One of his very first acts as a legislator, therefore, was to move a resolution to repeal the measure. On 20 March 1924, barely three months after his election, he argued on the floor of the house: "From whatever point of view—political, economic, or financial—this duty is viewed, one cannot help coming to the conclusion that the abolition of this impost is so imperative that it cannot be effected a day too soon. In the age we are living, Sir, political domination is sought to be utilized for economic domination of the subject race and the levy of the cotton excise is an instance in point. . . . This duty is a standing emblem of India's political subservience. It is not possible, Sir, for India to forget the history of this unfortunate impost, and the keen sense of injustice done to her by Britain." The industrialist quoted scholars like Romesh Chandra Dutt, Mahadev Govind Ranade, and Gopal Krishan Gokhale in his support and declared unhesitatingly that the levy had been imposed to please the Lancashire interests in the face of stiff Indian opposition. He concluded with a fervent plea to eliminate this source of "insult to our national sense of self respect."[53]

Kasturbhai was not alone in his fight against the contemptible duties. Stalwarts like Motilal Nehru, Purshotamdas Thakurdas and Mohammad Ali Jinnah gave him powerful and eloquent support. The government was eventually forced to announce the suspension of the duties in December 1925, and abolish them altogether in March 1926. All sections of the house greeted Sir Basil's announcement—"I have come to bury Caesar, not to praise him"—with satisfaction.[54] Jinnah made an impressive and forceful speech. Kasturbhai was less eloquent but perhaps more to the point when he drew the attention of the House that after the suspension of the duties in 1925, the cloth prices had gone down by 20 per cent. He thanked the government for "getting the historic wrong . . . righted", and hoped that Sir Basil "as the pall-bearer who is to give the statutory burial to the cotton excise duty, may intern the coffin sufficiently deep so as not to be discovered by any of the future archaeologists."[55]

The three-year Assembly term proved very fruitful to the young industrialist. He came in contact with many distinguished national leaders. Many life-long friendships were made during those years. Motilal Nehru was so impressed by Kasturbhai's performance in the Assembly that he declared that the mill-owner was a better Swarajist than many members of the Swarajist Party. *The Times of India* described Kasturbhai's speeches as "the most apposite".[56] Within a short period the young man had ceased to be a mere local millowner; he had attracted national limelight.

III

The Indian business community, in the meantime, was coming under a growing influence of the national movement. By the middle of the 1920s, a group led by Ghanshyam Das Birla and Purshotamdas Thakurdas had emerged which resented the dominant presence and influence of British interests on Indian business horizon. The nationalist businessmen were particularly irked by the supremacy of the British business houses in the Associated Chambers of Commerce (ASSOCHAM), a federation of regional and local chambers of commerce formed in 1920. The establishment of Federation of Indian Chambers of Commerce and Industry (FICCI) in 1927 was a natural nationalist response. It was the initiative of Ghanshyam Das Birla which resulted in the establishment of this body. Kasturbhai actively supported the move and was asked to be a member of the first executive committee along with some very prominent Indian businessmen of the times. Very soon his abilities came to be noticed by the FICCI leaders. In 1933, therefore, he along with two distinguished industrialists, Lala Shri Ram and Devi Prasad Khaitan, was chosen as a member of the FICCI delegation to a tripartite conference convened to consider the problem created by rising imports of Japanese textile goods.

Sir Homi Modi represented the Bomby Millowners' Association at the conference which was held at the initiative of the Government in Simla. Sir William Clare-Lees was the British representative. Modi and Clare-Lees both wanted the duties on British imports lowered to enable England to meet the Japanese challenge. Kasturbhai was willing to accept this proposal on the condidion that a ceiling was placed on imports from Britain to safeguard the interest of the Indian industry.

The British side was unwilling to accept the idea of ceiling and Khaitan for sometime remained ambivalent. The stalemate could not be resolved and a frustrated Kasturbhai did not see any purpose in prolonging his stay in Simla. The Modi-Lees Pact lowering the duty on British imports was signed in Kasturbhai's absence.

The Indian industrial circles which resented the provisions of the pact appreciated Kasturbhai's firm stand and rewarded him with the presidentship of the FICCI the very next year. A year later he was elected to head the Ahmedabad Millowners Association. Another honour that was conferred on him in 1936 was his inclusion in a seven-member committee of unofficial advisers attached to the official delegation appointed to negotiate the revision of the Ottawa agreement.

Signed in 1932, the agreement was the basis of trade relations between India and the United Kingdom. Heavily weighed in favour of the Imperial Government, the terms of the protocol had come under heavy fire. On the recommendation of the Central Assembly, therefore, the Indian Government decided to negotiate a new treaty. The official delegation was headed by Sir Zafarullah Khan, then the Commerce Member of the Viceroy's Council, and the Committee of unofficial advisers was supposed to assist him. It was a high power committee consisting of several luminaries of Indian industrial life including Ghanshyam Das Birla, Liaquat Ali Khan, and Sir Edward Benthal of the Bird and Company. The Zafarrullah Khan team drove a hard bargain and succeeded in achieving important modifications, favourable to India, in the earlier agreement. The Committee of unofficial advisers, including Kasturbhai, must share the credit for this achievement.

This was neither the first nor the last association of Kasturbhai with international negotiating teams or delegations to international conferences. Earlier he had attended the International Labour Conference at Geneva in 1929 as a member of the Indian delegation, and in 1940 he was adviser to the Indian team for Indo-Burma Trade negotiations. The Government of India conferred several other honours on him. He was appointed a director of the Reserve Bank of India in 1937 and a member of the board of governors of the Council of Industrial and Scientific Research in 1940.

Notwithstanding these official honours, Kasturbhai's nationalist sympathies and bonafides remained unquestionably intact. But none could have believed that he would go to the extent of conspiring to cause a labour strike to help the nationalist cause. This is exactly what he did after Gandhi's call of "Quit India" in 1942. He was in Bombay when the All India Congress Committee passed the historic resolution on 8 August 1942. Apprehending the consequences of Gandhi's and other Congress leaders' arrest, he left for Ahmedabad the same night. In the train he met Khandubhai Desai, the President of the Ahmedabad Textile Labour Association. The industrialist and the labour leader both agreed that they must do something to express their solidarity for the nation's cause. They decided, in the words of Kasturbhai, that it was "a desirable policy to send away workers to the villages so that the mills can't work and the British authourities cannot trace any person behind this move." On reaching Ahmedabad, Kasturbhai found that the workers had already decided to go on a three-day strike in protest against the Government action. Informed by Ambalal Sarabhai of the workers' decision, Kasturbhai replied: "It is going to be a protracted strike. Khandubhai and I have already taken a decision on this issue."

And a protracted strike it was. More than one lakh textile workers of Ahmedabad remained away from the mill premises for three months and a half. Their absence adversely affected production and seriously hampered the British war efforts in India. By 14 August, according to the *Gujarat Samachar*, thousands of workers had already gone to their villages and many thousands were leaving. The following day the railway authorities stopped all bookings for the local and express trains in order to prevent the millhands from leaving the city. But the exodus continued unabated. The strike made headlines all over the country and drew worldwide attention.

None knew that Kasturbhai had connived at the workers' resolve, and in fact encouraged them indirectly, to stop work. His role in the whole episode remained so secret that when Khandubhai Desai asked the workers on 14 November to resume duties, a group of citizens protested and twenty-one women observed fast at the residences of prominent millowners including Kasturbhai's. The millowners had some difficulty in convincing the protestors that there was no justification to continue the strike and the consequent prolongation of the sufferings of the workers.

It was at this time that the question of the appointment of the governor of the Reserve Bank of India cropped up following the sudden death of the incumbent, Sir James Taylor. Sir Chintamani D. Deshmukh, the Senior Deputy Governor, possessed all the qualifications except one to succeed Sir James: he was not an Englishman. It was Purshotamdas Thakurdas, another director, who took up the cudgel on Deshmukh's behalf. Some Indian members of the board hesitated but Kasturbhai gave solid support to Purshotamdas in his fight. So did Lala Shri Ram. It was the tenacity of these members which persuaded the board of the bank to recommend Deshmukh's name for the post—a recommendation which the government was forced to accept eventually. Kasturbhai legitimately deserved some credit for ensuring the appointment of the first Indian as the head of the most important financial institution in the country.

Another achievement at this time which must have brought Kasturbhai a great deal of satisfaction was his success in procuring Egyptian cotton for the Indian textile industry during the Second World War. The Indian industry had arranged for the import of one lakh bales of Egyptian cotton in 1942. The prospects of a large consignment to India upset the British textile interests as it was bound to increase the price of Egyptian cotton. Under pressure from Lancashire, the British Government imposed a ban not only on all future supplies of cotton to India but also on the shipment of the one lakh bales India had already purchased. The arbitrariness of the action naturally created a hue and cry among Indian millowners. An alarmed government sent a trade delegation to Cairo in August 1943 to negotiate a suitable agreement with the British trade representatives. Kasturbhai was a member of this team which was headed by an officer of the Indian Civil Service.

Discussions between the Indian and British teams began on a sour note. The British wanted the Indian delegation to agree to the need to stagger the purchase of Egyptian cotton with a view to checking the rise in prices. They also desired that all future purchase of the commodity be canalized through a

British firm. The Indians, however, refused to discuss anything until the fate of the cotton already purchased by India was settled to their satisfaction.

The stalemate resulting from the rigid positions of the respective delegations led to the walkout by the Indian team. The British eventually agreed to allow the shipment of the Indian order. Kasturbhai then assured on behalf of the Indian textile manufacturers that India would not buy more than 2,000 bales of Egyptian cotton per week. He, however, made it clear that the purchase must be effected through the normal trade channels and not through any single firm as the British delegation had suggested. He agreed that the prices would be fixed in advance based on the agreement between the two parties, and pointed out that the strict censorship of the cables, in force as a war measure then, would thwart any attempt to charge fraudulent rates.

Kasturbhai's plan was approved and the Egyptian cotton dealers were happy that their trade channels would remain undisturbed. However, a minor snag remained. The representatives of the Egyptian Cotton Association complained that they were hard hit by the charges for storage, demurrage, and insurance on the Indian consignment which was still awaiting shipment. Kasturbhai conceded that these charges should be borne by the Indian purchasers but emphasized that the benefits of decline in freight rate since the deal had been finalized must go to the Indians. The freight charges had gone down considerably on account of the war. Consequently in spite of the extra charges, the total cost to the Indian importers of the Egyptian consignments worked out to be slightly less. Kasturbhai's scheme proved successful and remained in force not only during the war but also for about three years after the conclusion of the hostilities in 1945.

Three years after his Cairo accomplishment, Kasturbhai salvaged another negotiation between India and a British firm. He was in the United States in 1946 in connection with his proposed dyestuffs project when he was asked by the Indian Government to join an Indian team in London which had gone there to negotiate an agreement with a well-known British firm, the Textile Machinery Manufacturers (TMM), for setting up a similar unit in India. Other members of the delegation including Krishnaraj Thackersey, Dharamsey Khatau, Sir Fred Stone, and Sir John Greeves were already in London. The TMM asked for Rs. 1 crore as goodwill and Rs. 50 lakhs as compounded royalties. The Indians, on the other hand, wanted the British company to subscribe for a part of the share capital of the proposed Indian venture. The two approaches were basically different and everyone seemed to have lost hopes. But not Kasturbhai. At a cocktail party, he inquired of Sir Kenneth Preston, the Vice-President of the TMM, when the two teams would meet again. Sir Kenneth saw no point in any future meeting as the two viewpoints were so far apart. "This may be so", Kasturbhai replied with his usual candour, "but we have not come five thousand miles to be told to go back empty-handed." It was largely due to his persuasiveness that the British firm scaled down its royalty demand to Rs. 25 lakhs. This was one of the most favourable deals negotiated for a public sector enterprise. Out of this agreement was born the National Machinery Manufacturers near Bombay.

That Kasturbhai helped promote a public sector undertaking was not at all surprising. Some time before India attained its independence he had clearly visualized the dominant role that the government of free India would play in the nation's economic life. This is clear from a document issued by a group of Indian industrialists in 1944. *A Brief Memorandum Outlining a Plan of Economic Development for India* was the result of a joint effort of eight luminaries of the Indian business world: Purshotamdas Thakurdas, J.R.D. Tata, Ghanshyam Das Birla, Lala Shri Ram, Kasturbhai Lalbhai, Ardeshir Dalal, A.D. Shroff, and John Matthai. The Bombay Plan, as it came to be popularly known, did not outline the role of the public sector; it, nevertheless, emphasized in no uncertain terms that after the advent of freedom practically every aspect of economic life will have to be so rigorously controlled by government that individual liberty and freedom of enterprise will suffer a temporary eclipse.[11]

IV

Though the alien Government of India recognized Kasturbhai's merit in ample measure, his known sympathies for nationalist cause, made him too unsafe to be entrusted with the leadership of any delegation. The Government of free India had no such reservation The Ahmedabad industrialist had all along been very close to prominent national leaders who held him in high esteem for his integrity, honesty, and qualities of leadership. It was no surprise, therefore, that after the advent of freedom, he was called upon to assume much more onerous responsibilities in national life than he had ever done before. He led a number of delegations sent to various countries to negotiate business affairs and he had to accept several official assignments relating to national problems. He acquitted himself creditably in all these tasks but his performance in a few specific instances merits special mention.

A variety of factors shot up the price of cotton in India in 1948. The tight supply position was a major reason. The principal aim of the Government behind sending a delegation headed by Kasturbhai to Cairo in 1948 was to arrange for the shipment of Egyptian cotton in return for Indian goods. Kasturbhai drew a blank because India was not in a position to supply what the Egytians thought they needed most—arms. Israel had just been created as an independent country and nothing to the Arab world seemed to be more valuable than the ability to deal with the new Jewish state.

Following the failure at Cairo, Kasturbhai proceeded to Kampala, the capital of Uganda, at the head of another team to negotiate the supply of East African cotton in December 1948. During the journey the Indian team missed the connecting flight at Cairo because of delay in the arrival of the flight from Bombay. Without caring for clearance from Delhi, he decided to charter a special plane in order to be able to reach his destination on time. When some members of the delegation expressed the fear that the Government might not sanction the special flight, Kasturbhai replied that in that case he would bear the additional expenses himself. The leader of the delegation attached utmost importance to the need to reach the venue of the negotiation on time.

Seventeen representatives of various East African countries participated in the discussions that centred round the purchase of three lakh bales of East African cotton, two lakh bales by India and one lakh by Great Britain. The greatest hitch was the price to be offered for the East African staple. The Government of India, nervous at the prospects of cotton scarcity, had authorized Kasturbhai to offer up to 33d. a pound. In Kasturbhai's judgment even 30d. for a pound was too high. He, therefore, offered to abide by an earlier agreement signed at New Delhi which had fixed the rate at 28.50d. The British, however, were not willing to go beyond 25d. It was the negotiating ability of the leader of the Indian team which broke the deadlock. As an honest broker between the governments of East African countries and Great Britain he suggested a price of 27.50 d. per pound. The East African representatives agreed to a further reduction of 0·40d. to accommodate the British viewpoint.

On behalf of India, Kasturbhai agreed to the purchase of two lakh bales at this price. But Great Britain wanted to link the price with that of Alexandria futures. This the East African representatives were unwilling to concede. Another deadlock resulted. Kasturbhai considered it unethical to let Great Britain down lest this should embarrass the cordial commercial relations between India and England. He, therefore, told the East African representatives that it had to be a package deal. India would not sign an agreement if Great Britain was left in the lurch. It was a gamble but Kasturbhai thought that the risk was worth taking. The East African representatives understood the implications of Kasturbhai's gentle threat and signed the agreement. The deal struck by the Ahmedabad industrialist benefited India by several crores of rupees as the cotton prices in India had shot up to 44 d. a pound by the time the shipment arrived. It was because of his success at Kampala that he was asked to head another delegation to Liverpool in 1952 to discuss the bulk purchase of East African staple. He also headed the Indian team to the Cotton Textile Industry Conference held at Manchester the same year.

It should not be assumed that in dealing with persons and governments abroad, Kasturbhai was always diplomatic and polite. Whenever the national honour and prestige was involved Kasturbhai's forthrightness and frankness came into full play no matter where he was. An experience during his Russian trip in 1954 is an excellent example. He had been drafted to lead a trade delegation to Russia in 1954 when Brij Mohan

Birla, the President of the FICCI, declined the invitation, apprehending that his close links with the United States might compromise the effectiveness of the Indian mission. The cold war was at its height and Birla's fears were not unfounded. Kasturbhai's delegation had a hectic time and enjoyed lavish hospitality in the Soviet Union. He, however, was not impressed by the quality of machinery in Russian factories. An exception was a textile mill in Tashkent. But even this unit did not, in his opinion, compare favourably with the better Indian mills as far as the card and blow room facilities were concerned. When the Russian manager proudly pointed to the dust-free blow room and other features of his establishment, the leader of the Indian delegation could not contain himself and politely informed his host about the superiority of the Indian textile factories in these spheres.

Kasturbhai's services as the chairman of the West-Coast Major Port Committee were unique in many ways. Partition had deprived India of the Karachi harbour. The new Government was naturally keen to locate another port suitably to serve the western and the northern regions. John Matthai, the Finance Minister, suggested to Sardar Patel the names of several distinguished persons to head the Port Committee. But the Deputy Prime Minister was not impressed and suggested Kasturbhai's name. Matthai knew Kasturbhai well and readily agreed to the Sardar's suggestion.

The newly appointed chairman of the Port Committee went about his job like a professional. He enlisted the services of eminent experts in the field and asked them for suggestions. Suggestions came from others as well. Balwantrai Mehta, who later became the Chief Minister of Gujarat, pressed the claim of his hometown, Bhavnagar, and the Jam Sahib of Jamnagar wanted Sika, lying on the northern coast of his erstwhile territory, to be selected. Kasturbhai politely told these influential claimants that Bhavnagar was open to heavy silt and the land adjoining Sika was nearly ten feet below the sea level. After weighing all pros and cons, the Committee unanimously selected Kandla in the Gulf of Kutch. As the site was near the Pakistan border, the opinion of the defence forces had to be sought. They gave a green signal.

Accepting the Kasturbhai report, the Government asked its

author to head the committee for the development of Kandla port. As soon as the committee started its work, it faced a major hurdle. It was necessary, in its judgment, to declare about 400 square miles of land around the port as the notified area but a private company had already acquired 11,000 acres of this area. With characteristic tenacity, Kasturbhai succeeded in persuading the company to surrender a major part of its property. A minor problem arose when Gopalswamy Iyengar, the Minister for Communication, showed slight reluctance to finance the study trip of the engineer associated with the committee to various European ports. Kasturbhai justified the small extra expenditure on the ground of the importance of the project and huge investment involved in it. After his return the engineer advised the committee to invite world wide tenders. The tenders were scrutinized with the help of a retired naval architect. A West German firm was given the contract to build the port with strict penalty clause for delay. The businessman in Kasturbhai dealt with a public project with the same care and thoroughness which he brought to bear on his private business. Unlike many public projects undertaken in free India, the port construction was completed within time and within budget.

An interesting public assignment that Kasturbhai handled was the chairmanship of a committee appointed by the Government of India to study the working of various ministries and suggest reduction in staff strength. A sub-committee was to hold initial discussion with each ministry with a view to generating alternatives for economy measures to be discussed later by the entire committee. The procedure was foolproof but the committee had to contend with bureaucratic resistance at every step. Kasturbhai was hardly used to this kind of intransigence. After 16 months of toil, the committee produced its report recommending drastic reduction of staff in several ministries. For instance, the strength of the purchase department of the Ministry of Commerce had grown from 400 before the war to about 7,000 in 1949; the committee averred that the department did not need more than 1,100 persons for efficient functioning. Kasturbhai viewed his involvement in this committee as the toughest job in his public life. This was also perhaps the least fruitful for the report was never implemented.

Among other public assignments which Kasturbhai handled after freedom was the chairmanship of the Industrial Committee of Mahatma Gandhi Memorial Fund. In this capacity he collected a sum which far exceeded Sardar Patel's expectation on whose initiative he had taken up the responsibility. In addition, he served, at various points of time, on a host of committees constituted by the Government. These included the Cotton Import Advisory Committee, Cotton Textile Fund Committee, Development Committee of Industries, Textile Advisory Committee, and Cotton Textile and Cotton Control Committee.

He remained active in unofficial agencies as well. He was the founder president of Gujarat Chamber of Commerce and Industry (Gujarat Vepari Mandal), established in 1949. In this capacity he led a determined fight against the decision of the Government of Bombay to make Marathi as the official language of the Dangs—a tribal region adjoining the present districts of Surat and Valsad in Gujarat. Kasturbhai considered the government decision unjust because Dangi, which the inhabitants of the region spoke, was a dialect of Gujarati. As the Chamber President he took up the matter with the Election Commission and presented a memorandum to the Government of India and President Rajendra Prasad. He also organized a Maha Gujarat Boundary Committee and organized meeting all over the Gujarat region to protest against the decision of the State Government. The Boundary Committee fielded its own candidates in the local elections and won a large majority of seats. Eventually the Bombay Government had to rescind its decision and the Dangs continued to be considered a part of the Gujarat region. But for Kasturbhai's efforts, the region would have gone to Maharashtra when the bilingual state was bifurcated in 1960.

In spite of heavy demands on his time and energy, Kasturbhai never forgot that it was the famine relief work which had brought him into public life. He continued to remain interested in relief work throughout his career. Gujarat suffered from natural calamities several times after India became free and Kasturbhai was at the vanguard of relief operation on almost all occasions. He was also associated with the operations to help other regions of the country affected by the wrath of nature. It was because of his long link with and genuine interests in such activities that he was asked to head the *Sankat Nivaran Society* set up jointly by the Gujarat Chamber of Commerce and Industries and the Ahmedabad Millowners Association in 1972 in cooperation with some other leading trade organizations in the State. Under Kasturbhai's leadership the Society became the principal forum in Gujarat for relief operations during the periods of social distress.

The Ahmedabad industrialist, thus, played a notable role in the nation's public life. Fields much beyond the chimneys of his factories and the headquarters of his business claimed his attention and felt the impact of his qualities of leadership.

CHAPTER X

Repaying the Social Debt

ACCORDING to some theorists, urge for profit, power, fame, and charity are the dominant motives behind an entrepreneur's pursuits at successive stages of his career. For Kasturbhai the urge to give away a part of his earnings for socially relevant causes seems to have been a compelling need almost from the beginning of his business life. Perhaps it was a part of his inheritance; perhaps it was the impact of his religion on him which stresses the need for charity; perhaps it was a plain and simple human desire to do something for the society. Almost all his ancestors had made donations for social causes. Kasturbhai went one step further; he institutionalized charity in his family and the enterprises.

He took the first step towards creating an institutional base for support to noble causes when under the Income Tax Law passed in 1922, tax exemption was granted to individuals on 50 per cent of the amount donated to charitable institutions approved by the Government. The same year Kasturbhai established a charitable trust in the name of his father, though he was still a back-bencher among the Ahmedabad industrialists. During the next five years, the members of the family donated more than Rs. 10 lakhs to the Lalbhai Trust which became a major outlet of family's support to deserving social demands. Several other trusts were established subsequently.

An opportunity to expand the institutional base for augmenting the quantum of assistance to public causes came when the Finance Act of 1948 brought the company donations also under the exemption provision. Kasturbhai did not lose time to take advantage of the change. All the textile companies in the group appreciated "the step taken in the right direction" and resolved "to make the fullest use of the chance now given to us to help deserving charitable institutions." Donations to various institutions started swelling immediately and the total contributions of the textile mills in the group and the Anil Starch rose to more than Rs. 174 lakhs by 1976. The Atul and associated companies from their inception up to the year of Kasturbhai's retirement from the active leadership donated an aggregate sum of Rs. 41.7 lakhs. The total assets of the famly trusts in the meantime continued to increase as a result of donations from the individual members and rose to Rs. 230.5 lakhs by the end of 1976. These trusts together granted more than Rs. 173 lakhs in support of noble causes between 1948 and 1976; the donations by individual members of the family during the same period exceeded 73 lakhs. Thus the Lalbhai family and the Lalbhai group of industries together gave out an aggregate figure of Rs. 477.7 lakhs during a short period of less than 30 years for the support of non-business purposes.

II

This is an impressive record indeed. But more impressive are the purposes for which the contributions were given. Education remained high on the list. Denied of the benefit of higher education himself, Kasturbhai did a great deal to expand the opportunities for higher learning in Ahmedabad. Educational facilities in the premier city and the most prominent industrial centre of Gujarat had developed very slowly even after the advent of the British rule. Between 1879, when the Gujarat College was established, and 1920, when Gandhi founded the Gujarat Vidyapith, only two other institutions of higher learning—the M.R. College of Science and the R.C. Technical

Institute—had been added. These institutions on one hand and the Vidyapith on the other represented two extreme points of view. While the government-controlled and government-managed Gujarat College and other two institutions were seen as an emblem of slavery by the nationalist elements, the ruling masters and their sympathisers regarded the Vidyapith as the hotbed of insurrectionists.

Several educationists and opinion leaders, who were against the British rule but saw great virtue in the modern system of education did not believe that the Vidyapith could really be an effective instrument of modern education, though none doubted its ability to strengthen the nationalist urge of the youth. They considered it necessary to establish educational institutions which provided facilities for modern education without blunting the nationalist sentiments of the pupils. They also felt the need to provide for a variety of instructional schemes. Kasturbhai was among such persons. Others who thought likewise included G.V. Mavalankar, Jiwanlal Diwan and Balwantrai Thakore. Diwan and Thakore were among the prominent educationists of their times.

The result was the establishment of the Ahmedabad Education Society in 1936. Kasturbhai was elected the Chairman of the Governing Body and became the most dominant figure in its administration. The academic leadership of the Society was entrusted to Anandshankar Bapubhai Dhruv, a retired Pro-Vice Chancellor of the Benares Hindu University and an educationist of great vision. The latter developed an integrated plan for expanding higher education in Gujarat through a series of institutions capable of imparting instruction in a number of disciplines. These institutions, according to his plan, were to evolve into a university. Gujarat then did not have a single university. The Society acquired a vast area of land around the present site of the Gujarat University—vaster than any other similar Society in the Bombay Presidency possessed then—to construct not only colleges but also hostels, teachers' quarters, and sports grounds.

Kasturbhai was not only one of the leading lights behind the formation of the Society but also one of its principal financiers. The major contribution for building the Lalbhai Dalpatbhai Arts College established in 1937 came from Kasturbhai and his brothers. The college was one of the first two institutions opened by the Society, the other being the H.L. College of Commerce. In later years, several other institutions were opened on the initiative of the Society and with the support of the Ahmedabad industrialists. These included M.G. Science Institute (1946), L.M. College of Pharmacy (1947), A.G. Teachers College (1952), M.K. Primary Training College, H.K. Primary School (both in 1956) and A.G. High School (1960). The Society also played a significant role in founding the Physical Research Laboratory in 1948 and the School of Architecture in 1962 which in due course earned an all-India reputation in their respective fields. The last institution to be started by the Society was the School of Urban Studies and Planning in 1972. The Society was not interested in merely adding institution after institution but also providing for facilities and opportunities for a variety of educational experiences geared to the changing needs of the community. It is largely due to the initiative of the Society that the entire area from the present location of the H.L. College of Commerce to the University and beyond has been converted into a veritable educational complex.

Kasturbhai's role in the affairs of the Society was crucial. He procured the services of the best available talents to head the institutions. Eminent scholars and experts nursed some of the institutions mentioned above in their formative years. Having placed competent men to assume the leadership role in these institutions, Kasturbhai thought it unnecessary to interfere in their working. But for the active guidance of the millowner in its affairs, it is doubtful that the Society would have achieved as much as it did, and but for his personal contribution and help in collecting funds, the Society would have remained financially crippled. On the occasion of its Silver Jubilee in 1962, the Society unhesitatingly acknowledged that about half of the total donations of Rs. 1,02,43,658 received by it till that date had been received "through Sheth Kasturbhai Lalbhai." Contribution from his own group of mills amounted to Rs. 28.5 lakhs between 1948 and 1976.

Several other educational and academic institutions benefited from Kasturbhai's munificence. The L.D. Engineering College, which is now controlled by the Government of Gujarat, would not have come into being but for an initial donation of Rs. 20

lakhs from Kasturbhai family. The Gujarat Vidya Sabha, a research institution founded in 1848 received a total amount of Rs. 35.57 lakhs and the Gujarat University Trust Rs. 6.64 lakhs from him. For the latter institution he collected funds from other donors and helped it in other ways too. It was because of his influence, for instance, that the Ahmedabad Education Society surrendered about 400 acres of its own land to the Gujarat University to develop its academic complex.

Among the institutions which gained immensely not only from Kasturbhai's generosity but also from his guidance were the Ahmedabad Textile Industry Research Association (ATIRA), Physical Research Laboratory (PRL) and the Indian Institute of Management (IIMA). The ATIRA was set up as a result of the initiative taken by the Ahmedabad Millowners Association. The Government of India had set up a committee in 1944 under the chairmanship of Shanmukham Chetty to suggest measures to encourage industrial research. The Millowners Association pointed out to this committee that there was no institution for textile research in the country even though it had a highly developed textile industry. The Association expressed its willingness to support a cooperative research organization provided the Government was willing to grant sufficient financial support. The Government accepted the proposal and the member mills of the Association, including Kasturbhai's mills, donated a sum of Rs. 52 lakhs.

In the meantime, Vikram Sarabhai, who later became the Chairman of the Atomic Energy Commission, had returned to India after completing his Ph.D. at the University of Cambridge. On the advice of Kasturbhai he had studied the organization and structure of industrial research institutions in the United Kingdom. The millowner had great affection and regard for the young scientist's commitment to research. They joined together to nurture the proposed institution—Kasturbhai as the Chairman of the Council of Administration, and Sarabhai as its Honorary Director. It was the combined vision of the researcher and the practical wisdom of the industrialist that resulted in the development of the ATIRA into a premier institution in its field. Referring to the impact of the combined leadership of the two institution builders, Kamla Chowdhry has rightly remarked: "Kasturbhai and Vikram represented a combination of science and practice, of the aspirations of two generations, of leadership styles significant to their respective groups—a combination of age, skills and experience which strengthened and enhanced the leadership of institutions like the ATIRA."[57]

Again it was the combined leadership of Kasturbhai and Sarabhai which resulted in the establishment of the PRL. Because of his academic background, Sarabhai had a keen interest in applying scientific knowledge and research to economic and social problems. On his initiative the Ahmedabad Education Society and the Karmakshetra Educational Foundaation, a charitable trust of the Sarabhai family, joined hands to set up the institution in 1947. Government support came in due course. As in the case of the ATIRA the governing council of the Laboratory was headed by Kasturbhai who continued to hold this position until a few years before his death. The first Director of the PRL was K.R. Ramanathan, an able scientist in his own right, who had just retired from the Metereological Department of the Government of India when the Institution came into being; Sarabhai took over the academic leadership after Ramanathan retired. The PRL which began its career in a small room of the M.G. Science Institute, has grown into one of the most prestigious institutions in its field. And for this the leadership that nursed the institution in its formative years must be given a great deal of credit.

Kasturbhai's role in the development of the Indian Institute of Management, Ahmedabad was of a somewhat different kind. The decision for setting up two institutions for management education was taken by the Government of India in 1959. Calcutta was chosen as the location for one of the proposed institutions. The second would have ordinarily gone to Bombay but for the timely intervention of Vikram Sarabhai and Jivaraj Mehta, the Chief Minister of the newly created State of Gujarat. Kasturbhai refused to be the Chairman of the Board of Governors but his role in nurturing the new institution was perhaps more important than that of any chairman in its history. Vikram Sarabhai, the Honorary Director of the Institute during the first three years of its life, leaned on Kasturbhai for advice and guidance; Sarabhai's successor, Ravi J. Matthai, needed his support in dealing with the Government of Gujarat and local industrialists. If the Ahmedabad Institute has attained a pre-eminent position in the field of management education in India and has won international recognition for its work, it is because it succeeded in maintaining its autonomous character against heavy odds. And in safeguarding the Institute's autonomy, Kasturbhai's role, Matthai unhesitatingly admits, was unique.

As the Chairman of Institute's Building Committee Kasturbhai was mainly responsible for developing the physical facilities which have attracted worldwide attention for their architectural design and grandeur. With an eye for details and economy and with a grasp of the intricate problems of construction, the industrialist won the epithet of "natural architect" from Louis Kahn, the internationally renowned architect who designed the Institute buildings. Kasturbhai also helped the Institute in fund collection and set an example for others by giving the largest financial contribution the Institute has ever received from any group of companies. In April 1975, he decided to retire from the Board of Governors of the Institute in conformity with his retirement plan. In a resolution passed on that occasion the Board characterized his services as "unparalleled", and his "support, advice, and assistance" in a variety of fields as "unstinting and invaluable". These tributes were truly deserved.

While giving attention to the problems of industrial, scientific, and management research, the millowner did not ignore the need to promote the study of Indian civilization. Genuinely proud of India's cultural heritage and acutely conscious that Ahmedabad did not have a single centre for research in this field, Kasturbhai decided to establish an institution exclusively committed to promoting the understanding and appreciation of Indian culture. The result was the birth of the Lalbhai Dalpatbhai Institute of Indology in 1963. Located in a single storeyed building with a spacious compound the Institute has a priceless collection of manuscripts, rare books, and microfilms dealing with Indian philosophy, religion, grammar, astrology, prosody, and linguistics. Recognized as a research centre by the Gujarat University, the Institute has published a number of books, brings out a quarterly journal, and organizes research seminars and lectures to promote interest in the study of India's past. Though the Institute receives small grants from the Central as well as State Governments for special projects, the major part of its expenses are borne by the revenue derived from the property of a defunct textile mill which the group had acquired to ensure a steady flow of support to the institution.

Another significant contribution of the industrialist to the life of the city is the Premabhai Hall, named after a Nagarsheth of Ahmedabad and one of Kasturbhai's ancestors. For long the millowner had realized the need for a suitable and spacious hall for holding cultural activities. The plan to construct a large auditorium with modern equipments and facilities was the outcome of this appreciation. Owing to a series of factors, the plan took a long time to materialize, but eventually a large air-conditioned structure with a seating capacity for about 1,000 persons was opened for public use in April 1976. Overlooking the historic Bhadra Fort and the Three Gates, the Premabhai Hall is an asset to the cultural life of the city. The Kasturbhai family and his group of companies donated about Rs. 35.5 lakhs out of the total construction cost of Rs. 52 lakhs.

III

Another cause, which remained very close to Kasturbhai's heart was his religion. Like several other traits of his personality, he had inherited his devotion to the Jainism from his parents, particularly from his deeply religious mother. Unlike his parents, however, he was more interested in the spirit rather than the ceremonial side of religion. He himself conceded to an interviewer in 1975 that his "religious outlook has been very different from that of my parents. My parents' religious outlook was more formal; mine is inward. . . . I am very much interested in the uplift of my soul. . . ." He was, however, conscious that his ancestors from the days of Shantidas Zaveri had all along occupied leadership position in the Jain community. None other than he himself could continue this tradition after the decline of the Nagarsheth branch.

It was this consideration perhaps that led him to accept the Chairmanship of the Anandji Kalyanji Trust as early as 1925. Symbolising the basic values of the Jainism in its name this institution had been patronized by the Svetambar Jains all over the country ever since its inception in the 1720s. Kasturbhai's father had played active role in the management of the Trust and had been its Chairman. After Lalbhai's death his mantle fell on Kasturbhai Manibhai of the Nagarsheth branch who was forced to resign because of certain disputes. Kasturbhai Lalbhai, then a youngman of about 30 years, took over the leadership from his more experienced namesake.

No sooner did the new Chairman take over than he faced a rather intricate problem to solve. The Anandji Kalyanji Trust had a large number of Jain temples under its management including the celebrated complex of shrines on the Shatrunjaya Hills, lying then in the territory of the princely state of Palitana. Under an agreement with the Thakore Saheb, the title by which the ruling prince of the state was known, the Trust used to pay him an annual sum of Rs. 15,000 by way of rent. When the time of renewing the agreement came in 1926, the prince desired the rent to be raised to Rs. 1,50,000, or else he would stop the flow of pilgrims to the temples. Knowing full well that for a large number of Jain devotees, an annual visit to the temples was more important than anything else, the Thakore Saheb was quite confident that he possessed a trump card. Kasturbhai, however, refused to be blackmailed and appealed on behalf of the Trust to the Jains all over the country not to visit the temples. His own grandmother was among a large number of faithfuls who discontinued their regular trek to the shrines. The firmness shown by the Trust and its leadership eventually paid off when the Thakore Saheb agreed, on Viceroy's intervention, to accept less than half the amount he had demanded earlier.

Having settled the dispute with the Palitana authorities, Kasturbhai gave his attention to the need to bring greater order in the working of the Trust. With his characteristic concern for details and efficiency and with his business-like attitude he introduced budgetary control, appointed a team of chartered accountants to audit the receipts and expenditures of the Trust, fixed the duration of the trustees' terms, and ensured that the elections were held at regular intervals. In other words, he brought his business experience to bear on the management of this religious institution. The impact of various reforms introduced by him was so remarkable that a committee appointed by the Government of India to study the working of religious trusts, headed by Sir C.P. Ramaswamy Aiyer, unequivocally testified in 1964 that the Anandji Kalyanji Trust was among the best managed in the country.

Under Kasturbhai's guidance, the Trust undertook the task of renovating a series of Jain temples in various parts of Gujarat and adjoining areas. Very little attention had been paid to the upkeep of the shrines and many were in a deplorable state. Under a temple renovation scheme launched by the Trust in 1932 the temples at Ranakpur, Dilwara, Girnar, Taranga, and Shatrunjaya Hills were repaired at a cost of more than 70 lakhs. Though the Chairman seldom neglected his usual concern for economy, he attached greater importance to the need to retain the original purity of the structures. In a particular instance when the renovation of the Ranakpur temple did not seem to be up to the mark in the eyes of an expert, Kasturbhai discarded the work and ordered it to be redone. Likewise there were serious problems in renovating the figurines on the walls which had been mutilated beyond recognition. The sculptors, therefore, recreated the damaged parts on the basis of details found in the scriptures. The result was that one can hardly detect difference between the original and renovated portions of these temples.

An example of the critical role that Kasturbhai played in renovating the Jain shrines is the manner in which he solved the difficulty in securing essential materials for renovating the Dilwara Temple at Mount Abu. In this temple a special variety of marble had been used which was available in the princely state of Dantia. The ruler of the state, however, refused permission to quarry the marble. Kasturbhai preferred to wait till India became free. After the merger of the state with the Indian Union, he used his influence with Morarji Desai, then the Chief Minister of Bombay, to acquire the marble of the desired quality.

Kasturbhai's role in renovating these temples was greatly appreciated by the lovers of India's past and the followers of the Jainism all over the country. There were widespread complaints about the moral laxity and rectitude among a section of Jain *sadhus*. Kasturbhai was perturbed that the misconduct of a few could bring the whole sect in disrepute. He decided to convene a conference in 1963 of Svetambar Jain representatives from all over the country to consider the problem and take corrective measures. A preparatory committee was appointed for the purpose and the Sheth, always particular about time, spent "lots of my precious time" discussing various problems. But he soon realized that none—"neither the Acharyas nor the heads of religious shrines"—was willing to offer him genuine support, though all of them paid lip service to the cause in the presence of the Sheth. Kasturbhai could not succeed in "a very important work . . . because of the lack of support from both the religious heads and laity."

He also felt sad on the question of the Harijan entry into the Shatrunjaya Hills temples. While the trustees of Anandji Kalyanji Trust could not think of permitting the Harijans to enter the shrines, Kasturbhai could not have kept them out without making a mockery of his convictions and his association with Gandhi, Patel, and Mavalankar. When no agreement could be reached, an indignant Chairman resigned from the leadership of the Trust. Realizing the gravity of the situation, the Trustees agreed to throw open the gates of the temples to all Hindus irrespective of their caste and religious background.

Kasturbhai served the cause of the Jainism not only by his time and energy but also by his money. The members of the family and he himself as well as the family trusts donated a large amount of money to the Anandji Kalyanji Trust and other Jain institutions. Because of his services to his religion, Kasturbhai achieved an unrivalled position among the Jains all over the country. Referring to Kasturbhai's position in the Jain community, Shantilal Shah, the editor of the *Gujarat Samachar* and himself an Oswal Jain, remarked that none among the Gujarat Jains since the days of Shantidas Zaveri could ever win the respect and esteem of his fellow religionists in the same measure as Kasturbhai had done. The fact, however, is that because of his services to a variety of public causes, Kasturbhai had become the undisputed leader of the entire city. His cooperation in any public cause was considered to be a *sine qua non* for its success; his reluctance to support a scheme often foredoomed it.

How did Kasturbhai look upon his own motives behind committing his time, energy, and resources to public causes. This is clear from an incident that Chinubhai Manibhai is very fond of recalling. A few years before his death the Sheth called Chinubhai and asked: "When you go out, don't people pay their respects? Don't they call you affectionately Sheth? Don't they offer you hospitality when you happene to visit them?" A flabbergasted Chinubhai, without any clue to the purpose behind these questions, answered that they did. "What have you done" shot back the older man, "what have you done to repay their debt?" Kasturbhai's charities, his concern for public causes, epitomized his way of repaying his debts to the society.

CHAPTER XI

Conclusion

IF Max Weber were to review Kasturbhai Lalbhai's career, he would find in the Sheth's performance an unfailing support for his explanation of Indian business behaviour. Writing more than half a century ago, the celebrated German sociologist attributed the slow growth of modern business enterprises in India to the so-called negative elements of the Hinduism and declared that the Jain ethics contained a truly great propelling force for business and economic achievement. He had earlier found the Protestant ethics of hard work, frugality, and simplicity to be the root of the rise of capitalist enterprises in the western world, and the values associated with the Jainism, in his opinion, approximated those of the Protestantism. His attempt to correlate the Jain ethics with business behaviour in India was induced by his desire to invest his theory with a general applicability. Weber and his followers may easily point to Kasturbhai's business success as a consequence of his commitment to the Jain values.

Another major theorist who might view Kasturbhai's career as an input to justify his construct is a more recent writer, Everette E. Hagen. His *On the Theory of Social Change*, published first in 1962, is, perhaps, the most *bravura* of all attempts made so far to explain the rise of business leadership. Through an extremely complicated process of reasoning, Hagen, an economist turned psychologist, concluded that major break-through in business occurs as a result of the efforts on the part of certain individuals to regain the status in the society which their families had lost earlier for one reason or the other. The loss of status respect, Hagen argued, leads the family into a state of limbo—which he calls a period of retreatism—which in turn creates conditions favourable to formation of creative, innovational personalities. He never attempted to apply his complex construct to India, but he could well have argued that the period immediately following the separation of the Motibhai branch from the illustrious Nagarsheth family constituted the era of retreatism for the splinter branch, and Kasturbhai symbolized the culmination of a strong urge on the part of his family to regain its lost status. Perhaps psychohistorians, who had strong influence on Hagen's way of thinking, would agree to this interpretation.

Yet another approach that can be invoked to explain Kasturbhai's entrepreneurial exploits is David C. McClleland's well-known thesis of achievement motivation. Did not, the supporters of this theory may point out, Kasturbhai set before himself moderately difficult goals, and show more initiative and exploratory behaviour, and did not his managerial style symbolize his readiness to assume personal responsibility for solving problems? These are the qualities, according to McClleland and his followers, associated with an entreprenurial personality imbued with high achievement motivation.

None can deny that the Jain values had considerable impact on Kasturbhai's behaviour. His fondness for reading Jain religious literature, his services to Jain institutions, and the beginning of his daily routine with an hour long prayer in a temple insideh is house all point to his deep devotion to his faith. We know of a host of businessmen whose business behaviour may not be said to conform to their religious beliefs and practices. In fact a series of empirical cases may be cited to suggest that businessmen normally do not see any serious contradiction between their religious and moral beliefs on one hand, and ruthless, and sometimes unethical, business practices on the other. The example of such contradictions in Kasturbhai's career would, however, be rare. In fact, even if business exigencies forced him to compromise his convictions, he did so with some degree of hesitation and only up to a limited extent. For instance, before deciding to launch the Atul complex, he felt somewhat uneasy about starting a line which entailed invisible loss of lives. A more revealing example of his steadfastness to his conviction was his rejection of a proposal to start a brewery in spite of the high profit potential of this business. His commitment to frugality, hard work, integrity, and fairplay thoughout his business career is well-known.

It is also probable that the awareness of the past heritage coupled with the relatively less important position of his family in the business and industrial circles of Ahmedabad at the beginning of his business career generated in him a sort of nostalgia and creative jealousy. And this induced him to consolidate the entrepreneurial initiative his father had taken and respond creatively to new opportunities for profit. After all, he was quite proud of his family's association with the line of Shantidas Zaveri and Nagarsheth Vakhatchand from his father's side and with the illustrious Hutheesing family from his mother's. Both these families had lost their previous lustre before he started his career and his own family was yet to carve out any significant place in industrial and business life of the city. Several families such as those of Ranchhodlal Chhotalal, Mansukhbhai Bhagubhai, and Mangaldas Girdhardas, with relatively less glorious heritage, were then in the forefront of the business and social life of the city. This discontent created by a sense of pride in his past on one hand and awareness of the existing inferior position of his family on the other must have created in him a desire to turn the tide in his favour. This could as well have been a significant element in his achievement motivation to expand his business enterprise.

And yet Weber's, Hagen's, or even McClleland's theories cannot explain all aspects of Kasturbhai's business activities and strategies. A host of writers have dealt with the weaknesses of Weber's and Hagen's basic constructs and it is not necessary for us to enter into a theoretical discussion about their general validity. It is sufficient to point out that by emphasizing a single factor to the neglect of other forces impinging on human behaviour, these theories attempt to present a unifactoral analysis of what essentially is a multifactoral phenomenon. The theory of achievement motivation also, though much more satisfactory than others, can only be a limited guide. While it can help us appreciate a significant force behind Kasturbhai's business dreams and aspirations, it cannot explain the factors affecting his strategies and structure. It cannot, for instance, explain why he refused to expand his business operations outside Gujarat even though his financial strength could have enabled him to do so easily or why his management structure remained paternalistic and centralized for the most part of his career in spite of his belief in more professionalized system as revealed in his support for management education. The concept of constellation of forces, as outlined in the introductory chapter, can answer these and similar other questions better.

The first phase of Kasturbhai's industrial career was marked by the expansion of his textile manufacturing concerns. What were the major constituents of the constellation of forces that influenced Kasturbhai's business behaviour during this phase of his life? At the time of his father's death, his social reference group was a community which had been traditionally associated with profit-making activities. He was brought up in a joint family tradition and a deeply religious environment. Conscious of his distinguished familial affiliation on the one hand and not so distinguished present on the other, he was aware of his deficiencies and lack of expertise and training to manage a young concern and prove worthy of his mother's expectation whom he devotedly loved. His initial urge, therefore, seems to have been to equip himself to consolidate the position of the Raipur Mills which he had inherited from his father. The First World War gave him an unexpected opportunity to do so.

The profits he earned during the war augmented his financial strength and confidence in his own ability to manage a manufacturing concern. Perhaps he became over-confident. The establishment of the Asoka Mills and the managerial naivete initially displayed by Kasturbhai in floating the new concern reflected his new attitude. The unexpected fall in the value of the Asoka's shares because of the reasons the young and impetuous promoter had not foreseen, and his success in pulling his new venture out of disaster added to his confidence but also tempered it with caution. Further expansion of manufacturing operations was marked by these two attributes. Though he added five more textile units to his group between 1924 and 1935, he never committed the kind of error which had brought the Asoka to the brink of ruin. Except for Ahmedabad New Cotton, which he acquired from another family, all other new companies were floated before the brunt of depression was acutely felt, and the investment in all these mills remained moderate.

The expansion programme exhibited, among other things, Kasturbhai's attachment to the concept of joint family system. It is significant that his concern for his extended family was the primary motive behind the establishment of as many as four out of the five mills added to the group after the Asoka. Three of these—the Nutan, the Aruna, and the Ahmedabad New Cotton—were floated to provide gainful employment to his sister's sons. The fourth, the Saraspur, was acquired to help Kasturbhai's two uncles out of disgrace and to ensure that a family company did not go out of the family's hands. Notwithstanding the bitterness of partition shortly before his father's death, Kasturbhai's faith in the efficacy of the joint family system had remained unshaken. The liquidation of the Saraspur Manufacturing Company gave him a unique opportunity to wipe an ugly scar off the face of the family unity.

Perhaps a hidden desire behind the expansion scheme was to put his family at the top of the business life of the city and thus bring the civic leadership back to Shantidas Zaveri's stock. Nagarsheths Hemabhai and Premabhai and their descendants had remained content with their commercial supremacy alone in the face of a rising industrial class in Ahmedabad. Consequently, the urban leadership was passing on to the industrial elite by the end of the 19th century. The only way to regain the lost position was to carve out a dominant place for the family in the industrial life of the city. Nothing epitomized this urge on the part of the rising star of the splinter branch more than the establishment of the Arvind Mills. In 1931, when the Arvind came into being, practically all the textile mills in Ahmedabad, except the Calico Mills controlled by the Sarabhai family, were geared to the production of relatively coarser counts of goods. By equipping his new mill with the manufacturing apparatus to produce finer materials, Kasturbhai symbolized his unconscious resolve to overtake the industrial leadership of the city. It is significant that most of his major industrial ventures, and all after the establishment of the Arvind, were given names starting with the first letter of the alphabet. Even though Arvindbhai and Ashokabhai, sons of Narottambhai and Chimanbhai respectively, were born before the companies bearing these names were floated, there was no relationship, Kasturbhai maintained, between the names of these individuals and those of the mills. In any case, the names of the Aruna, the Anil Starch, and the Atul referred to no individuals. The choice of these names signified, as it were, Kasturbhai's will to be at the forefront.

By the middle of the 1930s his ambition to become the largest producer of textile goods at the second largest centre of textile production in India had been fulfilled. He had also achieved a certain measure of social standing and national attention through his participation in public life. The result was a significant change in the constellation of forces which influenced his future plans. If the success in expanding his textile operations and the profits earned boosted his confidence in himself, his association with prominent business leaders of the country made him feel dissatisfied with his limited achievement. His involvement in the Central Legislative Assembly and the Federation of Indian Chambers of Commerce and Industry brought him in close contact with some of the most influential personalities in the Indian industrial and business life. The result was that his business reference group ceased to be the limited confines of the business world of Ahmedabad and assumed a national character. In other words, he began to measure his business achievements not in the context of the accomplishments of the industrialists in the city alone but those of the Birlas and the Tatas and the Shri Rams.

It is this change in the constellation of forces that led him to advise Chinubhai Manibhai to enter lines other than textiles. Kasturbhai himself did not look upon the Anil Starch as an entrepreneurial venture of great significance but simply as a source of gainful employment to a young member of the family seeking an opening to express his creativity. But the fact that his choice of the line for his cousin was different from the one he had selected for his nephews is not without significance. Nor can the choice of the new line be wholly explained in terms of the differing abilities and interests of his nephews and the cousin. After all Chinubhai had to train and orient himself into starch production before he was allowed to launch the venture; he did not possess any exceptional expertise for starch manufacturing when he approached the Sheth for advice on his career. It is also noteworthy that while the boards of directors of Kasturbhai's textile companies were largely composed of business and social figures in Ahmedabad, the Anil Starch from the very beginning had several well-known national figures like Chunilal V. Mehta, Sir Purshotamdas Thakurdas, Sir Cowasji Jehangir, and A.D. Shroff on its board. There is little doubt that by the end of the 1930s Kasturbhai had started looking upon himself in a wider rather than merely local perspective. It is this perspective that influenced Kasturbhai's entrepreneurial continuum in future.

The profits that his enterprises earned during the Second World War and the stature that he gained in the national life fortified the change in the constellation of forces and added to Kasturbhai's sense of discontent with his business accomplishments. The search for new avenues of entrepreneurial expression on his part was the inevitable consequence. The beginning of the Atul complex was the outcome of this search. Related though the new venture was, as the Anil Starch had been, with the field in which the family's industrial venture had originated, Kasturbhai's chemical and pharmaceutical venture was planned to be the single biggest enterprise in the group. Far more complex than any of his previous attempts, it demanded all the energy, imagination, foresight, and industry on the part of the founder and his associates. That they possessed these qualities in good measure admits of no doubt but the success of the new venture and its expansion was also ensured by the significant changes in the material environment. Notwithstanding some features of the national policy which the private enterprise resented, the Government of India offered positive encouragement to the attempts to reduce the country's dependence on imports; the exit of the British power attracted industrialists of other advanced countries to enter into collaboration with Indian industrialists; and the demand for dyes, the mainstay of the Atul and its associated companies, successively increased. By creating an industriul township, Kasturbhai joined a select band of Indian industrialists who had transformed a veritable wilderness into an industrial habitat pulsating with life. The emergence of the Atul as one of the biggest chemical and pharmaceutical complexes in the nation was the consummation of a hidden dream on the part of its founder to be counted among the most notable entrepreneurs of his times. As if to symbolize his affiliation with the nation's industrial leadership, he invited the members of the most well-known business families in the country including the Birlas to serve on its board.

It is somewhat surprising, however, that the location of Kasturbhai's all industrial undertakings remained confined to Gujarat. In fact none of the manufacturing units except the fertilizer division of the Anil Starch and the Atul group of companies were established out of his home-town. Admittedly, certain places out of Gujarat were considered for locating the dye and chemical companies, and if the present site of the Atul had not been found suitable, he would have certainly agreed to establish the Atul out of the Gujarat region. But it is well-known that throughout his career Kasturbhai was less than enthusiastic about locating his manufacturing facilities far away from the place of his residence. A few years before his death, he scoffed at a suggestion to participate in a joint sector company sponsored by the Government of Karnataka on the ground of the location being too distant from Ahmedabad. Unlike J.N. Tata or Lala Shri Ram, who consciously sought to establish their manufacturing plants out of their cities or regions or felt little inhibition against participating in business ventures away from their immediate surroundings, Kasturbhai displayed a great deal of preference for Ahmedabad and Gujarat. Why did an industrialist, who looked upon himself in a national perspective after the middle of the 1930s, remain confined to a specific geographical area?

Kasturbhai's attitude to management provides a clue to the understanding of this phenomenon. Belonging to a family of bankers and traders, he had inherited from his parents a managerial style which placed great premium on personal supervision of the business affairs by the owner manager. The scale of banking business under Dalpatbhai and Lalbhai, limited as it was, did not need any elaborate structure, and the size and complexity of his industrial operations made it possible for Lalbhai to give the same personal attention to his mills which he gave to his *pedhi*. Emphasis on personal supervision was not confined to Kasturbhai alone. It was a marked feature of the business behaviour of the Ahmedabad textile manufacturers in general. In other words, the managerial style with which Kasturbhai had any kind of interaction before entering his business career was centred around a belief that an undertaking to be well managed must fall within the range of the personal sight of the top leadership. Most of the Ahmedabad industrialists including Lalbhai had been used to managing their money-lending and trading operations from their '*gaddis*' or the seats, and they readapted this concept—which we may call the "*gaddi*" concept of management for the sake of convenience—for managing their industrial undertakings also. Incidentally the concept neatly conformed to the prevailing family structure.

Under these conditions Kasturbhai found the managerial form inherited from his father good enough for his purpose—a form which was woven around a personalized rather than institutionalized leadership. He had no reason to doubt the effectiveness of a managerial structure which had delivered the goods in the case of a number of industrial houses of the times. With little expertise and even less interest in the academic aspects of organization structure, he did not consider it necessary to bring about any major organizational innovation in his mills. For him concern for quality, a sense of fairplay in business dealings, and unfailing adherence to integrity and honesty were far more necessary for business success than a systematized structure. In any case, the organization theorists were yet to make any significant impact on Indian managerial structure. His childhood training and family atmosphere had instilled these qualities in him in good measure and the application of these qualities for business purposes created a feeling of trust towards his products and organizations among his customers and clients. As this approach bore fruit and preoccupied as he was with the building of more tangible aspects of his business, he gave little attention to the matters of managerial form almost up to the end of the 1950s. Even later, though some minor organizational changes were effected, Kasturbhai remained the central and most dominant figure in the management of his industrial undertakings.

In the light of the present-day organization theories, one may be tempted to pass a value judgment on Kasturbhai's perception of his own role in managing his enterprises. But the fact is that his business behaviour was consistent with the general historical experience. Entrepreneurial history offers very few examples of the first generation entrepreneurs paying great heed to organizational innovations or loosening their personal grip on their operations. Because of their own natural attachment to their creations and heavy dependence of their subordinates on their leadership, the personal values and experiences of the first generation entrepreneurs in most of the cases have been the single most important force behind the evolution of their managerial structure. Kasturbhai was no exception. Before coming to the helm of his business affairs, he had internalized the value of what we have called the '*gaddi*' concept of management, and his experiences and environment in later years did little to deflect him from his basic belief in the efficacy of this concept. And it is this factor more than anything else which inhibited the expansion of his industrial enterprises beyond the horizon of his personal ken and prevented the evolution of a less paternalistic management structure.

His personal background and experiences also explain the character of his major strategies. As a scion of a family of bankers and traders he had an essentially cautious approach to financial matters. His family did not possess a great deal of liquid capital at the time of his father's death. Practically all the textile mills in the city started with small initial investment and depended on public deposits for their working capital. These forces were at the root of his basically conservative attitude towards investment and dividend. His emphasis on moderate dividend, high reserve, ploughing back the profit, and increasing the capital of his companies through issuing right and bonus shares was the outcome of a basically conservative attitude. His marketing strategy was much more innovative and imaginative. The attempt to promote upcountry sales through the appointment of agents all over the country was a new experiment. But the insistence on prior payment for the goods before the agents were allowed to take delivery of the consigments was prompted by the desire to insulate his operations against price fluctuation and undue risk. He, however, honoured prior commitments about prices even if the prices of the goods rose after the contract was made. His sense of values would not let him gain at the cost of fairplay.

Kasturbhai's personnel policy, perhaps, is the most outstanding example of his financial conservatism informed by a sense of fairplay. It is no secret that the salaries of employees in his companies were comparatively low, but it is also well-known that very few, if any, of his executives or workers were ever lured away by the expectation or offer of higher emoluments elsewhere. This is because he all along remained an enlightened employer, and what his men lost in financial terms was more than compensated by the treatment they received. The distance that usually seems to separate different echelons of workforce in more professionalized organizations was hardly anywhere in sight in Kasturbhai's enterprises. In addition, a variety of welfare measures made the workers feel committed to the organizations they served. It is significant that all these measures were not adopted to satisfy statutory requirements; some were enforced much before the Government acted.

Kasturbhai's strategies and structure seem to have served his objectives well. When he entered the business life, he was nothing better than the owner-manager of a small textile concern. By the time he retired from active leadership, he presided over a sizable industrial empire comprising production facilities for a variety of goods. At the time of his father's death, the fate of the only company his family controlled was still uncertain. Under his leadership, the business underwent considerable expansion and consolidation with the result that a predominantly commercial family emerged as a prominent industrial house in the country. Whether different strategies and structures would have delivered better goods or resulted in greater expansion and consolidation is a question which cannot be answered adequately. After all, it is impossible to make the course of history return

Kasturbhai would have hardly deserved the mantle of Shantidas Zaveri and Khushalchand, had he remained content with winning a dominant position in the business field alone.

His more illustrious forebears had won a unique place in the life of the city through their support to public causes. In fact, Gujarat in general, and Ahmedabad in particular, had produced a large number of businessmen whose contributions to public life were no less significant than their success in business. As an heir to such glorious traditions, Kasturbhai was instinctively drawn into public life and felt impelled to support educational and religious causes. The nature of his activities in these spheres was understandably different from those of his forefathers as he was responding to the problems of a different age, but the concern for the society around him was as much a product of his heritage as the result of his interaction with his environment. However, like his business activities, his social concern also was best manifested in his services to his city and region.

Kasturbhai was, thus, essentially a regional entrepreneur. Lacking in the imaginative vision of J.N. Tata, the expansive aggressiveness of G.D. Birla, the acquisitive zeal of Lala Shri Ram, and technical expertise of Laxmanrao Kirloskar, he set before himself a more modest goal. Compared with several other business houses like those of the Thapars, the Mafatlals, and the Sarabhais, the growth of his group has been somewhat slower. It is not the quantum of profit and the size of his business so much as a managerial approach, informed by cautious thoroughness and enlightened business ethics, that won for him a place of honour in the Indian business world. The linkage effects of his business activities were confined essentially to the western region of India and his institution building efforts benefited Gujarat more than any other region. Few entrepreneurs gave as much to their region and community as Kasturbhai did. Among regional entrepreneurs he stands almost alone.

Postscript

THIS book was ready to go to the press when Kasturbhai unexpectedly passed away on 20 January 1980 at the age of 85. The event necessitated only minor changes in the narrative since the focus of the study is on his enterprises rather than himself, and that too for the period preceding his retirement from active management. The Sheth's death, however, is a milestone in the history of the group, warranting a pause to survey the state of his business during the period between his retirement and death. A detailed analysis of the working of the group during the period is beyond the scope of this study. What this postscript intends to present is a brief and qualitative account.

For one thing, the performance of the group during the short interregnum belied the impressions of many in Ahmedabad and elsewhere that the managerial structure developed by Kasturbhai could not be, like Ulysses' sword, handled by any other hands. Behind mute forebodings regarding the future of the group was the ignorance or inadequate appreciation of the subtle and slow manner in which Kasturbhai had developed the second line of leadership and paved the ground for transition to a new generation of decision-makers. It is a measure of the effectiveness of these steps that Kasturbhai's retirement had no detrimental effect either on the progress of his undertakings or the cohesiveness of the group.

This was due to the fact that by the time the new leadership assumed responsibility, the basic attitude and philosophy that underlay Kasturbhai's approach to management had come to pervade all levels of his organizations. The younger members of the family, who came to the helm following him, had internalized the basic values and beliefs that had guided the patriarch in his business career; the professional executives had come to appreciate that the concept of management that Kasturbhai had promoted was elastic enough to permit them to give full expression to their professional competence and win for them the status and role in no way inferior to that of the family members in managing the enterprises.

Kasturbhai's dissociation from leadership role, therefore, caused no dislocation in the managerial environment or business performance. The trends of sales and profits prevailing in the major part of the 1970s in various enterprises continued during the period after 1976. More significantly, the group expanded. A major development was the amalgamation of the Ahmedabad Laxmi Cotton Mills with the Arvind Mills. Established in 1914 by Amritlal Damodardas, a notable business personality of his times, the Laxmi Cotton had joined the ranks of sick units in the country, ill-equipped as it was to face the crises of the 1960s. Change in management did little to improve the situation and the mill eventually stopped its operations in 1977. About the same time, the Government of India introduced a provision in the Income Tax Act offering tax benefits to companies acquiring sick units. Taking advantage of this provision, the management of the Arvind Mills submitted a scheme of amalgamation in 1978 to which the Government and the courts accorded a quick approval so that the Laxmi Cotton, under a new name of Ankur Mills, became a division of the Arvind in April 1979.

The amalgamation scheme was marked by several noteworthy features. First, it was a measure of the reputation of the Arvind management that creditors agreed to wait for a period of 22 years for the settlement of their claims against the defunct company. And during this period only the secured ones would earn interest at a nominal rate. Secondly, the banks agreed to advance 75 per cent of the start-up capital and the entire working capital for 22 years on easy terms. And lastly, the Government agreed to allow tax deductions on the entire accumulated losses of the Laxmi Cotton, enabling the Arvind to eliminate its total tax liability for the year. These provisions collectively obviated the need for any substantial investment on the part of the acquiring unit to effect the acquisition. In creating the Ankur, thus, the Arvind, which had been a gift of the Raipur to its own shareholders, repeated a part of its own history.

Another significant expansionist activity of the group was the establishment of the Gujarat Aromatics as a joint venture in collaboration with the Government of Gujarat to manufacture cresol, a kind of petroleum-based resin used to enamel wire. The manufacturing operations were set up at Ankleshwar which had direct links with Baroda from where the raw materials came. The group contributed 25 per cent of the entire share capital, the Government took 26 per cent, and the remaining 49 per cent was left for public participation. Production started in 1979.

Though the younger generation of decision-makers played a leading role in these developments, or for that matter in managing the affairs of the enterprises in general, it is not quite correct to say that the Sheth led an entirely retired life during the years of his retirement. Temperamentally, he was not a retiring sort. For one thing, he continued to hold the chairmanship of the Arvind Mills till the end of his life. But he remained practically aloof from routine decisions even though he continued to attend his Arvind Mills office regularly and religiously as he had done for years. On major issues also he deferred to the views of the new leadership even if they sometimes ran counter to his own inclination. For instance, he was initially less than enthusiastic about the proposal to acquire the Laxmi Cotton but when the senior executives, armed with relevant statistical data and analysis, pressed for his concurrence the Sheth readily agreed.

Business, thus, claimed a small portion of Kasturbhai's hours during his retirement years. Having resigned from the managing boards of a host of organizations, he had no need to move out of Ahmedabad; his own enterprises in the city he rarely visited, unlike his practice before retirement. Most of his time was spent in reading religious literature or counselling social and cultural organizations. Nothing, however, was allowed to interfere with one schedule. For well over two decades a monthly visit to the Atul complex and Bombay had remained a part of Kasturbhai's routine. Without fail he would leave for Valsad at night of the first Sunday of each month, spend one day and a half at the Atul, and leave for Bombay the Tuesday afternoon. After spending one day and a half at Bombay he would take the train to Ahmedabad the Wednesday night to return home by the next morning. Not only the days were fixed for going from one place to the other but also the trains and hours. So inflexible was this routine that people close to him and his organizations all over India knew when he would be where on these days. The schedule remained undisturbed during the years of his retirement.

Kasturbhai would have ordinarily left for his Atul-Bombay trip in the evening of 6 January 1980 which was the first Sunday of the month. But the Jains in Broach, situated on the way to Valsad, had invited him to advise them on the renovation of a shrine and address their gathering on Sunday. The Sheth was keen to visit the Gujarat Aromatics, located only a few miles from Broach, which he had never visited since its inception. He, therefore, left Ahmedabad in the morning to avoid dislocation of his Atul Bombay routine. None at that time had any reason to suspect that this would be his last trip of this kind. His way of life marked by strict regularity, punctuality, and discipline had endowed him with a kind of health which many a younger man could envy.

The Sheth completed his engagements at Broach, felt satisfied at the progress of the cresol company, spent the usual one day and a half at the Atul, and reached Bombay according to his plan. He also completed the usual duration of stay at Bombay and returned to Ahmedabad the Thursday morning as he would have done in normal course. But unlike the previous occasions, he returned this time an ailing man. For, he had experienced some breathing trouble and congestion in chest the previous evening. Doctors, relatives, and friends suggested that he stayed on in Bombay, but he insisted on returning to his city. Whether he had any premonition of what was to happen is hard to tell but shortly before departing for Ahmedabad the Wednesday night, the Sheth, with tears peeping through his eyes, told one of his grandsons, who was leaving for the United States: "This is our last meeting. We will not meet again".

On reaching Ahmedabad, however, he felt better. In fact, he continued to assure his family members that all was well with him. On one occasion when he temporarily lost his speech, he rebuked one of his daughters-in-law for wasting good quality paper to communicate with him through writing. He even chided his elder son for remaining at home all the time and admonished him to call on B.K. Muzumdar, who was lying critically ill right at that moment. Muzumdar survived but not the Sheth. Through a ding-dong battle between life and death, lasting for the next 10 days, his condition generated more hopes than fears. But the fears had the last cruel laugh. The end came at 8 p.m. on 20 January 1980 almost unexpectedly—so unexpectedly that even the family members attending on him in his house at Shahibaug were taken aback. In the words of Shrenikbhai: "It was the kind of death my father would have liked to have".

Shrenikbhai is right. A sense of inner peace had been Kasturbhai's constant companion in his life: he left this world with the same sense of peace. Tributes flowed from all quarters. His loss was mourned not only because he was a "pillar of light among illustrious Gujaratis"[58] but also an "industrialist statesman".[59] His vision had a "very considerable versatility" and his "farsightedness and breadth of perspective" went far beyond the limited spheres of business. His accomplishments as a blender of old traditions and new approaches in management were indeed great but his greatness lay in "understanding the people and processes" and using this understanding "to bring out the best in a person". More striking than all this, however, was the fact that Kasturbhai, unlike many great persons, was "wholly unselfconscious of his greatness".[60]

A Note on Sources

We have avoided the practice of footnoting our sources. The substantive part of the work is primarily based on company records and interviews with key personalities. These sources are neither easily accessible to the reading public nor amenable to footnoting without needless repetitions. The references given in part I of this section relate only to direct quotations from sources other than company records and interviews. Quotations from company papers and interviews have been left unacknowledged, but their sources are clear from the context.

Descriptive bibliography in part II of this section mentions exhaustively the sources and authorities which have been used in writing different chapters.

I

REFERENCES

1. Alexander Gerschenkron, *Economic Backwardness in Historical Perspective* (Cambridge, Mass., 1962), 52.

2. R.K. Hazari, *The Structure of the Corporate Private Sector: A Study of Concentration, Ownership, and Control* (Bombay, 1967), 249.

3. W.T. Easterbrook, "The Climate of Enterprise" in *Explorations in Enterprise*, ed. by Hugh G.H. Aitken (Cambridge, Mass., 1967), 68-9.

4. S. Gopal, "Presidential Address", *Proceedings of the Thirty-ninth Session of the Indian History Congress* (Hyderabad, 1978), 3-4.

5. James Tod, *Annals and Antiquities of Rajasthan* (Delhi, 1971) II, 1193.

6. *Ibid.*, I, "Editor's Introduction", p. xxxi; Percival Spear; *India: A Modern History* (Ann Arbor, 1961), 87-9.

7. Tod, *Annals*, II, 929.

8. R.C. Majumdar (ed.) *History and Culture of the Indian People, V: The Struggle for Empire* (Bombay, 1966), 428.

9. B.G. Gokhale, "Ahmedabad in the VIIth Century", *Economic and Social History of the Orient*, XII-2 (April, 1969), 187.

10. Quoted in Ratnamanirao Bhimrao, *Gujaratnun Paatnagar: Amdavad* in Gujarati (Ahmedabad, 1929), 113n.

11. Abul Fazl Allama, *Ain-i-Akbari* translated by H.S. Jarrett and corrected by J.N. Sarkar (Calcutta, 1949) II, 247.

12. Ali Muhammad Khan, *Mirat-i-Ahmadi* translated in Gujarati by K.M.N.C. Farooqi (Ahmedabad, 1919). According to Nawab Ali and C.N. Seddon, *Haft Iqlim* written by Amin Ahmad-i-Razi in 1002 A.H. was a well-known geographical and biographical treatise. See their English translation of *Mirat-i-Ahmadi: Supplement* (Baroda, 1928), 8n.

13. William Foster (ed.) *The Journal of John Jourdain 1853-1619* (Oxford, 1912), 173.

14. ———*Early Travel in India, 1553-1619* (Oxford, 1921), 173.

15. ———*Voyage of Nicholas Downton* (London, 1939), 151-2.

16. ———*Early Travels in India*, 206.

17. P. Della Valle quoted in R. Bhimrao, *Gujaratnun Paatnagar*, 118.

18. Foster, *Voyage of Nicholas Downton*, 112.

19. M.S. Commissariat (ed.), *Mandelslo's Travels in Western India* (London, 1931), 26.

20. Foster, *Voyage of Nicholas Downton*, 151-2.

21. ———*Early Travels in India*, 173.

22. Faster, *English Factories in India, 1634-36.* (Oxford, 1911), 197-7; 258-9.

23. M.S. Commissariat, *Imperial Mughal Farmans in Gujarat* (Reprinted from *Journal of the University of Bombay*, IX-1, July 1940), 30.

24. Foster, *English Factories in India, 1624-29.* (Oxford, 1909), 188-9.

25. B.G. Gokhale, "The Merchant Community in the XVII Century India", *Journal of Indian History*, LIV-1 (April, 1976), 124.

26. Foster, *English Factories in India, 1634-36*, 314.

27. Commissariat, *Mandelslo's Travels in Western India*, 23.

28. Commissariat, *Imperial Mughal Farmans in Gujarat*, 39.

29. Ali Muhammad Khan, *Mirat-i-Ahmadi* translated by M.F. Lokhandwala (Baroda, 1965), 210.

30. *Ibid.*, 212.

31. *Ibid.*, 213.

32. Commissariat, *Imperial Mughal Farmans in Gujarat*, 51.

33. *Ibid.*, 52.

34. *Ibid.*, 49.

35. Commissariat, *History of Gujarat with a Survey of its Monuments and Inscriptions* (Bombay, 1959), II, 411.

36. *Ibid.*, 420-1. The original document is still available with Premvada K. Nagarsheth of Ahmedabad.

37. Khan, *Mirat-i-Ahmadi* translated by Lokhandwala, 505.

38. "Shri Shantidas Shethjino Raas", 23-4 in *Jain Aitihasik Raasmala* in Gujarati ed. by Mohanlal D. Desai (Ahmedabad, 1912).

39. *Prajabandhu*, 9 June 1912.

40. *Ibid.*, 9 June 1912.

41. S.D. Mehta, *Cotton Mills of India, 1854-1954* (Bombay, 1954), 196.

42. Quoted in India, National Committee on Science and Technology, *Report on Science and Technology: Plan for Chemical Industry* (Poona, 1973), 113.

43. India, Council of Scientific and Industrial Research, *Report of the Dyestuffs Exploratory Committee* (New Delhi, 1946), 35.

44. *Investors' Encyclopaedia, 1956-57*, 293.

45. *Gujarat Samachar*, 18 March 1952.

46. The index numbers for the industry are based on *Eastern Economist*, XXVIII-11 (15 March 1957), 400; those for Kasturbhai group are worked out on the basis of balance sheets for the appropriate years.

47. Michael Clapham to Manubhai Shah, 17 August 1979. Also see Roberi Kappeli to Manubhai Shah, 13 August 1979 (Arvind Mills Papers, Ahmedabad).

48. Peter Drucker, *Management: Tasks, Responsibilities, Practices* (London, 1974), 41-2.

49. India, *Legislative Assembly Debates*—5th March 1924, IV-24 (Delhi, 1924), 1172.

50. *Ibid.*, 11 March 1924, IV-27, 1344.

51. *Ibid.*, 26 February 1925, V-24 (Delhi, 1925) 1988.

52. *Ibid.*, 26 February, 1925, V-34, 1589.
53. *Ibid.*, 20 March 1924, IV-36 (Delhi, 1924) 2020, 2027.
54. *Ibid.*, 16 March, 1926, VII-33 (Delhi, 1926), 1567.
55. *Ibid.*, 15 March 1926, VII-32 (Delhi, 1926) 2533.
56. *Times of India*, 29 March 1926.
57. Kamla Chowdhry, *Change in Organizations* (Bombay, 1970), 143.
58. *Gujarat Samachar*, 21 January 1980.
59. Ravi J. Matthai, "Kasturbhai Lalbhai", *IIMA Alumnus* (May 1980), 9.
60. *Ibid.*, 10-11.

II

DESCRIPTIVE BIBLIOGRAPHY

Introduction

Because of underdeveloped state of business history in India, few works are available on the activities of Indian businessmen in the pre-British period. Some works that throw valuable light are: Ashin Dasgupta, "The Merchants of Surat, *c.* 1700-50" in Edmund Leach and S.N. Mukherjee, (eds.) *Elites in South Asia* (Cambridge, 1970), 201-22; S. Arasaratnam. "Indian Merchants and Their Trading Methods (*circa* 1700)", *Indian Economic and Social History Review* , III (March 1966) 85-95; Makrand J. Mehta, "Some Aspects of Surat as a Trading Centre in the 17th Century", *Indian Historical Review* I (September 1974), 247-61; J.H Little, *House of Jagat Seth* (Calcutta, 1967); D.R. Gadgil, *Origins of the Modern Indian Business Class: An Interim Report* (New York, 1959); M.N. Pearson, "Political Participation in Mughal India", *Indian Economic and Social History Review*, IX (June 1972), 113-131; D. Tripathi and M.J. Mehta, "The Profile of an Indian

Businessman in the 17th Century: Virji Vora", Case No. I-Eco 1707/R(Mimeo, Indian Institute of Management, Ahmedabad). W.W. Moreland, *India: From Akbar to Aurangzeb* (London, 1923) has also made references to the activities of some businessmen. Among the primary sources, perhaps the most valuable are the Factory records of the English East India Company edited by William Foster under the title *The English Factories in India* (Oxford, 1906-27), 13 Vols, and the accounts of travels by European travellers including *Early Travels in India, 1553-1619* (Oxford, 1921), *Voyage of Nicholas Downton* (London 1939), *The Journal of John Jourdain* (Cambridge, 1905), all edited by William Foster, and *Mandelslo's Travels in Western India* (London, 1931) edited by M.S. Commissariat. The records of the Dutch and French East India Companies are equally useful as shown by T. Raychaudhuri, *Jan Company in Coromandel 1605-1660* (The Hague, 1962) and Om Prakash, "The European Trading Companies and the Merchants of Bengal", *Indian Economic and Social History Review*, 1-3 (Jan. 1964), 37-63.

R.K. Hazari *The Structure of the Private Corporate Sector. A Study of Concentration, Ownership, and Control* (Bombay, 1967), which gives brief histories of the business houses covered in the study, is perhaps the single most important work to indicate that most of the families which are in the forefront of industrial life today did not occupy leadership position in the past. A number of company histories, cited exhaustively in Dwijendra Tripathi, "Occupational Mobility and Industrial Entreprenuship in India A Historical Analysis" *Developing Economics*, XIX (March 1981), 52-68 reveal the same thing. This article also indicates the nature of the existing works on Indian business history.

Works on entrepreneurial theories are galore and it is not necessary for our purpose to cite them exhaustively. We have basically drawn on Joseph Schumpeter, *The Theory of Economic Development* (Cambridge, Mass., 1949); Hugh G.J. Aitken, (ed.) *Explorations in Enterprise* (Cambridge, Mass., 1967); A H. Cole, *Business Enterprise in its Social Setting* (Cambridge, Mass., 1959), Amos Tuck School of Business Administration, "Proceedings of a Workshop on Entrepreneurship" (Mimeo, Hanover, 1969), and Divid C. McClleland, *The Achieving Society* (Cambridge, Mass., 1961).

CHAPTER I

Historical studies of castes and communities are very few. S.R. Bhandari, *Oswal Jati Ka Itihas*, in Hindi (Indore, 1937) 2 volumes, suffers from inadequacies but is still useful. James Tod's classic work, *Annals and Antiquities of Rajasthan* (Delhi, 1971) 3 volumes, corroborates Bhandari's account in many ways. Tod's work, based on his survey between 1818 and 1822 when he was the Political Agent of Western Rajputana, was first published in London during 1829-32. *Jain Aitihasik Raasmala* in Gujarati edited by Mohanlal L. Desai (Ahmedabad, 1912), woven around a kernel of historical facts, throws significant light on the background of the Oswal Jains.

A number of works, in addition to the ones mentioned above, makes reference to Osian as an ancient centre of the Jainism. Prominent among these are R.C. Majumdar et al. (eds), *History and Culture of the Indian Peaple V: The Struggle for Empire* (Bombay, 1966), and Gaurishankar H. Ojha, *Rajasthan Ka Itihas* in Hindi (Ajmer, 1927) 2 volumes. Interviews with a number of prominent Oswals, including Shantilal Shah, editor of the *Gujarat Samachar*, have supplemented the data collected from these sources.

Scholars have given little attention to the study of inland movement of races and people in India. Our account of the migration of the Oswals from the Marwar region to Gujarat and other parts of India is based on Gadgil, *The Rise of Modern Indian Business Class*; Tod, *Annals*; G.N. Sharma, *Social Life in Medieval Rajasthan, 1500-1800* (Agra, 1968); and Thomas A. Timberg, *The Marwaris* (Delhi, 1978).

The most useful source for the ancestry of Kasturbhai Lalbhai is *Jain Aitihasik Raasmala* edited by Desai which gives a geneology of the family. This is corroborated by a representation made by Nagarsheth Premabhai to the British Government in 1862. A copy of this document is available with Premvada K. Nagarsheth of Ahmedabad.

Any good work dealing with the early medieval social-cultural history of Gujarat and Rajasthan would throw light on the prosperity of Gujarat and the cultural integration between the two regions. For our purpose we have used K.M. Munshi, *Glory that was Gujarat Desa* (Bombay, 1955) 2 vols;

M.R. Majumdar, *Cultural History of Gujarat,* (Bombay, 1965); Sharma, *Social Life in Medieval Rajasthan*; and R.C. Majumdar, (ed.) *History and Culture of the Indian People V: The Struggle for Empire*. These works also throw light on the state of the Jainism in Gujarat during this period.

Source materials on the prosperity and grandeur of Ahmedabad under the Sultans and the Mughals are in abundance. Abul Fazl, *Ain-i-Akbari* translated by H.S. Jarrett and corrected by J.N. Sarkar (Calcutta, 1949) 2 volumes; Ali Muhammed Khan *Mirat-i-Ahmadi* translated in Gujarati by Kazi Muhammad Nizamuddin Chisti Farooqui (Ahmedabad, 1919) and in English by M.F. Lokhandwala (1965); *Mirat-i-Ahmadi* (supplement) translated by Syed Nawab Ali and C.N. Seddon (Baroda, 1928); *English Factories in India*; *The Journal of John Jourdain*; *Early Travels in India 1553-1619*; *Voyage of Nicholas Downton*, all edited by William Foster; *Mandelslo's Travels in Western India*, edited by Commissariat; *The Book of Duarte Barbosa: An Account of the Countries Bordering on the Indian Ocean and Their Inhabitants... completed about the year 1518 A.D.* Translated and edited by Mansel Longworth Dames (London, 1921); and Indrani Ray, "Of Trade and Traders in Seventeenth Century India: An Unpublished French Memoir by George Roques", Occasional Paper No. 26 (mimeo, Centre for for Studies in Social Science, Calcutta) are a few of the primary sources. Among the secondary sources, Ratnamanirao Bhimrao, *Gujaratnum Paatnagar: Amdavad* in Gujarati (Ahmedabad, 1929) is perhaps the most exhaustive. Maganlal Vakhatchand, *Amdavadno Itihas* in Gujarati (Ahmedabad, 1977), first published in 1851, is still useful, though outdated in many respects. B.G. Gokhale, "Ahmedabad in the XVIIth Century", *Economic and Social History of the Orient*, XII (April, 1969) (187-97) is an excellent concise account, and Bombay Government, *Gazetteer of the Bombay Presidency IV: Ahmedabad* (Bombay, 1879), throws valuable light. Kenneth L. Gillion, *Ahmedabad: A Study in Urban History* (Berkeley, 1968), though sketchy and deficient in many respects, also offers some insights.

CHAPTER II

Perhaps the most useful source for the careers of the ancestors of Shantidas is *Jain Aitihasik Raasmala* edited by Desai incorporating "Shri Shantidas Shethjino Raas". A recent Hindi work, Rishabhadas Ranka, *Tirtharakshaka Sheth Shantidas* (Bombay 1978) is based on legends. Uncritical acceptance of Jain traditions mars the value of Vakhatchand's account in *Ahmdavadno Itihas* but Bhimrao, *Gujaratnum Paatnagar* gives a more exhaustive and analytical account.

For the careers of Shantidas and his successors, our sources are much more satisfactory. In addition to the above sources we have a series of *farmans* issued by the Mughal rulers granting several privileges to the Sheth. Most important of these are compiled in M.S. Commissariat, *Mughal Farmans in Gujarat* (Reprinted from the *Journal of University of Bombay* IX, July 1940). *English Factories in India* edited by Foster makes frequent mention of the Jain magnate; Khan, *Mirat-i-Ahmadi* refers to his activities as well as those of his sons and grandson; *Mandelslo's Travels in Western India* edited by Commissariat throws light on the Chintamani Temple. A series of documents, known as *Khatapatras*, recording the sale and purchase of various kinds of properties in Ahmedabad in the 17th and the 18th centuries, help in resolving the controversy about Shantidas being the first Nagarsheth of Ahmedabad. These documents, written in old Gujarati, are preserved in the B.J. Institute of Oriental Research, Ahmedabad. The records of the Nagarsheth family in the possession of Premvada K. Nagarsheth, Ahmedabad are of inestimable ualue. A series of *Farmans* issued by the Gaekwads of Baroda and orders issued by the British Government, conferring various honours, titles, and privileges on the Nagarsheth family from time to time, are also useful. Copies of these are contained in *Jain Aitihasik Raasmala* edited by Desai.

A number of secondary works supplement these primary sources and also provide background information. The most important are M.S. Commissariat, *History of Gujarat with a Survey of Its Monuments and Inscriptions* (Bombay, 1959) 2 volumes and his *Studies in the History of Gujarat* (Bombay, 1935). Some other works include, H.G. Briggs, *The Cities of*

Gujarashtra (Bombay, 1849); E.W. Hopkins, *India: Old and New* (New York, 1901); B.M. Malabari. *Gujarat and the Gujaratis: Pictures of Men and Manners Taken from Life* (London, 1882); J. Houston, *Representative Men of the Bombay Presidency* (Bombay, 1900); B.K. Boman-Behram, *The Rise of Municipal Government in the City of Ahmedabad* (Bombay, 1937); and M.N. Patel, *Mahajan Mandal* in Gujarati (Ahmedabad, 1896). Dwijendra Tripathi and M.J. Mehta, "The Nagarsheth of Ahmedabad: History of an Urban Institution in Gujarat City", *Proceedings of the 39th Session of the Indian History Congress* (Hyderabad, 1978), 481-96 is perhaps the most comprehensive discussion of the subject.

The accounts of the Nagarsheth family have been strengthened by interviews with the surviving members particularly Premvada K. Nagarsheth.

CHAPTER III

M.L. Desai in his introduction to the *Jain Aitihasik Raasmala* has briefly referred to the careers of Dalpatbhai and Lalbhai. The story of speculation in India during the American War has been discussed in Dwijendra Tripathi, "An Echo beyond the Horizon: The Effect of the American Civil War on India", *Journal of Indian History*, Golden Jubilee Volume (1973), 635-65. Malabari, *Gujarat and Gujaratis* refers to Premabhai's loss during the share mania.

For environmental changes in the wake of the British rule see Dwijendra Tripathi, "Occupational Mobility and Industrial Entrepreneurship in India". S.D. Mehta, *The Cotton Mills of India*, 1854-1954 (Bombay, 1954), being the most comprehensive history of the Indian cotton textile industry, has provided perspective on the rise of the industry, and M.J. Mehta, "Ranchhodlal Chhotalal and the Ahmedabad Cotton Textile Industry: A study in Entrepreneurial History" (Ph.D. Thesis, Gujarat University, Ahmedabad, 1979) contains valuable data on the growth of the industry in Ahmedabad. Howard Spodek, "Manchesterization of Ahmedabad", *Economic Weekly*, XVII (13 March 1865), 483-90 is also a useful study.

Many vital facts about Lalbhai's career, character, and temperament have been gathered through interviews with those who knew him or of him, particularly Kasturbhai Lalbhai and Premvada K. Nagarsheth. The balance sheets and annual reports of the Saraspur Manufacturing Company and those of the Raipur Mills have been the major sources of information on the progress of Lalbhai's textile ventures during his life. S. Playne, *The Bombay Presidency, the United Provinces, the Punjab, etc.: Their History, People, Commerce, and Natural Resources* (London, 1917-20) contains useful data. Also helpful is a Gujarati publication entitled, *Amritamahotsava: The Saraspur Mills Limited, 1898-1973* brought out on the occasion of the platinum jubilee of the mill. Kasturbhai Lalbhai's personal narrative available in typescript with the family has also provided valuable insights. Old files of the *Prajabandhu*, a fortnightly published from Ahmedabad from 1898 to 1938, contain valuable data on Lalbhai and his enterprises. Information with regard to the Swadeshi Movement on the Ahmedabad industry has been gleaned from N.N. Desai, *Directory of Ahmedabad Mill Industry, 1929-1955* (Ahmedabad, 1958). Shirin M. Mehta, "Social Background of the Swadeshi Movement in Gujarat" presented at the 41st Session of the Indian History Congress, Bombay, 1980 has also been useful.

A commemorative volume presented to Kasturbhai Lalbhai on the occasion of his 75th birthday provides some useful glimpses into his early life. This unpublished work is available with the family. Also two books, A.D. Shroff Memorial Trust, *Kasturbhai Lalbhai* (Bombay, 1978), and Dhirubhai Thakar, *Parampara ane Pragati: Kasturbhai Lalbhainun Jeevancharitra* in Gujarati (Bombay, 1980) throw light on his personality traits. For our basic insight, however, we have depended on interviews with Kasturbhai Lalbhai including the ones he had granted to an American scholar, Howard Spodek, a few years ago. The data on the performance of the mills are collected from the balance sheets and annual reports for the appropriate years.

CHAPTER IV

This chapter is primarily based on the data collected from

the balance sheets and annual reports of the Raipur, Asoka, Saraspur, Aruna, Arvind, Nutan, and Ahmedabad New Cotton Mills for the appropriate years. Interviews with Kasturbhai Lalbhai and B.K. Muzumdar have supplemented the documentary materials. Background information pertaining to business environment has been gleaned from Government of India, *Report of the Tariff Board*, (New Delhi, 1926); S.D. Mehta, *Cotton Mills of India, 1854-1954*; M.J. Mehta, "Ranchhodlal Chhotalal and the Ahmedabad Cotton Textile Industry"; N.N. Desai, *Directory of Ahmedabad Mill Industry 1929-1955*; and M.D. Joshi, "Currency" in V.B. Singh (ed.) *Economic History of India, 1857-1956* (Bombay, 1965), 374-413.

CHAPTER V

This chapter is primarily based on the balance sheets and annual reports of the Anil Starch Limited for the period 1938-1946, of the seven textile companies, which comprise the Kasturbhai Lalbhai group of mills, for the same period, and of the Atul Products Limited for the period 1948-1952, The Articles of Association of the Atul, available in the office of the Registrar of Companies, Ahmedabad has also been consulted. Extensive interviews with Chinubhai Manibhai, Kasturbhai Lalbhai, B.K. Muzumdar, and B.V. Shah have been helpful in reconstructing the early histories of the Anil Starch and the Atul.

The Investors' Encyclopaedia, for 1952-53 has yielded crucial background data regarding the Anil Starch; S.D. Mehta, *Cotton Mills of India 1854-1954*; V.B. Kulkarni, *History of the Indian Cotton Textile Industry* (Bombay, 1979); N.N. Desai, *Directory of Ahmedabad Mill Industry 1929-1956*; and the *Annual Reports of the Ahmedabad Mill Owners' Association* for the appropriate years have provided perspective and supporting data for the textile side of business.

Supplementary data for the Atul have come from diverse sources such as the *Investors' Encyclopaedia, 1956-57*; Council of Scientific and Industrial Research, *Report of the Dyestuffs Exploratory Committee* (New Delhi, 1946): Government of India,

Department of Industries and Supplies, *Report of the Panel on Fine Chemicals, Drugs, and Pharmaceuticals* (Delhi, 1949); Government of India, Planning and Development Department, *Report of Heavy Chemicals and Electrochemical Industries Panels* (Delhi, 1949); and National Committee on Science and Technology, *Report on Science and Technology: Plan for Chemical Industry* (Poona, 1973). J.P. De Souza, *History of the Chemical Industry in India* (Bombay, 1961) and a number of brochures and pamphlets published by the company have also been useful. Government of Great Britain, Board of Trade, *Report of the Dyestuffs Industry Development Committee on the Present Position and Development of the Dyestuffs Manufacturing Industry in Great Britain* (London, 1930); United States Tariff Commission, *Dyes: War Changes in Industry Series*, Report No. 19 (Washington, 1946); and United States Tariff Commission, *Synthetic Organic Chemicals: United States Production and Sales, 1954*, II Series, Report No. 196 (Washington, 1955) have provided information on some of the developed countries.

CHAPTER VI

In addition to the balance sheets and annual reports of the textile companies in the Kasturbhai Lalbhai groups of mills and the Anil Starch from 1647 to 1977 and related papers, the following works have been used for writing this chapter. J.N. Bhagawati and Padma Desai, *India: Planning for Industrialization and Trade Policies since 1951* (London, 1970) and H. Venkatasubbiah, *Indian Economy since Independence* (New York, 1961) for government policies; S.B. Agrawala, *Price Trends in India since 1951* (Delhi, 1971) for price movement, S.D. Mehta, *Cotton Mills of India, 1854-1954* and Kulkarni, *History of the Indian Cotton Textile Industry* for general understanding of the textile industry; the *Annual Report of the Ahmedabad Millowners' Association* for the years 1947 to 1977 for insights into the problems of the Ahmedabad mills.

Among the official reports which have provided supportive data on various aspects are: Government of India, Ministry of Commerce and Industry, *Report of the Working Party for the*

Cotton Textile Industry (Delhi, 1952); Government of India, Ministry of Commerce, *Reports of the Indian Tariff Board on the Cotton Textile Manufacturing Industry* (Bombay 1947; 1957) Government of India, *Reports of the Indian Tariff Board on the Starch Industry* (Bombay 1947; 1951); Government of India, *Report of the Indian Tariff Board on the Continuance of Protection to the Starch Industry*, (Bombay 1949; 1955); Government of India, *Report of the Indian Tariff Board on the Glucose Industry* (Bombay, 1947); Government of India, Tariff Commission, *Reports on the Continuance of Protection to the Glucose Industry* (Bombay, 1953; 1955)

Supportive data for units other than Kasturbhai Lalbhai's are taken from *Kothari's Economic and Industrial Guide of India*, (published as *Investor's Encyclopaedia* up to 1959-60 and as *Kothari's Economic Guide and Investors' Handbook of India* from 1961 to 1970), for the years 1946-47 to 1977.

Data and information provided by the company records and other published sources are supplemented by interviews with Kasturbhai Lalbhai (including the one he had granted to a member of the faculty of the Indian Institute of Management, Ahmedabad in 1964 record of which is available with the IIMA), Shrenik Kasturbhai, Manubhai D. Shah, and Chinubhai Manibhai.

CHAPTER VII

The annual reports and balance sheets of the Atul Products, from 1952 to 1977 and those of Atic Industries from 1956 to 1977 and Cibatul from 1961-1977 form the backbone of source materials for this chapter. In addition, the following official reports have provided crucial data and background information; Government of India, Tariff Commission, *Report on the Dyestuff Industry* (Bombay, 1954); *Reports on Review of Protection to the Dyestuff Industry* (Bombay, 1964; 1968): *Report on Half-yearly Review of the Dye-Intermediates Industry* (Bombay, 1970); *Reports on the Continuance of Protection to the Dye-Intermediates Industry* (Bombay, 1972; 1974; 1975); *Reports on the Continuance of Protection to the Plastics Industry*

(Bombay, 1956; 1959; 1962); and Government of India, Ministry of Commerce, *Report of the Indian Tariff Board on the Plastics Industry* (Bombay 1949).

Besides, a series of brochures brought out by the Atul and its associated companies and newspaper articles and supplements have been useful. Important among the latter kind of materials are "Story of Atic Industries Limited", *Chemical Age of India*. XXII (January 1972); a Silver Jubilee Supplement on the Atul in *Hindustan Times*, 17 March 1977 and a comprehensive analytical review of the Atul in *Financial Express*, 2 July 1979. N.S. Johary, "A Fifteen-year Perspective Plan for Dyestuffs and Intermediates Industry" presented at the ICMA Seminar on Perspective Plan for Chemicals held at Bombay on 10 December 1976, and Council of Scientific and Industrial Research, *Report of the First Get-together of Research and Industry* (New Delhi, 1966), particularly those of the working groups 2, 4, and 5 have also been helpful. *Kothari's Economic and Industrial Guide of India* for the years 1952 to 1977 has provided information on general industrial situations. K.M. Kapadia & S.D. Pillai, *Industrialization and Rural Society: A Study of Atul Bulsar Region* (Bombay, 1972) has a comprehensive discussion on the social impact of the Atul.

Supplementary information has been collected through interviews with Kasturbhai Lalbhai, B.K. Muzumdar, Siddhartha Kasturbhai, Shrenik Kasturbhai, B.V. Shah, N.S. Johary, A.R. Naik, and R.H. Acharya.

CHAPTER VIII

A number of works have dealt with the rise and growth of the managing agency system in India such as P.S. Loknathan, *Industrial Organization in India* (London, 1935); Raj K. Nigam, *Managing Agencies in India* (Delhi, 1957); S.K. Basu, *The Managing Agency System* (Calcutta, 1950), Radhey Shyam Rungta, *Rise of Business Corporations in India, 1851-1900* (Cambridge, 1970); Blair B. Kling, "The Origin of the Managing Agency System in India," *Journal of Asian Studies* XXVI (November 1965) 37-47; Andrew F. Brimmer, "The Setting for

Entrepreneurship in India". *Quarterly Journal of Economics,* LXIX (November 1955), 551-76; and Vera Anstey, *Economic Development of India* (New York, 1952). None of the existing works, however, has referred to the relationship between the joint family system and managing agency structure. For a sample of early attack on the managing agency system see "The Bombay Cotton Mills: Their Defects in Management and How to Remedy Them", *Indian Textile Journal* V (November 1894 to June 1895). Between 1898 to 1903, the *Prajabandhu* of Ahmedabad published a series of articles alluding to the alleged misdeeds of the mill agents.

On the changing structure and strategies of Kasturbhai Lalbhai's enterprises, exhaustive interviews with Kasturbhai Lalbhai, B.K. Muzumdar, Siddhartha Kasturbhai, Shrenik Kasturbhai, Chinubhai Manibhai, M.D. Shah, B.V. Shah, N.S. Johary and a number of employees, both past and present, of the Arvind Mills and the Atul provided crucial inputs. The accounts of interviews have been cross-checked with the help of data available in the balance sheets and annual reports and related papers of the Kasturbhai Lalbhai's enterprises.

CHAPTER IX

An idea of the social concerns of Kasturbhai Lalbhai's ancestors can be had from *Jain Aitihasik Raasmala* edited by Desai; Bhimrao, *Gujaratnun Paatnagar*; D. Tripathi and M.J. Mehta, "The Nagarsheth of Ahmedabad" and Commissariat, *History of Gujarat*, II. Probably the best written account of Gandhi's role in organizing the Ahmedabad textile labour is Mahadeo H. Desai, *A Righteous Struggle* (Ahmedabad, 1951). Kasturbhai Lalbhai's non-business activities have been dealt with in A.D. Shroff Memorial Trust, *Kasturbhai Lalbhai* and Dhirubhai Thakar, *Parampara and Pragati*. Some aspects of Kasturbhai's participation in the formation and development of the Federation of Indian Chamber of Commerce and Industry (FICCI) have been discussed in H. Venkatasubbiah *Enterprise and Economic Change: 50 years of FICCI* (New Delhi, 1977); and Stanley Kochanek, *Business and Politics in India* (Berkeley,

1974). Frank Moraes, *Sir Purshotamdas Thakurdas* (Bombay 1957); and Arun Joshi, *Lala Shri Ram: A Study in Entrepreneurship and Industrial Mangement* (New Delhi, 1973) throw some light on two of Kasturbhai's contemporaries with whom he had close contacts. On Kasturbhai's role as a legislator, Government of India *Legislative Assembly Debates*, IV-VIII (Delhi, 1924-1926) are an indispensable guide.

Interviews with Kasturbhai Lalbhai have supplemented the knowledge gleaned from published sources with regard to his non-business activities.

CHAPTER X

The data for the chapter have been collected from the records of the family trusts, balance sheets, and annual reports of Kasturbhai Lalbhai's enterprises, and of the Ahmedabad Education Society. Also Kasturbhai's correspondence with the authorities of various institutions has been consulted. Interview with Kasturbhai Lalbhai, B.K. Muzumdar, Ravi J. Matthai, and Shantilal Shah have yielded supplementary information. Among the secondary sources Arthur H. Cole, *Business Enterprise in its Social Setting* (Cambridge, Mass., 1959) has provided insight into the dominant motives behind an entrepreneur's action at various stages; Kamla Chowdhry, *Change in Organizations* (Bombay, 1970) has dealt with Kasturbhai's role in developing the Ahmedabad Textile Industry Research Association (ATIRA); and A.D. Shroff Memorial Trust, *Kasturbhai Lalbhai* has given the account of his support for educational and religious causes.

CHAPTER XI

In this chapter an attempt has been made to apply the theory of constellation of forces, discussed in the introductory chapter, to Kasturbhai Lalbhai's career. For other theoretical constructs discussed in this context see *From Max Weber: Essays in Sociology* edited by H.H. Gerth and C. Wright Mills

(New York, 1958); Everette E. Hagen, *On the Theory of Social Change* (Homewood, Ill., 1962); and McClleland, *The Achieving Society*. Morris. D. Morris, "Values as an Obstacle to Economic Growth in South Asia: An Historical Survey", *Journal of Economic History*, XXVII (December, 1967), 588-607; and D. Tripathi, *Occupational Hobility andIndustrial Entrepreneurship in India* are major attacks on Weber's Indian thesis. Alexandar Gerschenkron, "How Economic Growth Begins" in his *Continuity in History and Other Essays* (Cambridge, Mass., 1968), 368-74 is a masterly critique of Hagen.

References to leading families in the Ahmedabad textile industry at the beginning of Kasturbhai's industrial career are found in M.J. Mehta, "Ranchhodlal Chhotalal and the Ahmedabad Cotton Textile Industry". For the careers of J.N. Tata, Lala Shri Ram, and Laxamanrao Kirloskar see F.R. Harris, *Jamsetji Nusserwanji Tata: A Chronicle of His Life* (London, 1959); Arun Joshi, *Lala Shri Ram: A Study in Entrepreneurship and Industrial Management*; and Kirloskar and Sons, *Yantrikanchi Yatra* in Marathi (Kirloskarvadi, 1958).

POSTSCRIPT

The chapter is based on the balance sheets and related papers of the enterprises in the group and interviews with Shrenik Kasturbhai, Vimla Siddharthabhai, and Manubhai D. Shah. N.N. Desai, *Directory of Ahmedabad Mill Industry, 1929-1955* contains a short history of the Ahmedabad Laxmi Cotton Mills. The Ahmedabad edition of the *Times of India* of 21, 22, and 25 January 1980, and the *Gujarat Samachar* of 21, 22 and 24 January 1980, have been used for news relating to Kasturbhai's death and tributes paid to him.

Index